## VALUING BUREAUCRACY

To be effective, government must be run by professional managers. When decisions that should be taken by government officials are delegated to private contractors without adequate oversight, the public interest is jeopardized.

Verkuil uses his inside perspectives on government performance and accountability to examine the tendencies at both the federal and state levels to "deprofessionalize" government. Viewing the turn to contractors and private sector solutions in ideological and functional terms, he acknowledges that the problem cannot be solved without meaningful civil service reforms that make it easier to hire, incent and, where necessary, fire career employees and officials. The indispensable goal is revitalize bureaucracy so it can continue to competently deliver essential services. By highlighting the leadership that already exists in the career ranks, Verkuil senses a willingness, even eagerness, to make government, like America, great again.

Paul R. Verkuil is President Emeritus of the College of William & Mary, and served as Dean of both Cardozo School of Law and Tulane University School. He served over five years in the Obama Administration as Chairman of the Administrative Conference of the US. He is the author of *Outsourcing Sovereignty* (Cambridge, 2007).

# Valuing Bureaucracy

## THE CASE FOR PROFESSIONAL GOVERNMENT

PAUL R. VERKUIL

CAMBRIDGE
UNIVERSITY PRESS

CAMBRIDGE
UNIVERSITY PRESS

University Printing House, Cambridge CB2 8BS, United Kingdom

One Liberty Plaza, 20th Floor, New York, NY 10006, USA

477 Williamstown Road, Port Melbourne, VIC 3207, Australia

4843/24, 2nd Floor, Ansari Road, Daryaganj, Delhi - 110002, India

79 Anson Road, #06-04/06, Singapore 079906

Cambridge University Press is part of the University of Cambridge.

It furthers the University's mission by disseminating knowledge in the pursuit of education, learning and research at the highest international levels of excellence.

www.cambridge.org
Information on this title: www.cambridge.org/9781107176591
DOI: 10.1017/9781316817063



First published 2017

Printed in the United States of America by Sheridan Books, Inc.

*A catalogue record for this publication is available from the British Library.*

ISBN 978-1-107-17659-1 Hardback
ISBN 978-1-316-62966-6 Paperback

*Dedicated to my colleagues at ACUS,*
*especially Shawne, Matt, and Harry,*
*and, as always, to Judy.*

# Contents

# Acknowledgments

This book reflects my continuing effort to connect academic ideas and constitutional norms to practical and political realities. Ten years ago *Outsourcing Sovereignty* was published on this premise. Since then I have served five and a half years at the Administrative Conference of the United States (ACUS), which gave me a close-up view of government. As one who works in the broad field of public law and administration, it is hard not to be jarred by the many contradictions that emerge from it, among them why it is so hard to do government well and why doing so is such a controversial proposition. I'm not talking policy choices, which are meant to be contested, but implementation of agreed-upon policies, which are inevitable, if not ministerial, acts. But controversy is the territory that bureaucracy inhabits. The fact that bureaucrats exercise discretion, if not autonomy, explains some of the criticism and introduces my theme.

The title *Valuing Bureaucracy* acknowledges the reality of governance and the importance of professional management. While that might seem an obvious proposition, it is an increasingly contested one. Efforts to deregulate and reduce regulations have created parallel incentives to "deprofessionalize" government by hiring alternative actors who supplant career managers. This is part of a larger movement to revalue bureaucracy, inspired by political forces who want to shrink the administrative state if not dissolve it altogether.

Admittedly, bureaucrats can be aggravating, if not overbearing, and bureaucracy can be tedious, if not oppressive. The painting on the cover, *Red Tape* by Maurice Sterne, captures these feelings. This is one of 20 panels painted by the artist during the 1930s for the main library reading room of the Department of Justice (DOJ) in a series entitled "The Search for Truth." Sterne depicts Justice Holmes as Don Quixote fighting bureaucratic entanglements.[1] There

[1] My first acknowledgment is to Dennis Feldt, the DOJ librarian, who was kind enough to provide a photograph for the book cover. He also explained the painting, as follows: "The Sterne panels

is no specific reason (or judicial opinion) to explain why Holmes was chosen as the Don, but he is the perfect character for the role. Holmes had enormous influence over the United States government, fought bravely for it in the Civil War, and left his residual estate to it. But while Holmes is pictured fighting red tape, which is a product of government, he did not oppose government itself. Holmes recognized that "taxes are what we pay for civilized society."[2] (Like Holmes, I confess to feeling a little quixotic as I make the case for professional government in these contentious times.)

Numerous people helped this project, specifically, Reeve Bull, Cary Coglianese, John DiIulio, Francis Fukuyama, Paul Joskow, Don Kettl, Alan Krueger, Dave Lewis, Jon Michaels, Nira Olson, Norm Ornstein, Anne O'Connell, Ricky Revesz, Jim Tozzi, Adrian Vermeule, Matt Wiener, Amber Williams, and Stephen Williams. Many of them read the manuscript and all provided invaluable comments. Thanks also to Steve Croley and Raj Shaw for being candid about their agencies (Department of Energy (DOE) and Agency for International Development (USAID)), Shaun Donovan for sharing thoughts about his two agencies (Department of Housing and Urban Development (HUD) and Office of Management and Budget (OMB)), and Beth Cobert for doing the same (OMB and Office of Personnel Management (OPM)). In addition, Matthew Blum of OMB led me through the intricacies of inherent government functions. The Comptroller General, Gene Dodaro, and Chris Mihm of the Government Accountability Office (GAO) were very generous in finding, sharing, and explaining numerous GAO reports. Ray Limon and Jeff Neal (expert human capital leaders at several agencies), provided deep perspectives on their craft. Stan Soloway and Rich Wilhelm, a senior official at Booz Allen Hamilton, generously explained how the government contractor community operates.

I also gained many insights from Paul Volcker, Shelley Metzenbaum, and Tom Ross of the Volcker Alliance, which is on a comparable mission to explain and restore quality professional leadership to government, and from Max Stier, who is President of the Partnership for Public Service.

are in the surrealistic style, so there is a lot of meaning in them that is known only to the artist. The description of the 'red tape' painting is that it shows a huge spider web of red tape with an animal head and squirrel in the middle; the skull possibly signifying the death of many things due to red tape. The web also has the roman numerals of a clock which suggests the passage of time . . . The despondent and pleading people are caught in the web and the interpretation is that they are being released by Justice Holmes as a Don Quixote type figure." Email to author, July 18, 2016.

2 See *Compañía General de Tabacos de Filipinas* v. *Collector of Internal Revenue*, 275 U.S. 87, 100 (1927). The Internal Revenue Service has this quote over its building on Constitution Avenue.

John DiIulio, Don Kettl, and Paul Light whose work in this field is so influential, were also of great assistance in many ways. Secretary George Schultz, who understands government deeply and from many perspectives, generously provided his time.

Institutional arrangements in Washington were offered by ACUS (where I have reverted to senior fellow status), the Center for American Progress (thanks to Neera Tanden, Carmel Martin, and Liz Kennedy), and the National Academy of Public Administration (thanks to director Dan Blair). I was also invited to serve as a visiting scholar at the New York University (NYU) Wagner School of Public Service while preparing the manuscript.

Finally, I want to acknowledge my editor at Cambridge, John Berger, for launching and then encouraging this project throughout, and Kevin Bell, a recent NYU law graduate and the first Jerre Williams Fellow at ACUS, for his research, drafting, editing, and resolute managing of this complicated project.

The last word goes to my wife Judy, my children Tara, Gibson, and Alex (also a White House staffer) and grandchildren Lucy and Orrin, who make my life so fulfilling.

# 1

# Introduction and Overview

A feeble execution is but another phrase for a bad execution; and a government ill executed, whatever it may be in theory must be in practice, a bad government.

Alexander Hamilton, *Federalist* 70

The title of this book urges that bureaucracy be valued, and makes a case for professionalism in government. But since millions of people are employed by federal, state, and local governments, many of whom are hard-working professionals, this proposition may not seem obvious or even logical. How is it possible that government at all levels, the leviathan that is the modern state, could be weakened by a lack of professionalism? Aren't there professionals among these numbers of government employees who do the job of managing the bureaucratic state? Of course, many are at work doing their jobs effectively. But their numbers are shrinking relative to the size of government, and contractors and other workers are growing in proportion. Clearly bureaucratic size need not equate with bureaucratic energy, and the energy that professionals provide ensures directed, purposeful, and accountable government. When government is "deprofessionalized," this energy can be lost, and the structure is hollowed out.

Bureaucracy exists in both the government and private sectors for a reason: for all its faults, it is the most efficient way to organize large functions.[1] So we cannot "banish" bureaucracy,[2] even if we wanted to. Bureaucracy alone is

[1] See Richard Posner, *Bureaucracy and Efficiency*, The Becker–Posner Blog (Jan. 12, 2014), www.becker-posner-blog.com/2014/01/bureaucracy-and-efficiencyposner.html (questioning bureaucracy's failures, but concluding "it must be on balance an efficient means of administration or it wouldn't be so pervasive in both the public and private sectors").

[2] See David Osborne & Peter Plastrik, Banishing Bureaucracy: The Five Strategies for Reinventing Government (1997) (proposing strategies to "reinvent" government by making it more efficient).

not the problem; the problem lies with the quality of management that determines its energy and its efficacy. Alexander Hamilton's quote above equates ill execution with bad government. Hamilton saw an energetic executive branch as "essential to the steady administration of the laws." Paul Light has deepened Hamilton's insights by identifying the characteristics that his words encompass.[3] Light's view is that through the growth of contractors the federal service has been so depleted it cannot live up to Hamilton's vision for it.[4] This book builds on these insights.

And energetic execution is not just an Executive branch problem. Since it is the dictates of Congress that agency officials administer under our constitutional system, a deprofessionalized Executive branch leads to problems for the First branch as well. Ill execution of laws hurts both branches. Government administration has always been the Executive's role,[5] and its effectiveness has been critiqued since the beginning of the Republic.

In today's terms, administration is meant to be performed by professional managers, largely career officials who devote their lives to executing government, supervised by political appointees and overseen by congressional committees. Professionalism reflects competencies and skills along with a degree of independence. But current criticisms make the idea of professionalism controversial or even illegitimate. Rhetoric about the size of bureaucracy overwhelms concerns about its quality. As Don Kettl has shown, America seems to have lost its commitment to competence in government.[6] Those at the management levels, where Hamilton's "energetic" government operates, are finding their positions more precarious as duties and missions expand without additional support and contractors assume more responsibility. This is where bureaucracy is being devalued. The powers of government are meant to be exercised by political appointees and career officials acting on instructions from Congress and the President, but when others perform their tasks, the question of who is in charge arises. I earlier identified this issue metaphorically as one of "outsourcing sovereignty," the process of devolving government responsibilities

[3] See Paul C. Light, A Government Ill Executed: The Decline of the Federal Service and How to Reverse It (2008); see also Paul C. Light, *A Government Ill Executed: The Depletion of the Federal Service*, 68 Pub. Admin. Rev. 413, 413–19 (2008).

[4] Light puts the federal workforce at risk due to impending retirements and the excessive use of private contractors and grantees to manage it. See Light, 68 Pub. Admin. Rev. at 417.

[5] See Jerry Mashaw, Creating the Administrative Constitution: The Lost One Hundred Years of American Administrative Law (2012).

[6] See Donald F. Kettl, Escaping Jurassic Government: How to Recover America's Lost Commitment to Competence 56–57 (2016) (hereinafter Jurassic) (Kettl notes that performance problems are piling up "as competent professionals are overwhelmed by complicated tasks").

from professional managers to surrogates and subordinates whose connections to the sovereign can be attenuated or even conflicted.

## A. THE IMPACT OF THE ELECTION

The manuscript for this book was submitted in October 2016, before the election. Thus, I completed the bulk of the work behind a veil of political ignorance. My thought is that what is said here is good for both parties; for the goose and the gander. Now the veil has been lifted and the gander won. Many more surprises are undoubtedly in the offing.

A Clinton presidency would have provided a predictable relationship to the bureaucracy from someone with long service in the executive and legislative branches. A Trump presidency is unpredictable and many federal bureaucrats are nervous.[7] But he also seems willing to reconsider rash statements, which may be necessary if professional government is to be strengthened. However, policy expertise, what professionals embody, may be something that Trump's appointees do not value.[8]

Early indications on this score are mixed at best. On the one hand, he has nominated several former military officials to key positions.[9] Whatever their policy views, these career officers are the product of one of our most successful bureaucratic enterprises. They are inclined to respect service, civilian or military, and appreciate the value of professionalism. They may help the President better appreciate what Peter Wehner calls the "craft of governing,"[10] which has increasingly become undervalued. If Trump listens to these voices and adapts to the spirit of the "professional amateur" that George Plimpton imbued[11] then maybe he will respect and benefit from the career professionals in government.

7 See Jessica Schulberg, *The Last Line Of Defense: Federal Bureaucrats Wait Nervously For Donald Trump*, Huffington Post (Dec. 6, 2016), www.huffingtonpost.com/entry/federal-bureaucrats-trump_us_5846d516e4b02f60b024d483 (federal employees view Trump's "unpredictability" as a challenge to agency policies).

8 See Neil Irwin, *Donald Trump Is Betting That Policy Expertise Doesn't Matter*, N.Y. Times (Dec. 1, 2016), www.nytimes.com/2016/12/01/upshot/donald-trump-is-betting-that-policy-expertise-doesnt-matter.html (recurring theme of Cabinet appointments is each of policy or political experience).

9 James Mattis for Secretary of Defense and John Kelly for Secretary of Homeland Security are notable nominees.

10 Peter Wehner, *In Defense of Politics, Now More Than Ever*, N.Y. Times Op-Ed (Oct. 29, 2016), www.nytimes.com/2016/10/30/opinion/campaign-stops/in-defense-of-politics-now-more-than-ever.html?_r=0 ("Our low regard for politics is leading us to undervalue the craft of governing . . . ").

11 See Liam Smith, *Plimpton! The Professional Amateur*, Huffington Post Blog (Aug. 18, 2016), www.huffingtonpost.com/liam-smith/george-plimpton-documentary_b_5682745.html.

On the other hand, Trump's nominee to the Environmental Protection Agency (EPA), Scott Pruitt, appears not to believe in the missions of the agency he is proposed to head. Additionally, his pick to lead the Office of Management and Budget (OMB), Rep. Mick Mulvaney, has been a prominent leader in House Freedom Caucus efforts to shut down the government over Planned Parenthood and the Affordable Care Act, and an advocate of cutting the federal workforce and privatization.[12] This puts the career employees in difficult territory. A president is entitled to latitude in selecting his team, but they act for the President and must demonstrate a clear commitment to the fundamental mission of the agency they seek to lead.[13] That is the lesson of the "Take Care" clause of Article II of the Constitution.

Another troubling development involves inquiries from Trump's transition team at the Department of Energy (DOE) about the names of career employees and contractors who participated in climate change initiatives and activities.[14] This action led Senator Edward Markey to write Mr. Trump that "civil servants should never be punished for having executed policies with which the new administration disagrees."[15] This lesson may be a good one for Trump to receive even though it may have been the result of his overzealous DOE transition officials.

An interesting side note to the transition involves the suggestion that a Commission be established (similar to the Hoover Commission during the Truman Administration) to "modernize and shrink the federal government."[16]

[12] See Katherine McIntire Peters, *Trump's Pick to Lead OMB Supports Privatizing Some Federal Operations, Cutting Workforce*, Government Executive (Dec. 17, 2016). www.govexec.com/management/2016/12/trumps-pick-lead-omb-supports-privatizing-some-federal-operations-cutting-workforce/133995/.

[13] See Cass R. Sunstein, *There's One Main Job Requirement to Lead a Federal Agency*, Bloomberg View (Dec. 9, 2016), https://www.bloomberg.com/view/articles/2016-12-09/there-s-one-main-job-requirement-to-lead-a-federal-agency; see also Jane Mayer, *Scott Pruitt, Trump's Industry Pick for the EPA*, The New Yorker (Dec. 7, 2016), www.newyorker.com/news/news-desk/scott-pruitt-trumps-industry-pick-for-the-e-p-a (Trump has outsourced environmental policy to GOP donors).

[14] Steven Mufson & Juliet Eilperin, *Trump Transition Team for Energy Department Seeks Names of Employees Involved in Climate Meetings*, Wash. Post (Dec. 9, 2016), https://www.washingtonpost.com/news/energy-environment/wp/2016/12/09/trump-transition-team-for-energy-department-seeks-names-of-employees-involved-in-climate-meetings/.

[15] Letter from Sen. Edward J. Markey to Donald Trump, Dec. 9, 2016.

[16] The *Wall Street Journal* proposed the idea. Some have suggested that Newt Gingrich should lead it. See Tom Shoop, *A Gingrich Commission to Reorganize Government?*, GovExec Blog (Dec. 2, 2016), www.govexec.com/federal-news/fedblog/2016/12/gingrich-commission-reorganize-government/133605/.

If Mr. Trump finds it appealing, this could be a timely undertaking. Civil service reform, which this book advocates, has a better chance of success in a bipartisan and Commission-like setting, where workable reforms can be debated and proposed. If this Commission, or Mr. Trump and his advisors directly, were to look closely at the management problems brought about by the unchecked use of contractors, government might be modernized and shrunken under the Trump Administration. Not a bad legacy.

It is surely too early to chart the direction of the next administration. But there are some troubling signs, and even fears of a "kakistocracy" have been expressed.[17] It may be that Trump's early appointments, like those of Ronald Reagan before him (e.g. Anne Gorsuch at EPA and James Watt at Interior), will not fairly express his governing course. At all events, the need for a robust career service has never been greater.

## B. WHY THE TOPIC OF CONTRACTING CONTINUES TO EXPAND

*Outsourcing Sovereignty*[18] was written ten years ago, but since then its subject has grown and spread – metastasized really – throughout government. Chapter 2 brings the reader up to date on the many academic and legal developments that have occurred over the last decade. It shows the connection between professional government and constitutional government that is essential to the arguments presented here. Chapter 2 also describes the field of contractor studies in law and economics that has burgeoned during the last decade. The focus of *Outsourcing Sovereignty* was largely upon the use of private military contractors during the Iraq War. But the fate of Blackwater and similar entities (which will be updated) now becomes the starting point for a broader inquiry. To understand the rise of the private military, the relationship of contractors to government had to be addressed in legal and constitutional, as well as operational, terms. As use of contractors has grown, problems are created for government at all levels. Professionals charged with running the government are finding their numbers static or even shrinking as the number of contractors and other surrogates grows apace. Government has long been run by career officials, but the centrality of their role increasingly hangs in the

[17] See Ryan Lizza, *Donald Trump's First, Alarming Week as a President Elect*, THE NEW YORKER (Nov. 16, 2016), www.newyorker.com/news/daily-comment/donald-trumps-first-alarming-week-as-president-elect (calling Trump's proposed appointees a "Kakistocracy" – government by the least qualified).

[18] See PAUL R. VERKUIL, OUTSOURCING SOVEREIGNTY: WHY PRIVATIZATION OF GOVERNMENT FUNCTIONS THREATENS DEMOCRACY AND WHAT WE CAN DO ABOUT IT (2007).

balance and professionalism is an oddly endangered concept in the current environment.

### C. THE HUMAN INFRASTRUCTURE ANALOGY

The case for professionalism is really about rebuilding infrastructure, something President Trump understands. Infrastructure has, however, human as well as physical dimensions. The physical side is well known. The deterioration of bridges, roads, water systems, and other facilities has reached crisis levels due to a lack of capital investment.[19] There seems to be an increasing consensus politically that infrastructure must be invested in and upgraded.[20] But infrastructure also consists of human capital: the investment in those whose careers are devoted to running government. In fact we cannot fix one without the assistance of the other; indeed, in some cases, the physical and human needs are identical.[21]

These thoughts crystallized during my many commutes between New York and Washington, DC. One involves the need to replace two Hudson rail tunnels that are almost a century old, a project that has been planned for over 40 years.[22] What has held the project up is not a comedy, but a tragedy, of errors. The problem was almost solved in 2010, when it was presented to Governor Chris Christie by a bipartisan group of New Jersey political leaders who had secured federal funding. But Christie balked, pulling New Jersey's contribution and shifting the state's share to gas tax reductions. The federal match transferred many billions to projects in other states instead. For New Jersey, the physical infrastructure needs remain unaddressed because political

[19] See American Society of Civil Engineers, The American Infrastructure Report Card 2013 (2013), www.infrastructurereportcard.org/executive-summary/; Ray LaHood, *Why are We Letting our Infrastructure Fall to Pieces?*, Governing (Apr. 11, 2016) (noting that $1 billion is needed to repair the DC Metro, and the gross domestic product will suffer $3.1 trillion in losses if we fail to repair infrastructure by 2020).

[20] See Conor Dougherty, *Coming Soon, Economists Hope: Big Spending on Roads, Bridges and Ports*, N.Y. Times (Sept. 18, 2016), http://www.nytimes.com/2016/09/19/business/economy/coming-soon-economists-hope-big-spending-on-roads-bridges-and-ports.html (noting that infrastructure funds would lift the economy no matter where they are spent because the needs are nationwide).

[21] The relationship between human and physical infrastructure can be seen in the problem government has with replacing and updating its technology systems. As Chapter 8 shows, replacing outdated computer systems is essential if the government, through its officials, is going to perform effectively.

[22] See Jim Dwyer, *Less Talk, More Action on Hudson Rail Tunnels, Before It's Too Late*, N.Y. Times (May 17, 2016), http://www.nytimes.com/2016/05/18/nyregion/long-delayed-hudson-rail-tunnels-delayed-delayed-and-delayed-again.html.

officials, very likely over the objections of professionals in state government, permitted expediency to trump long-term planning. The tunnel planning process has now been restarted as some 20 different agencies struggle to move through the endless permit process (and without the federal funds yet appropriated). It is difficult to overstate the devastation to the local, regional, and national economy if one of the old tunnels goes out, as it did temporarily in the aftermath of Hurricane Sandy.[23]

The other infrastructure crisis involves the DC Metro system, which connects to Amtrak at Union Station. Proudly inaugurated 50 years ago by President Johnson, deferred maintenance on the Metro has brought it to the edge of disaster.[24] Current plans to restore it to full service will require billions of dollars and entail single-tracking and shutting down whole lines for months at a time. The Metro system carries millions of passengers every day, many of whom are federal workers. To adjust, the government must maximize the use of workplace flexibilities (e.g. teleworking) and Congress has even suggested that federal employees be able to use their transit benefits for ride-sharing programs like Uber and Lyft.[25] It is difficult to understand how government could have reached the point where the Metro system has become a dangerous operation. Certainly, the private sector or most state-regulated public utilities understand the need to plan ahead. Deferred maintenance is a cost that must be accounted for in the budget or rate base. The Metro situation connects the need to rebuild physical infrastructure with the need to overcome deficiencies in human infrastructure. Since most federal employees ride the Metro, their efficiency is reduced whether by delays or alternative work arrangements, making government less effective for a considerable time. This is an outcome that only a public sector cynic could applaud.

How did we get in this predicament? I thought about this while flying by helicopter over the Hoover Dam on the way to the Grand Canyon last summer (and shot the picture below). America built the Hoover Dam, one of the great

[23] See generally Sarah Kaufman, Carson Qing, Nolan Levenson & Melinda Hanson, Rudin Center for Transportation, NYU Wagner Graduate School of Public Service, Transportation During and After Hurricane Sandy (2012), https://wagner.nyu.edu/files/rudincenter/sandytransportation.pdf (explaining a timeline of transportation infrastructure impacts felt in the region as a result of the storm).

[24] See James Surowiecki, *System Overload*, The New Yorker (Apr. 18, 2016), www.newyorker.com/magazine/2016/04/18/inside-americas-infrastructure-problem.

[25] See H.R. 6008, 114th Cong., 2d Sess., Transit Benefits Modernization Act § 3(a) permitting federal transit benefits to be used for alternative transportation to Metro while it is under reconstruction. Forty percent of Metro's 2.3 million annual peak load passengers are federal employees.

The Hoover Dam, author photograph.

wonders of the world. There was no political divide on making this investment. It was conceived and completed under a Republican president, Herbert Hoover, in 1931, before the New Deal began. And it was constructed by a consortium of government contractors, led by the Bechtel Group.[26] Where are the comparable figures to Hoover and FDR who could rebuild this country again? And when we find them, as we must, energetic government professionals will be needed to manage the process. Infrastructure can't be fixed just by passing laws and appropriating moneys, necessary as those acts of Congress are. To manage the process effectively, we have to invest in human resources as well. Bureaucratic human capital is needed for several reasons. First, infrastructure investment requires contracting with firms in the private sector to do the work. This process calls for professional officials at all levels of government. Without them, billions will be lost on fraud, waste, and abuse in government contracting, and projects will be unnecessarily delayed. The value of competence in government, therefore, is measurable and demonstrable. But the second reason we need to invest in bureaucratic human

[26] See SALLY DENTON, THE PROFITEERS: BECHTEL AND THE MEN WHO BUILT THE WORLD (2016) (hereinafter PROFITEERS).

capital is that, more broadly, everything government does should be done well. QED.

## D. THIS IS PERSONAL

In *Outsourcing Sovereignty*, the research design was largely created through case and statutory analysis of legal norms and dictates, internet and library searches – usual tools of administrative law and regulation scholarship. But this time around, that academic perspective has been supplemented with an observer dimension. For five and a half years I served as a federal agency head – the Chairman of the Administrative Conference of the United States (ACUS) – a perch from which to view government from the inside. ACUS was restarted (having been defunded for 15 years) when I was confirmed by the Senate in April 2010.[27] "Standing up" an agency is an experience that makes one realize how complicated and often frustrating government work can be.[28] ACUS is an agency notably concerned with legal questions, especially those emanating from the Administrative Procedure Act (APA). But the revived Conference also looked at public management issues like ethical rules about government contracting, efficiency standards set by the Government Results and Performance Modernization Act, and how to do retrospective rulemaking. ACUS recommendations on these subjects are discussed in later chapters.

President Obama called ACUS a "public–private partnership designed to make government work better," because our 101 members include officials representing many agencies and private citizens (public members) who brought enormous experience, having served in every administration since Lyndon Johnson was President.[29] So we were able to leverage the private sector experience as well as the public sector. An ideal mix. This remarkable collection of astute government officials and alumni taught me a lot about government professionalism. In addition, I was granted access to numerous agency officials, White House staff, and congressional leaders who taught me some of the techniques and realities of administration that often do not get discussed publicly. It was these professionals, exhibiting the energy Alexander Hamilton

[27] See *Verkuil Confirmed As Head Of Administrative Conference*, THE FLAT HAT (Mar. 23, 2010), http://flathatnews.com/2010/03/23/73111/.

[28] See Paul R. Verkuil, *ACUS 2.0: Present at the Recreation*, 83 GEO. WASH. L. REV. 1133 (2015); see also Paul R. Verkuil, *What the Return of the Administrative Conference of the United States Means for Administrative Law*, 1 MICH. J. ENVTL. & ADMIN. L. 17 (2012).

[29] This is appropriate since it was President Johnson who signed the Administrative Conference Act in 1964. Pub. L. No. 88–499, 5 U.S.C. §§ 591–96.

required for good government to happen, who made me understand the need to write this book once I left government.

## E. THE ADMINISTRATIVE LAW AND POLICY DIVIDE

Administrative law is a venerable field of study,[30] but it is too limited a frame from which to view the practice of government. Of more salience are fields like public policy and public administration, management disciplines with different starting points.[31] Public policy relies heavily on economics and related disciplines (with law as one) to critique administration. Public administration, while less theoretical, better focuses on how administrators act. Obviously, these disciplines are connected. As Richard Keevey notes, "administration breathes life into policy."[32] This experience has made me appreciate both public policy (grounded in cost–benefit analysis) and public administration (grounded in management).[33] One of public administration's founders was Louis Brownlow,[34] one of the great figures of the New Deal. The famous Brownlow Report submitted to President Roosevelt[35] is often referred to by administrative lawyers today. At that time, the big players in government management at all levels grew out of the public administration field and they even questioned the role of lawyers in public management.[36] But the lawyers are hard to contain; they came and multiplied. During the New Deal, top university law school graduates were eager to work in Washington. Brought to Washington by mentors like Felix Frankfurter and Jerome Frank, they populated agencies like the Agricultural Adjustment Administration and the National Labor Relations Board and litigated major cases.[37]

30 See RICHARD J. PIERCE, JR., SIDNEY A. SHAPIRO, & PAUL R. VERKUIL, ADMINISTRATIVE LAW AND PROCESS (6th ed. 2014).

31 Of course, sometimes lawyers do broader work in public administration as well. See Eloise Pasachoff, *The President's Budget as a Source of Agency Policy Control*, 125 YALE L. J. 2182 (2016) (describing how OMB's budgeting functions manage regulatory agencies).

32 Richard F. Keevey, *Public Policy vs. Public Administration: Different in Character, Both Critical for Success*, PA MAGAZINE (Winter 2015–16) at 2.

33 Serving as a Senior Fellow at the National Academy of Public Administration (NAPA) has allowed me to continue working on subjects like civil service reform that are central themes of this book.

34 LOUIS K. BROWNLOW, A PASSION FOR ANONYMITY: THE AUTOBIOGRAPHY OF LOUIS BROWNLOW (1959).

35 PRESIDENT'S COMM. ON ADMIN. MGMT., REPORT WITH SPECIAL STUDIES 37 (1937) (known as the Brownlow Report).

36 See Fritz Morstein Marx, *The Lawyer's Role in Public Administration*, 55 YALE L. J. 498 (1946) (a public administration scholar queries how well lawyers are able to run federal agencies).

37 See PETER H. IRONS, THE NEW DEAL LAWYERS (1982) (documenting the accomplishments of young government lawyers).

The New Deal regulatory enthusiasm that motivated the field of public administration waned during the Eisenhower years of the 1950s[38] but was reignited with John Kennedy's famous inaugural address to his fellow Americans: "ask not what your country can do for you – ask what you can do for your country." These words renewed public service commitments to government and led to initiatives like the Peace Corps. They also triggered a gift to Princeton University that provides a relevant metaphor for the present divide between the goals of public administration and public policy. In 1961, Charles Robertson (a Princeton graduate) and his wife Marie, inspired by Kennedy's words, made a $35 million gift to Princeton's Woodrow Wilson School for Public Policy and International Affairs for the purpose of sending young graduates into the Foreign Service and other government agencies.[39] Over the decades, the endowment grew to over $850 million, but the cause it was to support – sending top graduates into government – waned. Much of the money was used to fund an outstanding economics department with theoretical brilliance but little interest in government service.[40]

The inability of Princeton's Woodrow Wilson School to produce graduates who go into the public sector is mirrored in other top public policy programs like Harvard's Kennedy School where the majority of students go into the private sector.[41] Ironically, as Bill Moyers has noted,[42] the training received at public policy schools often lands graduates with jobs at consulting firms, who contract their services to government agencies, rather than having government hire them directly. To reverse this relationship has been the goal of the Volcker Alliance (led by Tom Ross) and Paul Volcker himself, who serves as the ultimate model of a government professional.

38 President Eisenhower was, however, a deft political manager, often behind the scenes. See Fred I. Greenstein, The Hidden-Hand Presidency: Eisenhower as Leader (1982).

39 See Douglas White, Abusing Donor Intent: The Robertson Family's Epic Lawsuit against Princeton University (2014).

40 The Robertson lawsuit was settled with Princeton paying the $90 million in legal fees for both sides and establishing a $50 million Robertson Foundation for Government that is independent of the university and will help prepare students for government service. *Id.*

41 The difficulty of sending talented graduates trained in public policy to government is a concern of this book. In order to fix it, both the schools and government need to provide better connections to the public sector. See Richard Brand, *Graduates; Saying No to Public Service*, N.Y. Times (Jan. 7, 2001), www.nytimes.com/2001/01/07/education/graduates-saying-no-to-public-service.html; James Pierson & Naomi Schaefer Riley, *The Problem with Public Policy Schools*, Wash. Post (Dec. 6, 2013), www.rockinst.org/newsroom/news_stories/2013/2013-12-06-Washington_Post.pdf.

42 See Zaid Jilani, *The Privatization of Public Service*, BillMoyers.com (Nov. 21, 2013), http://billmoyers.com/2013/11/21/the-privatization-of-public-service (noting that Syracuse's Maxwell School sends graduates to Deloitte Consulting).

All of this suggests that there are many obstacles to getting the same degree of talent to serve in government that was possible in the past. The private sector scoops up bright young lawyers and pays them well. Investment banking houses pay even better than law firms. But, while the New Deal talent flow is not likely to return, there are still attractions to government service. Paul Volcker, who has long fought for better talent in government, continues to press public policy schools, including his own Woodrow Wilson School, to do a better job. And my experience suggests that graduates from law, public policy and public administration schools are still eager to get into government. They can even be dislodged from law firms and are willing to take lower salaries (once their loans are paid off). The demand for public service can be tapped effectively, as it was at my agency, but more effort is required. Working for consulting firms is not the answer.

## F. THE NEW FOURTH BRANCH?

As noted in *Outsourcing Sovereignty*, contractors have been labeled the "Fourth Branch of Government."[43] For administrative lawyers, that phrase is confusing. It originally derived from Louis Brownlow's report to FDR, which applied the term to independent agencies the President was trying to rein in.[44] That it now refers not to government agencies insulated from Presidential control, but to those outside government hired to serve agencies, is quite ironic. It takes the mythical Fourth Branch idea to a whole new dimension. How is it now possible to declare those employed to serve a branch of government as a branch of government themselves? A rhetorical question, perhaps, but one that needs careful consideration.

Contractors have become forceful players at all levels of government. And this is true not just at the federal level. State and local governments, where the bulk of government officials work, are increasingly turning to contractors to perform, and even oversee, critical public services.[45] Chapter 5 shows the

43 See Scott Shane & Ron Nixon, *U.S. Contractors Becoming a Fourth Branch of Government* (Feb. 4, 2007), available at www.nytimes.com/2007/02/04/world/americas/04iht-web.0204contract.4460796.html.

44 President's Comm. On Admin. Mgmt., Report With Special Studies 37 (1937). The "fourth branch" has become a standard way of describing the bureaucracy, not just the independent agencies, in textbooks as well as in judicial opinions. See, e.g., J. Rohr, To Run a Constitution 153 & n.77 (1986); *Process Gas Producers Group* v. *Consumer Energy Council of Am.*, 463 U.S. 1216, 1218–19 (1973) (White, J., dissenting).

45 See *Standing Guard: How Unaccountable Contracting Fails Governments and Taxpayers, Report by In The Public Interest* (2014). The report concludes: "Do Not Outsource Contract Oversight." *Id.*, at 17.

problem of quality government in the states is driven by both contractor and professionalism issues. Many states have seen a drop in experienced agency personnel due to two factors. The first is that the loss of experienced workers is accelerating due to baby boomer retirements.[46] The second is the rise of the "at will" public employment movement that makes experienced state workers vulnerable to replacement when administrations change. Chapter 4 discusses competence and professionalism issues that must be corrected for states to operate programs effectively. The temptation to use contractors is highest when there is a lack of confidence in the professionals running government. Sometimes this is seen in the use of outside overseers to replace appointed or elected officials (this is in effect a variation on the contractor theme) in cities like Flint or Detroit. Much like the federal government, states have moved away from career officials in management positions and undermined professionalism in government.

Ultimately, the power of contractors to assist in achieving government ends, either well or poorly, derives from broad skepticism about government capacity and the notion that government is "broken." This has profound consequences for energetic and professional government. Francis Fukuyama warns that "the belief that government is unfixable will draw us into an equilibrium where poor quality government becomes a self-fulfilling prophesy."[47] When professionalism is not seen as an essential condition for well executed government, the ability to control contractors is lost. The problem is not using contractors to assist government officials; the contractor "problem" comes into play when they displace, or act without adequate oversight from, government professionals – in effect, when they become a branch of their own.

### *The Connection between Contractors and Civil Service Reform*

At the federal level, the role of contractors has grown with minimal recognition or resistance. One task this book assumes is to understand why that should be. There are several likely reasons, political influence among them, but one is particularly uncomfortable: perhaps government officials believe contractors are the lesser of two evils, the first evil being the civil service itself. In my experience, the level of frustration among agency heads over the inability to hire or fire civil servants is almost palpable. On the hiring side, the civil service

46 See Mike Maciag, *The 'Silver Tsunami' Has Arrived in Government*, GOVERNING MAGAZINE (May 31, 2016), www.governing.com/topics/mgmt/gov-government-retirement-survey-center-state-local.html.

47 Francis Fukuyama, *Governance: What Do We Know, and How Do We Know It?*, 19 ANNUAL REV. POLIT. SCI. 6–1, 6–12 (2014).

system puts obstacles in the way of efficient employment. On the firing side, the obstacles discourage effective management. Just consider the congressional testimony of Jonathan Jarvis, Director of the National Park Service (NPS), responding to his agency's Inspector General's report on sexual harassment by employees in the Grand Canyon region. He begged Congress for more firing authority,[48] in the course of testimony that led some members to call for his resignation.[49] Civil service reform is discussed in Chapter 8. If it is correct that there is a connection between the use of contractors and the weakness of the civil service system then the latter must be fixed before the former can be effectively controlled. Until then we will see the federal government using contractors in circumstances that are head-scratchers.[50]

Put yourself in the shoes of a newly confirmed agency head. You come into government with a limited time horizon after a lengthy confirmation process.[51] You have a high-achieving background and want to make a difference. Each day in office counts and you soon realize that the rest of government does not move at the pace you set. You want to hire and appoint assistants who share your desire to achieve, but bringing them on is no easy matter. The time necessary to hire staff is complicated by Office of Personnel Management (OPM) regulations and protocols; the security clearance process alone can take about a year. So you face something of a Hobson's choice: pursue new government employees, whom you have difficulty hiring, or engage contractors who are readily available (and come with security clearances). Not only is hiring easier, but firing is also, since contractors are replaceable if they don't

48 See Eric Katz, *NPS Chief Asks for More Firing Authority as Lawmakers Deride Agency for Employing 'Scum'*, Government Executive (June 14, 2016), www.govexec.com/oversight/2016/06/nps-chief-asks-more-firing-authority-lawmakers-deride-agency-employing-scum/129074/.

49 The Interior Secretary, Sally Jewel, emphasized the importance of agency leadership to combat sexual harassment, but did not endorse Jarvis' call for more firing authority. See Lisa Rein, *Jewell: Park Service Must Examine Its 'Culture' After Harassment Claims*, Washington Post, Jul. 13, 2016, at A17.

50 One example is the recent decision of GSA to outsource its human resources (HR) systems services to IBM. GSA provides HR services for a fee to 40 smaller agencies (ACUS is one) and recovers fees for services. But rather than turning its business line over to other federal agencies (like USDA) who do similar work, it chose to outsource to IBM. I'm sure small agency heads are wondering in which direction the charges will go now. See Jason Miller, *What Message Does GSA's Decision to Outsource Its HR Systems Send to Rest of Government?*, Federal News Radio (Dec. 5, 2016), http://federalnewsradio.com/reporters-notebook/2016/12/message-gsas-decision-outsource-hr-systems-send-rest-government/.

51 Matthew Dull & Patrick S. Roberts, *Continuity, Competence, and the Succession of Senate-Confirmed Agency Appointees, 1989–2009*, 39 Presidential Studies Quarterly 436 (2009) (finding a median tenure of 2.5 years for appointees who served under President George H. W. Bush or President Clinton)

work out. When this choice is available, the cost implications are minimized and you move forward. There are even contractor "body shops" that let you name the qualifications or even the individuals you seek (which is not quite kosher).[52] When I tried this scenario out on savvy government officials (and contractors), I got many knowing nods.

This was not, however, my experience at ACUS. One of the privileges of restarting an agency is that you are able to hire all the employees. By using workarounds and taking advantage of the "excepted" service (more on that later), I was able to bring into government a highly motivated group. Many of them are still at ACUS or working effectively in other agencies. If they could be multiplied throughout government, professionalism would surely be heightened. So the techniques for improving the hiring process short of statutory reform are worth noting. This is what Chapter 8 discusses.

## G. WHEN DID CONTRACTORS BECOME SO ATTRACTIVE?

The use of contractors grew significantly during the Reagan Administration, for policy and political reasons. In many ways, President Reagan came into office looking for a fight with government employees. In his first inaugural address he memorably declared: "government is not the solution to our problem; government is the problem."[53] Suspecting the civil service was full of entrenched Democrats, or at least determined obstructionists, President Reagan sought to limit its influence.[54] "Every once in a while," he said, "somebody has to get the bureaucracy by the neck and shake it loose and say, stop doing what you're doing."[55] He was given a political gift when the air traffic controllers went on strike illegally. By refusing to back down and removing 11,000 controllers,[56] Reagan built public support for his fight against the bureaucracy. He appointed confrontational agency heads (like Anne Gorsuch at EPA) who "acted like an

[52] The term "body shop" generally refers to a government contractor which sells the expertise of highly talented individuals. While there are rules governing the hiring of specific individuals for contracted work, a dedicated and clever agency procurement officer can effectively hire given individuals as contract employees by writing the requirements for a post in such a way that they are carefully tailored to fit an individual's resume. For an example, see Donald L. Barlett & James B. Steele, *Washington's $8 Billion Shadow*, VANITY FAIR (Mar. 2007), www.vanityfair.com/news/2007/03/spyagency200703.

[53] Jan. 20, 1981, available at www.presidency.ucsb.edu/ws/?pid=43130.

[54] See Stephen Barr, *Civil Service Will Remember Reagan as the Anti-Government President*, WASHINGTON POST, June 8, 2004, at B02, www.washingtonpost.com/wp-dyn/articles/A23306-2004Jun7.html.

[55] RONALD REAGAN, SPEAKING MY MIND: SELECTED SPEECHES 392 (1989).

[56] See Joseph A. McCartin, *The Strike That Busted Unions*, N.Y. TIMES (Aug. 2, 2011), www.nytimes.com/2011/08/03/opinion/reagan-vs-patco-the-strike-that-busted-unions.html.

invading army who did not trust their new subjects."[57] While the negative views of bureaucracy he engendered continue to this day, in fact many civil servants during the Reagan years were working effectively and responsibly.[58] And even his appointees mellowed. William Ruckelshaus replaced Anne Gorsuch at EPA and rallied the career civil servants. The Reagan Administration contained iconoclasts who had experience as government contractors and were equipped to challenge complacency and incompetence in the career ranks. For example, George Schultz, who became a four-time Cabinet Secretary, had been President of Bechtel Group.[59] Bechtel is one of the most famous government contractors.[60] As earlier noted, it led the coalition that built the Hoover Dam. Bechtel also sent Cap Weinberger to the Reagan Administration, another business-oriented leader of strong will, who often clashed with Schultz.[61] But they both believed in getting things done, and had academic as well as business credentials to back them up.[62] Schultz claims he didn't care whether his appointees were Republicans or Democrats, so long as they achieved.[63] In this environment, contractors were viewed as problem-solvers who could deliver superior results and shake up a recalcitrant bureaucracy. I tested my thinking on the influence of contractors during the Reagan years in an interview with George Schultz.[64] To my surprise (satisfaction, really), Schultz was in favor of career staff over contractors "so long as they were A players."[65] He worked closely with career officials while preparing the federal budget at the Office of Management and Budget (OMB). As Secretary of State, he favored the use of marines over military contractors at embassies. So while contractors grew during the Reagan presidency, and Bechtel remained a big player,[66] Schultz, for one, agreed that developing a quality civil service

57 See MARISSA M. GOLDEN, WHAT MOTIVATES BUREAUCRATS?: POLITICS AND ADMINISTRATION DURING THE REAGAN YEARS (2000).

58 See *id.*, at 151–59 (contradicting views of bureaucratic intransigence).

59 See PROFITEERS.

60 See Stephen Labaton, *Government by Bechtel*, N.Y. TIMES (May 22, 1988) (reviewing Laton McCartney, *Friends in High Places – The Bechtel Story: The Most Secret Corporation and How It Engineered the World* (1988).

61 See PROFITEERS, at 114–15.

62 Schultz had been Dean of the University of Chicago Business School and is still a Senior Fellow at the Hoover Institution.

63 See GEORGE P. SCHULTZ, ISSUES ON MY MIND (2013) (Schultz appointed highly qualified officials, whether Democrat or Republican, as his deputies at the Department of Labor. He believed that "experience matters").

64 The interview took place at Secretary Schultz's home in San Francisco on Aug. 16, 2016 [hereinafter Schultz Interview].

65 He had more trouble with NSC staff at the White House while at State than with private contractors.

66 The Bechtel family owes its entire fortune to the federal government. See PROFITEERS, at 11.

was "right on the mark." Still, Bechtel and other contractors[67] were expert practitioners of the revolving door process discussed in Chapter 4. And many of them surely viewed themselves as problem-solvers and bureaucracy as the problem to be solved.

Another critical event during the Reagan period was the creation of Americans for Tax Reform (ATR) by Grover Norquist. In fact, Norquist says he established this group at the behest of President Reagan.[68] Today 95 percent of Republicans in Congress have subscribed to Norquist's no new taxes pledge along with numerous governors and state legislators. His famous statement "I just want to shrink [government] down to the size where we can drown it in the bathtub" inspired the anti-bureaucracy movement. The "starve the beast" strategy animates the sequester solution in Congress that freezes discretionary spending and cripples agencies' abilities to manage programs effectively.[69] In this setting, the use of contractors to provide short-term fixes becomes the only way to get government to function, even if they cost more than their civil service counterparts.

But Reagan was not the only recent president to question the bureaucracy. The notion of a bloated government unable to function effectively crossed party lines when the Clinton years began. By declaring "the era of big government is over,"[70] President Clinton struck a further blow against bureaucracy. Equating the size of government with inefficiency, Clinton effectively encouraged the use of private contractors, since government employee full-time employee head counts (or FTEs) became the focus of attention.[71] As a result, the number of government employees, which has been steady since the 1960s at 2 million, went down by 351,000 during the Clinton years, something that had not even

67 Halliburton and its CEO Dick Cheney are also revolving-door experts. See Conor Friedersdorf, *Remembering Why Americans Loathe Dick Cheney*, THE ATLANTIC (Aug. 30, 2011), www.theatlantic.com/politics/archive/2011/08/remembering-why-americans-loathe-dick-cheney/244306/; see also Wil Hylton, *The People v. Richard Cheney*, GQ MAGAZINE (Feb. 13, 2007), http://www.gq.com/story/richard-cheney-vice-president-impeachment.

68 See ABOUT AMERICANS FOR TAX REFORM, www.atr.org/about (last visited Aug. 25, 2016). Ironically, President Reagan "violated" the no new taxes pledge of the ATR.

69 See JURASSIC, at 16.

70 President William Clinton, Address Before a Joint Session of the Congress on the State of the Union (Jan. 23, 1996), available at www.presidency.ucsb.edu/ws/?pid = 53091. This message was reinforced (much to President Clinton's dismay) later in his administration when Newt Gingrich's Contract with America asked "Isn't it time we got Washington off our backs?" See NEWT GINGRICH, CONTRACT WITH AMERICA 125 (1994).

71 The focus on FTEs, rather than budget dollars that support them, is still a prominent cry in Congress. For example, whether employees of the Transportation Security Administration (TSA) should be contractors or government employees led to an extended fight in Congress. See OUTSOURCING SOVEREIGNTY 57–77 (2007).

happened under Reagan.[72] Reducing government head count only added to the demand for contractors, who were called upon to fill the gap, and their numbers grew to untold proportions.[73] John DiIulio calls this "proxy administered government" which Chapter 3 takes up in more detail.

Another point about the Clinton years bears noting. To his credit, President Clinton appointed Vice President Gore to "reinvent government."[74] Seizing on a popular idea that "government should steer, not row,"[75] the reinventing movement sought to reduce the size of government by rethinking how it operates. Much of continuing value was learned from this undertaking,[76] but it again implied the need for contractors, since the "steerers" needed "rowers." In many situations, the rowers were either private contractors or state or local government employees, or both.[77]

## H. WHAT ARE INHERENTLY GOVERNMENTAL FUNCTIONS?

The dichotomy between rowers and steerers is a useful way to view the contractor situation. Rowers can be either contractors or government employees, and in many cases contractors can compete more effectively for these jobs, especially if their responsibilities are carefully defined and subject to competitive bidding. Since rowers do not exercise leadership roles, they are not exercising "inherent government authority" under applicable law.[78] It is the steerers this book worries about.[79] These are the officials that perform inherent government functions, which are defined as activities "so intimately related to the public interest as to mandate performance by government personnel."[80]

[72] See JURASSIC, at 47.

[73] Paul C. Light, *The Real Crisis in Government*, WASHINGTON POST (Jan. 12, 2010), available at www.washingtonpost.com/wp-dyn/content/article/2010/01/11/AR2010011103255.html (Light has estimated government contractors at about 7.5 million).

[74] John M. Kamensky, *Role of the "Reinventing Government" Movement in Federal Management Reform*, 56 PUB. ADMIN. REV. 247 (1996).

[75] See David Osborne & Ted Gaebler, *Reinventing Government: How the Entrepreneurial Spirit is Transforming the Public Sector* 25 (1992).

[76] Reinventing alumni still populate government or important advisory bodies like the National Academy of Public Administration (NAPA).

[77] See John J. DiIulio, Jr., BRING BACK THE BUREAUCRATS: WHY MORE FEDERAL WORKERS WILL LEAD TO BETTER (AND SMALLER!) GOVERNMENT (2014) (hereinafter BUREAUCRATS), at 16–18.

[78] See OMB Circular A-76 discussed *infra*.

[79] I earlier compared steerers to foxes, and rowers to hedgehogs. See OUTSOURCING SOVEREIGNTY at 159–61 discussing the famous Isaiah Berlin polarity: the fox knows many things, the hedgehog one big thing.

[80] *OMB Circular A-76: Performance of Commercial Activities* Attachment A § B.1.a.; OMB, *Work Reserved for Performance by Federal Government Employees*, 75 Fed. Reg. 16,188, 16,190 (Mar. 31, 2010).

This is hardly a self-explanatory category. The OMB Policy Letter describes the contours of inherently governmental in more detail:

> (a) The term includes functions that require either the exercise of discretion in applying Federal Government authority or the making of value judgments in making decisions for the Federal Government, including judgments relating to monetary transactions and entitlements. An inherently governmental function involves, among other things, the interpretation and execution of the laws of the United States so as –
>
> (1) to bind the United States to take or not to take some action by contract, policy, regulation, authorization, order, or otherwise;
> (2) to determine, protect, and advance United States economic, political, territorial, property, or other interests by military or diplomatic action, civil or criminal judicial proceedings, contract management, or otherwise;
> (3) to significantly affect the life, liberty, or property of private persons;
> (4) to commission, appoint, direct, or control officers or employees of the United States; or
> (5) to exert ultimate control over the acquisition, use, or disposition of the property, real or personal, tangible or intangible, of the United States, including the collection, control, or disbursement of appropriations and other Federal funds.
>
> (b) The term does not normally include –
>
> (1) gathering information for or providing advice, opinions, recommendations, or ideas to Federal Government officials; or
> (2) any function that is primarily ministerial and internal in nature (such as building security, mail operations, operation of cafeterias, housekeeping, facilities operations and maintenance, warehouse operations, motor vehicle fleet management operations, or other routine electrical or mechanical services).[81]

The difference between "providing advice, opinions, and recommendations" and exercising judgment and discretion is a conceptual line that is hard to manage or control. In addition, contractors who provide long-term support may be encroaching on "critical functions" that should be reserved to the agency.

[81] Publication of the Office of Federal Procurement Policy (OFPP) Policy Letter 11–01, Performance of Inherently Governmental and Critical Functions, 76 FR 56227–01.

Based on assessments required by the FAIR Act,[82] about one-third of government employees, some 700,000 civil servants, are reported by agencies to be performing inherent or critical government functions. While that category is larger than the number of professional leaders of most concern here, it does set some parameters, one of which is the number of government officials whose work cannot be outsourced. This means there is a wide field where government employees conceivably could have contractor proxies.[83] But many contractors go after jobs that fall into the inherently governmental category. Major government consulting firms like McKinsey and Booz Allen do not provide lower-echelon workers to government. They specialize in high-level managers, especially in the national security field. As a result, government by contractors has created a "multisector" workforce, which is analyzed in Chapter 8.

## I. RADICAL REFORM IN THE STATES: A NEO-SPOILS SYSTEM?

While *Outsourcing Sovereignty* was directed at the federal level, this book also explores comparable problems at the state and local levels here and in Chapter 5. Deprofessionalization of government is a phenomenon at both the federal and state levels, but for different reasons. The challenge at the federal level is to preserve the role of career officials against the growth of contractors, when the civil service itself remains unreformed. The challenge for the states is to preserve a professional workforce in the face of political movements that are radically changing civil service rules and practices. Twenty-eight states have gone to "at will" public employment,[84] a decision which ends tenured employment and frees states to hire and fire more liberally. Led initially by Georgia and Florida, the movement has spread to states like Wisconsin where public

[82] Under the Federal Activities Inventory Reform (FAIR) Act of 1998, Public Law 105–270, agencies are required to identify those who do inherently governmental functions. About 730,000 of government's 2 million employees are so identified.

[83] When George W. Bush was elected he pushed for outsourcing competitions under the Circular A-76 process in order to expand the contractor role in government, while not crossing the inherent government function line. President Obama reversed the Bush Order and that is where things stand today. See *Memorandum for the Heads of Executive Departments and Agencies – Subject: Government Contracting* (2009), www.whitehouse.gov/the-press-office/memorandum-heads-executive-departments-and-agencies-subject-government-contracting.

[84] See Jung In Kim, Civil Service Reform in Six States: Examining Perceptions of State Human Resource Professionals in Colorado, Florida, Georgia, Kansas, Missouri, and South Carolina 9–10 (2010) (dissertation prepared under direction of J. Edward Kellough), available at https://getd.libs.uga.edu/pdfs/kim_jung-in_201008_phd.pdf; see also Steven W. Hays & Jessica E. Sowa, *A Broader Look at the "Accountability" Movement: Some Grim Realities in the State Civil Service Systems*, 26 REV. OF PUB. PERS. ADMIN. 102–17 (2006) (documenting 28 states).

sector unions have been reined in.[85] The consequences of the at will movement have yet to be fully understood. On the one hand, freedom to remove underperforming public employees is desirable (and would be welcome at the federal level as well). On the other hand, the remedy may cut too deep, putting effective as well as ineffective state employees at risk. In several states the loss of knowledgeable professionals has had very negative consequences. This is especially true in the states discussed in Chapter 5. In Wisconsin, the "at will" idea led to a revision of the civil service system that has produced what amounts to a statutory scheme for nonprofessional government.

### *The Wisconsin "Reforms"*

Wisconsin has a strong history of progressivism under Governor Robert La Follette and became the third state to enact civil service reform in 1905.[86] As Chapter 7 discusses, the spoils system was entrenched in state and federal governments. It was Teddy Roosevelt and allies like La Follette who brought the "spoilsmen" down. Now, under Governor Scott Walker, civil service protections that apply to 30,000 public workers have been severely restricted.[87] The statute Walker signed into law replaces merit-based competitive examinations with "competitive procedures," a resume-based system managed by the Division of Personnel Management, an executive agency.[88] The Act also reduces reinstatement and restoration rights for existing employees and lengthens probation periods for those in supervision and management positions from one to two years. It expedites grievance procedures for those subject to removal and gives the governor's administrative office a bonus pool to distribute to effective workers. Not surprisingly, the law has had a negative effect on Wisconsin's public sector unions,[89] long Governor Walker's bête noire. But whether the statute

85 Many of the 28 states are considered "right to work" regimes where union dues may not be checked off, but Wisconsin has a long tradition of public sector unionization. Public sector unions have been attacked for mandatory dues practices (agency shops) that allegedly violate workers' First Amendment rights. See *Friedrichs* v. *California Teachers Association*, 136 S. Ct. 2545 (2016) (*per curiam* 4–4); see also *Abood* v. *Detroit Bd. Of Educ.*, 431 U.S. 209 (1977) (permitting agency shops).

86 See Dan Kaufman, *The Destruction of Progressive Wisconsin*, N.Y. Times Op-Ed (Jan. 16, 2016), www.nytimes.com/2016/01/17/opinion/campaign-stops/the-destruction-of-progressive-wisconsin.html.

87 See Editorial, *Governor Walker Resumes His War on Workers*, N.Y. Times (Feb. 20, 2016), available at www.nytimes.com/2016/02/21/opinion/sunday/gov-walker-resumes-his-war-on-workers.html.

88 Wisc. Assembly Bill 373 §§ 25, 32, 41 (Oct. 7, 2015) [cite to sections].

89 See Monica Davey, *With Fewer Members, a Diminished Political Role for Wisconsin Unions*, N.Y. Times (Feb. 27, 2016), available at www.nytimes.com/2016/02/28/us/with-fewer-members-a-diminished-political-role-for-wisconsin-unions.html.

brings a newly invigorated civil service or retrogressively permits politics to reenter the appointment system remains to be seen. While a true spoils system may not return, the potential to shift substantial numbers of state employees based on politics makes it possible for a "neo-spoils" system to emerge.[90]

Beyond the politics of the Act, what does it do for professional government? By making it easier to replace established employees and managers, it favors newcomers who can be appointed on largely subjective factors (resume, interviews). This can help agency managers who want to select superior candidates expeditiously, but it also opens the way for politics to reenter the appointment process. If it is assumed that experience can be a good thing and that expertise and institutional memory are necessary things, then jettisoning experienced personnel may not be in the state's long-term interests. The other side of "reinvigorating" the civil service by new appointees is the potential "brain drain" of knowledgeable professionals from state government.

Some aspects of the Act are positive: longer probationary periods and shorter removal hearing times are something the federal system could benefit from. But giving Wisconsin's Governor's Office clout in hiring, replacing, and rewarding public workers, creates a power that in the wrong hands could undermine the fair and objective hearing principles of the civil service system. Absent evidence that the spoils system has returned, state radical reform efforts will continue to expand.[91] These efforts undermine the cause of professional government and Walker is vying to bring them to the Trump Administration. The traditional trade-off between lower salaries (at least at the management level) for job security and tenure protections has been broken. Unless salaries rise, which is unlikely to happen except for contractors, the radical-reform states stand to lose valuable experience and institutional knowledge, while gaining some rejuvenation from newcomers. But who is to teach them how to run government?

## J. PROFESSIONAL GOVERNMENT CAN BE INNOVATIVE AND COLLABORATIVE

Alexander Hamilton's phrase about a "government ill executed" is a powerful reminder that from the beginning of our Republic there were those who understood the consequences of bureaucratic ineptitude. We have come a long way since that time to depoliticize and professionalize government. And

[90] See Paul R. Verkuil, *Save the Bureaucrats*, REGBLOG (Sept. 8, 2016), www.regblog.org/2015/09/08/verkuil-save-the-bureaucrats/.

[91] See Stephen E. Condroy & R. Paul Battaglio, *A Return to Spoils? Revisiting Radical Civil Service Reform in the United States*, 67 PUB. ADMIN. REV. 425 (2007) (surveying several "at will" states, Georgia, Florida, and Texas, and finding no clear evidence of political hiring).

more change based on innovative ideas is needed. Certainly on the civil service front, rules and regulations that were once protective have become rigid and even paralyzing. So we have a baby-in-the-bathwater problem. How can we innovate without sacrificing a civil service system that, for all its faults, is the envy of the world?[92] Meritocratic government was our first innovation. Collaborative government may be our next.

### 1 *Public–Private Collaborations*

Given the demands on government and the budgetary restrictions at the federal and state levels, we must be open to new ways of delivering public services that involve the private sector as well. This collaboration does not eliminate the need for professional government, in some ways it requires more of it. Two examples show the opportunities and pitfalls of collaboration. Since the 2008 financial crisis, private equity has taken over much of the ambulance services in America. At a time when local governments are strapped for cash, this has been a welcome infusion of capital. But it is still a public service that must be managed. Private equity is interested in returns on investment and aggressively pursues individuals for payment of ambulance services without full awareness of the consequences.[93] Public ambulance services are more attuned to these vulnerable situations and write off charges where appropriate. Public managers must make these decisions for private services to work properly.

At the federal level, corporate donors have invested in the National Parks which have a $12 billion backlog in maintenance.[94] With 307 million visitors annually, the National Parks Service, which celebrated its 100th anniversary in 2016, is stretched too thin to manage effectively. But do we want Yosemite brought to you by Apple? While "a little commercialism can help,"[95] a lot of

[92] Meritocracy, long the hallmark of the United States civil service system, has gone international. Fifty-five of 62 countries followed by Global Integrity (an NGO) had rules against "nepotism, cronyism, and patronage." See *Mandarin Lessons*, THE ECONOMIST (Mar. 12, 2016), www.economist.com/news/international/21694553-countries-are-trying-harder-recruit-best-bureaucrats-not-hard-enough-mandarin.

[93] See Danielle Ivory, Ben Protess & Kitty Bennett, *When You Dial 911 and Wall Street Answers*, N.Y. TIMES (Jun. 25, 2016), www.nytimes.com/2016/06/26/business/dealbook/when-you-dial-911-and-wall-street-answers.html?_r=0.

[94] See PUBLIC GOODS POST, OUR PROFITIZED NATIONAL PARKS, http://myemail.constantcontact.com/Our-Profitized-National-Parks.html?soid=1123831197794&aid=mgTDOcq4g2w (last visited Aug. 26, 2016) (collecting sources).

[95] Editorial, *A Little Commercialism Can Help National Parks*, BLOOMBERG VIEW (Jun. 7, 2016), https://www.bloomberg.com/view/articles/2016–06–07/a-little-commercialism-can-help-national-parks; see also Toluse Olorunnipa, *Hurting for Cash, U.S. National Parks Turn to Companies*, BLOOMBERG (Jun. 17, 2016), www.bloomberg.com/politics/articles/2016–06–17/hurting-for-cash-u-s-national-park-service-turns-to-companies. As one who walks in

it might offend public sensibilities. These are matters of judgment and degree that professionals need to manage for this exercise in collaborative governance to work effectively.

John Donahue and Richard Zeckhauser, in their recent book *Collaborative Governance*,[96] provide other federal, state, and local examples where smart government involves the private sector to achieve public ends. The authors see collaborative governance as a "force multiplier" to achieve greater public goods. They identify the key ingredient as one of "shared discretion" between the two sectors. Since the exercise of discretion is the hallmark of inherent government functions, government professionals need to do the sharing. The use of social impact bonds is another way to fund government services without adding to the public budget.[97] But, again, to make this form of financing work, the government must define the expectations and returns properly.[98]

## 2 *The Need for Capacity*

Whether it is done collaboratively or not, the capacity of government to provide and deliver public services must be bolstered. Jacob Hacker and Paul Pierson argue in *American Amnesia* that we have forgotten the universal benefits of a robust public infrastructure and that "we need to increase the capacity of government to act."[99] And June Sekena reminds us that the public economy – the producer of public goods – is in crisis.[100] Since government acts through agents, the public goods deficiency needs both human and physical infrastructure investment.

Manhattan's Central Park, I can appreciate the work of the Central Park Conservancy. As a board member of the Statue of Liberty – Ellis Island Foundation, a public–private collaboration, I also understand what a difference private funds can make.

96 See John D. Donahue & Richard J. Zeckhauser, Collaborative Governance: Private Roles for Public Goals in Turbulent Times 4–6 (2011) (discussing delivery of health and education services).

97 See Judith Rodin & Margot Brandenburg, The Power of Impact Investing – Putting Markets at Work for Profit and Global Good (2014) (describing ways governments can encourage social investing).

98 Many consider the City of Chicago's 2008 decision to grant a 75-year lease of parking meters at an upfront payment vastly below its value to be one of failed public management. See Romy Varghese, *Harrisburg's Parking Bond Sale Avoids Chicago Regret*, Bloomberg (Oct. 15, 2013), www.bloomberg.com/news/articles/2013–10–15/harrisburg-s-parking-bond-sale-avoids-chicago-regret.

99 Jacob Hacker & Paul Pierson, American Amnesia – How the War on Government Led Us to Forget What Made America Prosper 343 (2016).

100 See June Sekena, The Public Economy in Crisis: A Call for a New Public Economics (2016). Sekena is chair of the Public Goods Institute.

Increasing government capacity by involving the private sector in a collaborative way also has political advantages. Motivating the private sector to participate in (and profit from) government investment may be one way to counter the nihilistic view of those like Grover Norquist who want to shrink government to the vanishing point. That view is far from our conservative traditions. Remember it was Herbert Hoover who mustered the government capacity to build the Hoover Dam through the work of contractors. Our need to produce infrastructure accomplishments today is less grand by comparison. Fixing bridges, roads, tunnels, and updating technology are manageable investments with a high potential return to the economy. Investment in infrastructure like transportation networks only government can do effectively because of coordination problems that stymie the private sector acting alone.[101] When it comes to human infrastructure – professional government – the investment is much smaller by comparison, but the returns can be equally positive.

What is needed is not more money for government but more government for the money. Shrinking a federal civil service that has been flat for 50 years and replacing it with contractors will neither save money nor create competent government. Investing in the professional workforce creates value on several levels. One is to get better government for the money. Another is to help restore public trust in government, which creates its own value chain.

## K. THE CONNECTION BETWEEN TRUST IN GOVERNMENT AND PROFESSIONALISM

Most surveys show that trust in government is at an all-time low. At the end of 2015, Gallup reported that only 19 percent of Americans expressed trust in government.[102] And Jim Clifton, the CEO of Gallup, stated that "a staggering 75 percent of the American public believe corruption is 'widespread' in the U.S. government, not incompetence, but corruption. This alarming figure has held steady since 2010."[103] So something is surely wrong with how government is perceived, whether what is measured is trust, corruption, or competence.

[101] See Noah Smith, *Don't Lowball the Upside of Fixing Roads and Bridges*, Bloomberg (Aug. 23, 2016), https://www.bloomberg.com/view/articles/2016–08–23/don-t-lowball-the-upside-of-fixing-roads-and-bridges.

[102] See Gallup, *In Depth: Trust in Government*, www.gallup.com/poll/5392/trust-government.aspx (last visited July 6, 2016).

[103] Jim Clifton, *Explaining Trump: Widespread Government Corruption*, Gallup Blog (Jan. 6, 2016), www.gallup.com/opinion/chairman/188000/explaining-trump-widespread-government-corruption.aspx.

But to understand the relationship between professionalism and trust, we must know what aspects of government are of the most concern to the public. Polls look separately at the courts, Congress, and the President; but the bureaucracy, within the Executive branch, doesn't often receive separate scrutiny.[104] It is necessary, therefore, to drill down in the polls to find out how bureaucracy is doing in the public's view.

Clearly corruption and Congress go together. Gallup surveyed for confidence in institutions from 2006 to 2016, and among the 14 institutions Americans lost the most confidence in were banks, organized religion, news media, and Congress, with Congress dead last at a 9 percent confidence level.[105] It is not hard to see why Congress has fallen so far. Consider that 85 percent of Americans call it corruption when financial supporters have more access and influence with members of Congress than average Americans and 90 percent of Americans believe it is corruption when a member does a business or individual a favor because they received financial support.[106] You might call this the Citizens United "dividend."

The Pew Research Center has polled trust in government by analyzing specific government activities and agencies.[107] The following chart shows that the public is remarkably discerning in evaluating agency performance. Thirteen agencies on this list are viewed more favorably than the US Supreme Court (i.e. above 50 percent), including controversial ones like the CIA and EPA. And even the Internal Revenue Service (IRS) and Veterans Affairs (at 42 and 39 percent)[108] rank higher than Congress (at 27 percent). These agencies are among those with whom the public has the most contact. In the case of the Postal Service (USPS), contact is daily, and National Parks receive 307 million visitors annually. In these cases familiarity breeds respect, not contempt.

[104] The Gallup Blog suggested that the high corruption numbers in the last ten years could be attributed to two sources: the US Attorney political firings during the Bush Administration and the IRS political manipulation of the 501(c)(4) organization approvals under Obama. While these were subject to separate surveys, they were not directly part of the corruption survey. Gallup also shows that the US is perilously close to being listed in the top ten most corrupt countries in the world, a status it has never before approached.

[105] See Jim Norman, *Americans' Confidence in Institutions Stays Low*, Gallup Blog (June 13, 2016), www.gallup.com/poll/192581/americans-confidence-institutions-stays-low.aspx.

[106] See Liz Kennedy, *Citizens Actually United: The Bi-Partisan Opposition to Corporate Political Spending and Support for Common Sense Reform*, Demos (Oct. 25, 2012), www.demos.org/publication/citizens-actually-united-bi-partisan-opposition-corporate-political-spending-and-support.

[107] See Pew Research Center, Beyond Distrust: How Americans View Their Government 58 (2015).

[108] VA's favorability plummeted after the problems with its health care services, falling from 68 percent favorable in 2013 to 39 percent in 2015. See *id.*, at 60.

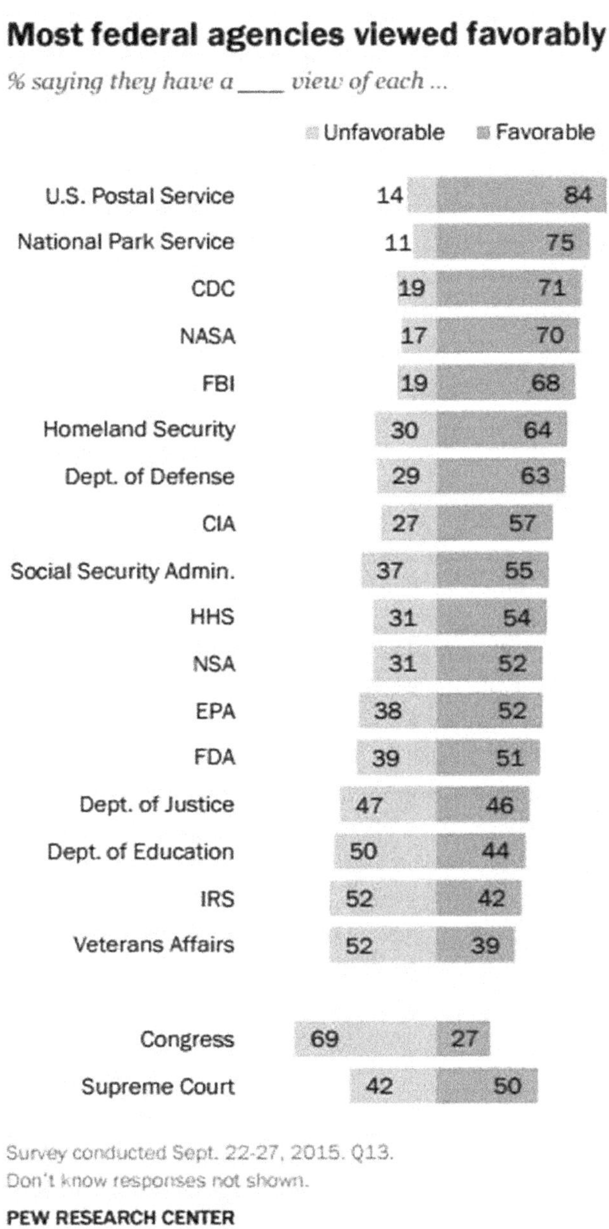


"Ratings of Federal Agencies, Congress and the Supreme Court" Pew Research Center, Washington, DC (November, 2015) www.people-press.org/2015/11/23/4-ratings-of-federa;-agencies-conmgress-and-the-supreme-court/agencies-1/.

So while agency officials are swept up in the public's general lack of trust in government, they are not measured as severely as Congress on Gallup's corruption scale and they do quite well on Pew's favorability scale. As one who has lived among them, it is not hard to see why agency officials are rarely corrupt. The Rules of Ethics require detailed and burdensome financial disclosures, for example.[109] The annual reporting requirements for Presidential Appointed Senate Confirmed (PAS) officials on stock holdings require professional assistance to complete and receive extensive review within and outside the agency. On a much broader scale, contact with lobbyists is less overt in the agency setting (although it exists) and there is no equivalent in rulemaking to drafting proposed legislation for members of Congress, often with contributions expected. Rulemaking is not the Wild West in this regard, although outside contact happens before the Notice of Proposed Rulemaking (NPRM) process begins and the Office of Information and Regulatory Affairs (OIRA) review process invites lobbyists to discuss proposed rules.

At the state level there are much fewer ethical controls of agency officials or politicians. The impact of Governor McDonnell's case,[110] where the Supreme Court defined an "official act" narrowly to exclude meetings and receptions where favors are given (e.g. Rolexes) exposes state politicians to lobbying pressure that may call for stricter laws in the future.[111]

Thus, agency officials are not at high risk of corruption. When it comes to competence, however, it is another story. Lack of adequate staffing at crucial agencies like Social Security and IRS means phone calls go unanswered, regional offices are closed, and response times expand to an unconscionable degree.[112] With retirements accelerating and replacements rationed, we may be facing a government performance shortfall and trust in career officials could plummet. Higher professional performance standards would surely help ensure higher trust in the bureaucracy. But for all its faults, the bureaucracy is unlike Congress, which remains the broken branch.[113]

Because Congress has become gridlocked over partisan bickering which Thomas Mann and Norm Ornstein document (and lament), the executive

[109] See Eric Katz, *New Rule Would Exclude Non-Manager Feds from Financial Disclosure Requirements*, Government Executive (Oct. 6, 2016), www.govexec.com/pay-benefits/2016/10/new-rule-would-exclude-non-manager-feds-financial-disclosure-requirements/132173 (the Office of Government Ethics proposes eliminating requirements on employees who are GS-13 or below).

[110] See *McDonnell* v. *United States*, 579 U.S. __, No. 15-474 (Jun. 27, 2016).

[111] See the discussion in Chapter 2 at notes 77–80.

[112] See the discussion of the million case backlog at the ALJ stage of the Social Security disability process discussed in Chapter 4.B.2.

[113] See Thomas E. Mann and Norman J. Ornstein, The Broken Branch (2014).

branch has stepped into the vacuum. President Obama left the White House as "one of the most prolific authors of major regulations in presidential history."[114] The truth, of course, is that under our system the President is not the "author" of regulations. In fact, it is the bureaucracy that writes and approves regulations under congressional delegations (subject to presidential oversight through the OIRA review process). The executive branch consists of both political and career officials, who engage in professional government. Congress has a big stake in effective bureaucratic performance since its laws are being implemented.

President Trump has issued 20 executive orders in his first ten days, "more than any incoming President in the modern era."[115] And Congress has stood by mutely waiting for more to come.[116] While ahead on ukases, the Trump Administration is behind in appointing sub-Cabinet policy officials to most agencies, who are the professionals expected to run the agencies and carry out his orders. Trump is preparing an executive order to require agencies to plan ways to reorganize government.[117] Reorganization not only requires professionals to implement, it needs legislation to be implemented. As of now, President Trump is out front of Congress and his bureaucratic capacity.

When one factors in his unprecedented ethics problems,[118] it is hard to see how the Trump era can do anything but create new lows in the public's view of government and its beleaguered bureaucracy. This does not have to be the case. Even though the President's chief strategist, Steve Bannon, contemplates the "deconstruction of the administrative state,"[119] the new regime will have to learn to live with it. The bureaucracy does necessary things, and even the Trump Administration will want to do those things well. After all, they own it now.

114 Binyamin Appelbaum & Michael D. Shear, *Once Skeptical of Executive Power, Obama Has Come to Embrace It*, N.Y. TIMES (Aug. 13, 2016), www.nytimes.com/2016/08/14/us/politics/obama-era-legacy-regulation.html.

115 Editorial, USA TODAY, *If Obama was the imperial president, what does that make Trump?* (Feb. 1, 2017). ("Members of Congress need to show more spine . . . ").

116 *Id.*

117 Jason Miller, *White House prepping government reorg executive order*, FEDERAL NEWS RADIO (Feb. 15, 2017).

118 See Alfred R. Hunt, *Trump Ethics: A Job Program for Washington Lawyers*, BLOOMBERG VIEW (Feb. 19, 2017).

119 See Max Fisher, *Bannon's Vision for a "Deconstruction of the Administrative State,"* N.Y. TIMES (Feb 25, 2017, at A13).

# 2

# The New Learning on Outsourcing Sovereignty

*Outsourcing Sovereignty* articulated the legal principles at stake in government's use of private contracting to demonstrate that outsourcing uniquely challenged democratic governance and the sovereignty of the people under the Constitution. By applying various aspects of the Constitution (the Appointments Clause, Take Care Clause, oath requirement, due process, separation of powers and nondelegation), the case was made for "constitutional governance." On the administrative side, statutes like the Sub-Delegation Act and OMB's Circular A-76 were viewed as innovative opportunities to stem the tide of contractor governance. Since then, many superb scholars have analyzed the use of government contractors in terms of the constitutional values at stake. This chapter will discuss developments at the intersection of contractor studies and governance, as well as judicial decisions that sharpen the meaning of public versus private governance, the definition of official behavior, and the role of public ethics. Contractor studies is an established field in economics, as the Nobel Committee recognized in awarding the 2016 memorial prize to Oliver Hart and Bengt Holmstrom for their analysis of contractual arrangements in private and public relationships. Professor Hart was quoted on his work in words that bear on the legal issues central to this book: "A government wouldn't contract with a private company to carry out its foreign policy because it's just too difficult to specify in a contract how to carry out foreign policy. That would be crazy."[1] Welcome, economists, to the world of inherent government functions.

[1] Binyamin Appelbaum, *Oliver Hart and Bengt Holmstrom Win Nobel in Economics for Work on Contracts*, N.Y. Times (Oct. 10, 2016), www.nytimes.com/2016/10/11/business/nobel-economics-oliver-hart-bengt-holmstrom.html.

As a scope note, it is useful to distinguish the broader "privatization" movement from contracting-out of government services. Both developments assume a preference for private sector alternatives.[2] But while contracting out (outsourcing) relates to privatization, the premise between them is different. Outsourcing assumes that the government retains control of certain functions, but performs them through private subordinates. The functions themselves remain public. Privatization is about the functions the market should do without any direct role of government. Sometimes the government and the private sector meet halfway and a collaboration between the sectors occurs,[3] or "public–private partnerships" emerge.[4]

It is entirely consistent to believe that government functions should be privatized, but still believe that government jobs should not be contracted out. We are dealing with different levels of analysis. If Congress wants to privatize certain functions, it makes a substantive decision based on efficiency reasons. Of course, it may not be efficient to privatize public goods (infrastructure) since the private market by definition does not provide them. The remaining government functions could also be managed privately. A professional government can still be a small government and preside over the privatization of many of its functions. In fact, in a privatizing environment, quality government officials are especially needed. They must negotiate effectively with the often high-priced talent in the private sector or be embarrassed by the results.[5] When Margaret Thatcher pushed privatization of government programs in the United Kingdom during the Reagan years, she still needed government officials to manage the process.[6] The career officials in Her Majesty's Civil Service (permanent secretaries) pushed back against her proposals but ultimately carried them out. Thatcher's relationship to her civil servants reflects similar tensions during President Reagan's administration discussed in Chapter 1. One can only imagine the degree of tension that will occur between the career and political camps during the Trump Administration.

[2] See Rubin, *The Possibilities and Limitations of Privatization*, 123 Harv. L. Rev. 890 (2010) (reviewing Government by Contract: Outsourcing and American Democracy (2009); see *infra* note 7).

[3] See Donahue & Zeckhauser, *supra* Chapter 1, at note 96.

[4] See World Bank, What are Public Private Partnerships?, http://ppp.worldbank.org/public-private-partnership/overview/what-are-public-private-partnerships (last visited Aug. 26, 2016).

[5] Consider the City of Chicago officials who basically gave away the parking rights to city streets in a long-term deal at 10 percent of their value, discussed in Chapter 1.

[6] See Charles Moore, Margaret Thatcher: The Authorized Biography ch. 17 – "Cuts" (2015).

## A. A DECADE OF NEW OUTSOURCING SCHOLARSHIP

A watershed event of 2008 was a symposium that brought a multidisciplinary approach to the subject. In a three-day conference at Harvard, scholars gathered to debate and analyze the unprecedented use of private contractors to perform government work.[7] Accelerating since September 11, 2001, this movement affected national security, disaster relief, prison management, environmental monitoring, and many other functions of government. In particular, "where contractors once provided support, they now play a significant role in planning and operational decision making."[8] The consequence is that the "ubiquity of governance-by-private-contractors outstrips our legal and political capacities of oversight. . . ." The conference assessed these developments, which were central to my contribution,[9] as they were for many others.

Two questions at the heart of that conference and this book are the constitutional and democratic limits on government outsourcing and how are they to be enforced. The former question is theoretical, but the latter is quite practical; it asks whether government officials are professional enough to oversee and control the contractor state, thereby fulfilling the role assigned to them in our democracy.

An insightful contribution came from Jack Donahue, who asked whether government workers have been "warped" in the sense that "commodity" tasks (repetitive, delegable ones) have been retained while "custom" tasks, those that require professional employees,[10] have been delegated. The irony, for Donahue, was that the government/private-contractor divide has been stood on its head: routine jobs (e.g. post office functions) continue to be performed internally, whereas complex assignments involving matters of judgment and supervision have been given over to contractors. There are practical explanations for this inversion, public sector unions among them, but when it occurs, i.e. when custom tasks are contracted out, bigger problems arise. For one thing, the inherent government function requirement of Circular A-76 has been undermined, as Matthew Blum explained.[11]

7 Government by Contract: Outsourcing and American Democracy (2009) (Jody Freeman & Martha Minow eds.), hereinafter Government by Contract.

8 *Id.*, at 2. See also Dan Guttman, *Contracting United States Government Work: Organizational and Constitutional Models*, 3 Pub. Org. Rev. 281, 281 (2003).

9 See Paul R. Verkuil, *Outsourcing and the Duty to Govern*, in Government by Contract at 310.

10 John D. Donahue, *The Transformation of Government Work*, in Government by Contract at 42; see also John D. Donahue, The Warping of Government Work (2008).

11 See Matthew Blum, *The Federal Framework for Competing Commercial Work between Public and Private Sectors*, in Government by Contract at 63, 66 (noting that in 2006, in a

Potentially the jobs being outsourced are of those responsible for overseeing other contractors doing commodity tasks. This creates the dilemma of contractors evaluating contractors noted by the editors of the conference, with the consequence that government professionals play a backup role inconsistent with their public responsibilities. When contractors perform contractor evaluation tasks they can produce a double negative – assuming nondelegable assignments and then self-validating the effectiveness of their services.

Nina Mendelson provided important practical ideas about how to improve oversight of contractors in her contribution to the Harvard conference.[12] She focused on subjecting contractors to the kinds of transparency requirements that apply to public employees and providing for review of contracting decisions under the Administrative Procedure Act (APA). There is much to be said for leveling the playing field between contractor and government official obligations, especially in circumstances where contractors perform what amounts to inherent governmental responsibilities. Her work helps ameliorate some of the difficulties with contractor use, and better adjusts us to the inevitability of the "blended" workforce, which is explored in Chapter 8.

What Mendelson's work does not do, of course, is address the demand for government contractors in the first place. This task is assumed by Sharon Dolovich, in the context of private prisons.[13] Her view is that contractors prevail by changing the public–private debate to one dealing exclusively with "comparative efficiency" where the direct costs of prison operations become the exclusive focus of debate, overriding other values such as humanitarian concerns. Dolovich's insights are elaborated in Chapter 4, where the private prison phenomenon is discussed in terms of regulatory capture.

The Harvard conference highlighted several scholars working in the emerging field of outsourcing sovereignty, led by the editors of the volume, Jody Freeman and Martha Minow.[14] No one has broadened the theoretical inquiry more than Gillian Metzger who followed up her article in the Harvard volume[15]

civilian workforce of 1.8 million FTEs, 720,000, or 41 percent, were defined as inherently governmental); see also Chapter 8 dealing with Circular A-76.

12 Nina A. Mendelson, *Six Simple Steps to Increase Contractor Accountability*, in *id.* at 241.

13 Sharon Dolovich, *How Privatization Thinks – The Case of Prisons*, in GOVERNMENT BY CONTRACT at 128.

14 See note 2, *supra*; see also Martha Minow, *Outsourcing Power: How Privatizing Military Efforts Challenges Accountability, Professionalism, and Democracy*, 46 B.C. L. REV. 989 (2006); Jody Freeman, *Extending Public Law Norms through Privatization*, 116 HARV. L. REV. 1285 (2003).

15 Gillian E. Metzger, *Private Delegation, Due Process, and the Duty to Supervise*, in GOVERNMENT BY CONTRACT at 291.

with a deep dive into the government's duty to supervise.[16] Metzger lamented the fact that "constitutional law stands largely aloft from the reality of administrative governance," and showed the central importance of *supervision* to the constitutional scheme. I view supervision as a nondelegable duty under the Constitution[17] and as one way to prevent government from becoming "ill executed," in Hamilton's terms. Ensuring that officials fulfill their duty to supervise deprives contractors of any oversight role. But how is this requirement to be enforced? As Metzger acknowledges, the development of an "active supervision" constitutional norm invites the courts to employ heightened administrative review. This poses challenges of institutional competence and separation of powers that make courts reluctant to act. The question of who supervises the supervisors is one fraught with open-endedness and subjectivity and is why the courts have rendered the nondelegation doctrine largely nonjusticiable since the 1930s.[18]

Thus the "duty to supervise" as an antidote to contractor control of policy comes with some caveats. While the Constitution is central to this debate, it may have to be resolved by a stronger executive role rather than a judicial one. In some respects, this is what the extended debate over the *Chevron*[19] doctrine has been all about. The acceptance by the courts that executive branch agencies should decide issues of regulatory policy is a recognition of the courts' backup role. It is premised on the assumption that in situations where legal/policy issues are interconnected, Congress impliedly delegates decision authority to the agencies, not the courts. Congress has been debating this implied delegation in recent legislative activity that restores active judicial review.[20]

Unrelated to the Harvard Conference, Daniel Ernst's recent *Tocqueville's Nightmare*[21] explores how leading lawyers during the Progressive Era moderated the impact of the New Deal through the courts and created "rule

16 Gillian E. Metzger, *The Constitutional Duty to Supervise*, 124 YALE L. J. 1836 (2015); see Leslie Green, *The Duty to Govern*, 13 J. LEGAL THEORY 165–85 (2007) (discussing the duty to supervise from a legal philosophical perspective).

17 See OUTSOURCING SOVEREIGNTY at 102–04.

18 See Eric Posner & Adrian Vermeule, *Nondelegation: A Post-Mortem*, 70 U. CHI. L. REV. 1331 (2003).

19 See *Chevron U.S.A., Inc.* v. *National Resources Defense Council, Inc.*, 467 U.S. 837 (1984).

20 See H.R. 4768, The Separation of Powers Restoration Act of 2016, 114th Cong. (2015–16), which seeks to "overrule" *Chevron* by requiring under the APA *de novo* judicial review of agency interpretations of rules and statutes. See also Paul R. Verkuil, *Properly Viewed, Chevron Honors the Separation of Powers*, THE HILL (Jun. 23, 2016), http://thehill.com/blogs/congress-blog/judicial/284643-properly-viewed-chevron-honors-the-separation-of-powers.

21 DANIEL R. ERNST, TOCQUEVILLE'S NIGHTMARE: THE ADMINISTRATIVE STATE EMERGES IN AMERICA, 1900–1940 (2014).

by lawyers," which included short-lived techniques like nondelegation. Ernst makes a persuasive case for how lawyers stymied the more radical moves of the New Deal era. Jeremy Kessler's review of Ernst's book creatively connects this historical case to the present and shows us why process can still have a decisive effect over substance.[22]

Jon Michaels' numerous works on outsourcing deserve close attention. Michaels' work began in the national security arena where contractors bear an increasing burden of mission conception and implementation. In *Privatization's Progeny* he has broadened his focus to what he calls the "marketization of bureaucracy" and the use of bounty and prize initiatives in government.[23] In a recent book review,[24] Michaels also considers the results of privatization efforts on the civil service and sets out a central inquiry of this book. Relatedly, Anne O'Connell has made major contributions to the outsourcing debate by looking at agencies that sit at the boundary between public and private institutions.[25] O'Connell's training as a lawyer and political scientist provides her with the tools to classify agency activities and expose the fault line between public and private governance. This work is crucial to the outsourcing debate since "borderline" agencies often have statutory structures that may make them freer and more inclined to use contractors in decisionmaking roles.

Nicholas Parrillo, a legal historian, has produced a path-breaking study of how professional government began and from where it emerged. In *Against the Profit Motive*,[26] Parrillo traces the evolution from officials who received commissions and bounties for their government activities to the modern, salaried civil service. By divorcing pecuniary self-interest from a public official's motivation for service, a shift Parrillo calls "the civic Republican dream of the revolutionary era," the possibility of "trust" in government arose. This shift also helped realize the promise of the civil service originally introduced by the Pendleton Act of 1883[27] and maturing in the next

[22] Jeremy K. Kessler, *The Struggle for Administrative Legitimacy*, 129 Harv. L. Rev. 718 (2016) (book review of *id.*); see also James O. Friedman, Crisis and Legitimacy: The Administrative Process and American Government (1978).

[23] See Jon D. Michaels, *Privatization's Progeny*, 101 Geo. L. J. (2013); see also Anne O'Connell, *Public Agencies Going Private, Jotwell* (June 17, 2013), available at http://adlaw.jotwell.com/public-agencies-going-private/ (reviewing *Privatization's Progeny*).

[24] See Jon Michaels, *Running Government Like a Business . . . Then and Now*, 128 Harv. L. Rev. 1152 (2015).

[25] Anne Joseph O'Connell, *Bureaucracy at the Boundary*, 162 Penn. L. Rev. 841 (2014).

[26] Nicholas Parrillo, Against the Profit Motive: The Salary Revolution in American Government, 1780–1940, at 9, 35 (2013).

[27] Ch. 27, 22 Stat. 403 (1883) (amended 1978).

century.[28] The hard-fought victory for the merit system and professional government over the spoils system will be discussed in Chapter 6.

Ironically, as Jon Michaels has pointed out,[29] the profit motive has now returned to government in the form of private contractors. While contractors work under strict guidelines, Michaels sees "contemporary privatization [as] in part a neoliberal reversion to the presalarization era."[30] In reality, government and contract workers often sit side-by-side doing the same work. One has the benefits of tenure, the other has the benefit of higher salary. The dividing line (or "boundary" in Anne O'Connell's terms) between the two is often hard to discern, which is another theme of this book.

John DiIulio, Don Kettl, and Paul Light, public administration academics who have made fundamental contributions to the outsourcing field, deserve final mention.[31] Their work appears in several of the chapters in this book. It serves to unify and broaden much of the legal scholarship and shows how much the fields of law and public administration relate to each other.[32] They really personify the point made in Chapter 1 that law alone is an inadequate lens through which to view the administrative state.

## B. UPDATE ON PRIVATE MILITARY CONTRACTORS: FROM SECURITY TO TORTURE TO DRONES

*Outsourcing Sovereignty* focused on the use of military contractors in Iraq (principally Blackwater) and the difficulties they posed to constitutional accountability mechanisms. But that became the starting point. Laura Dickinson continues to do extensive work on military contracting,[33] and Allison Stanger has connected outsourcing to the future of American foreign policy.[34] We all

[28] For a good study of how Teddy Roosevelt helped eliminate the spoils system as Civil Service Commissioner, see DORIS KEARNS GOODWIN, THE BULLY PULPIT: THEODORE ROOSEVELT, WILLIAM HOWARD TAFT, AND THE GOLDEN AGE OF JOURNALISM (2013), at 134–57.

[29] Michaels, *supra* note 23. [30] *Id.*, at 1171.

[31] See DiIulio, *supra* Ch. 1, note 77; Kett, Ch. 1, note 6; Paul C. Light, A GOVERNMENT ILL-EXECUTED – THE DECLINE OF THE FEDERAL SERVICE AND HOW TO REVERSE IT (2008).

[32] See, e.g., Paul C. Light, *Back to the Future on Presidential Appointments*, 64 DUKE L. J. 1499 (2015); *Good Government Requires Good People*, REGBLOG (Sept. 8–11, 2015), www.regblog.org/2015/09/08/series-good-government-good-people/ (a series on recruiting and retaining professionals in government featuring submissions by several scholars on professionalism in government).

[33] See Laura A. Dickinson, *Public Values/Private Contract*, in GOVERNMENT BY CONTRACT at 335; see also Laura A. Dickinson, *Regulating the Privatized Security Industry: The Promise of Public/Private Governance*, 63 EMORY L. J. 417 (2013); *Outsourcing Covert Activities*, 5 J. NAT'L SECURITY L. & POL. (2012).

[34] See ALLISON STANGER, ONE NATION UNDER CONTRACT (2009).

build off the work of Peter W. Singer who gave the first systematic look at the military contractor problem.[35]

Any update of the contractor story must include the criminal convictions of the Blackwater employees who were contracted by the State Department for security in Iraq.[36] Undoubtedly, lack of adequate oversight by government officials contributed to the reckless behavior of Blackwater employees that led to the deaths of innocent Iraqis.[37] That many Blackwater employees were former military was itself an embarrassing fact for the government. Their aggressiveness exceeded the contractual requirements their roles contemplated. But they were not alone in this regard. Active military as well as contractors were involved in the torture of Iraqis at Abu Ghraib prison. A compelling account of the torture that took place at Abu Ghraib is provided by Eric Fair, who participated as a contractor. Fair acknowledges his personal responsibility, but notes that he was overseen by a one-star general from behind a two-way mirror.[38]

The biggest revelations on torture came from the Senate's decision to publish in redacted form the CIA's Torture Report.[39] Finding 13 of the Findings and Conclusions section of the Report describes how two contract psychologists devised the CIA's "enhanced interrogation" program:

> the psychologists carried out inherently governmental functions, such as acting as liaison between the CIA and foreign intelligence services, assessing the effectiveness of the interrogation program, and participating in the interrogation of detainees in held in [sic] foreign government custody.

These two contractors (who held academic positions and received $81 million for their efforts) explicitly violated the inherent governmental function test[40] but they were only part of the picture. The CIA report states that contractors made up 85 percent of the CIA's Rendition, Detention, and Interrogation group. It is difficult to read this report and accept how government officials could have let contractors run amok in the way they did.

35 See Peter W. Singer, Corporate Warriors – The Rise of the Privatized Military Industry (2001); see also Peter W. Singer & Allan Friedman, Cybersecurity and Cyberwar 206 (2014) (connecting the private/public roles of cybersecurity).

36 See Matt Apuzzo, *Blackwater Guards Found Guilty in 2007 Iraq Killings*, N.Y. Times (Oct. 22, 2014), available at www.nytimes.com/2014/10/23/us/blackwater-verdict.html.

37 See CNN, *Iraq: 'Blackwater Must Go'* (Oct. 17, 2007), www.cnn.com/2007/WORLD/meast/10/16/iraq.blackwater/index.html?eref=ib_world.

38 See Eric Fair, Consequence: A Memoir (2016).

39 Committee Releases Study of the CIA's Detention and Interrogation Program, www.intelligence.senate.gov/press/committee-releases-study-cias-detention-and-interrogation-program (collecting declassified documents not fitting traditional committee print forms).

40 John Rizzo, former General Counsel of the CIA, in his book Company Man, called them "sadistic and terrifying."

It would be a mistake to conclude that the Blackwater convictions or the CIA torture report have led to a cutback in military contractors. Contractors are very hard to banish from government. The latest use of contractors is by the Air Force as drone pilots.[41] They are told to line up, but not to fire at, targets to avoid performing inherent government functions, but as Laura Dickinson has concluded it is virtually impossible for them not to cross the line, if indeed it is a line at all.[42] The Obama Administration was no more successful in curtailing military contractors than it was in closing Guantanamo Bay.[43] To sort out the respective responsibilities of contractors and military officials in these situations requires a close look at the chain of command in each situation. Clearly the military has a much better accountability mechanism through the Code of Military Justice. The victims of military contractors are left to the civil justice system, which, despite the Blackwater judgments, hardly seems an adequate remedy. The military outsourcing problem and its many manifestations are still being analyzed by the Department of Defense which to its credit brought Laura Dickinson in as an advisor.

Through it all, it seems, private contractors march on whether in military or civilian settings, propelled by market and political forces that are hard to counter. But the scholars discussed here continue to question the limits of military contractors in government and study the negative effects upon the public sector. Ultimately, the problems of military contractors are just one aspect of contractor government this book explores. The contractor/civil servant divide is at the heart of responsible government.

## C. NOTABLE SUPREME COURT CASES ON CONTRACTING, GOVERNANCE, AND PUBLIC ETHICS

*Outsourcing Sovereignty* illuminated ways the Constitution might be applied to outsourcing decisions through nondelegation and separation of powers principles as well as the Take Care, Due Process, Appointments clauses, and the

41 See Paul R. Verkuil, *The Case for Bureaucracy*, Op-Ed, N.Y. Times (Oct. 3, 2016), www.nytimes.com/2016/10/03/opinion/the-case-for-bureaucracy.html.

42 See Laura Dickinson, *Drones and Contractor Mission Creep*, Just Security (Aug. 5, 2016), https://www.justsecurity.org/25223/drones-contractors-mission-creep/; Laura Dickinson, *Drone Contractors: An Oversight and Accountability Gap*, Just Security (Jul. 21, 2015), https://www.justsecurity.org/24795/drone-contractors-oversight-accountability-gap/.

43 See Spencer Ackerman, *Despite Clinton Pledge, State Dept. to Pay out Billions More to Mercs*, Wired (Sept. 29, 2010), https://www.wired.com/2010/09/despite-clinton-pledge-state-department-ready-to-pay-mercs-billions/.

oath requirement under Article VI.[44] At the state level, where federal constitutional questions are more limited, the use of public–private partnerships was explored extensively.[45] Several recent cases update these issues in notable ways. Like the scholarly literature, these cases are helping to define the field of outsourcing studies, even if the judges involved are not always aware of their role in this effort.

The definition of a government agency and how it operates was revisited in *Department of Transportation* v. *Association of American Railroads* (*Amtrak*).[46] The question of whether Amtrak was a government agency under the First Amendment had earlier reached the Court,[47] but the issue here was broader: whether Amtrak was "public" for the purpose of regulating private railroads. Amtrak had the statutory power through "metrics and standards" decisions[48] to modify the scheduling of private freight routes, but were they constitutionally authorized to do so? The DC Circuit reversed a district court decision and held that under nondelegation and separation of powers analysis Amtrak was in effect a private entity that could not be granted or delegated public powers.[49]

The DC Circuit noted Amtrak's private character (i.e. it was supposed to be a for-profit enterprise) and its absence from the statutory list of government agencies[50] and concluded it could not exercise coercive powers over private entities. Remarkably, the circuit court relied on New Deal nondelegation cases like *Carter* v. *Carter Coal Co.*,[51] which forbade delegations under the Bituminous Coal Conservation Act to private companies and unions to set wages. *Carter Coal* is a fascinating precedent highlighted in *Outsourcing Sovereignty*,[52] so its use here is hard not to appreciate. But while several DC Circuit judges have had an affinity for New Deal nondelegation cases in recent years, the Supreme Court is having none of it.[53]

In a functionalist opinion by Justice Kennedy, the Supreme Court dismissed the formalist reasoning of the DC Circuit and restored Amtrak to constitutional status. Citing the political control of the Congress and the executive

44 See Outsourcing Sovereignty 102–20 (2007); see also *id.* at 140–57 (chapter 7 connecting nondelegation cases to contract law).

45 See *id.* at 169–74.

46 135 S. Ct. 1225 (2015).

47 See *Lebron* v. *Nat'l R.R. Passengers Corp.*, 513 U.S. 374 (1995); OS at 97.

48 5 U.S.C. § 207, etc.

49 See 721 F.3d 666 (D.C. Cir. 2014) (vacated and remanded).

50 See 49 U.S.C. §24301(a)(3) (Amtrak "is not a department, agency, or instrumentality of the United States Government").

51 298 U.S. 238, 56 S. Ct. 855, 80 L. Ed. 1160 (1936).

52 See Outsourcing Sovereignty, 105–120.

53 See, e.g., *Whitman* v. *Am. Trucking Assns., Inc.*, 531 U.S. 457 (2001), *reversing* 175 F.3d 1027 & 195 F.3d 4 (D.C. Cir. 2000) (the circuit court had used the nondelegation doctrine to remand an EPA rule).

over Amtrak's stock, its Board (mostly presidentially appointed and Senate confirmed[54]), the fact that Amtrak receives $1 billion in subsidies annually and its supervision by other federal entities, the Court produced a unanimous opinion in favor of government status. The Court's analysis showed how connected Amtrak is to government, unlike the situation in *Carter Coal*, which involved a bald delegation of public authority to private entities. Justice Kennedy emphatically concluded, "Amtrak was created by the Government, is controlled by the Government, and operates in the Government's benefit."[55]

This would be the end of it for separation of powers and nondelegation purposes if not for two remarkable concurrences by Justices Alito and Thomas. Justice Alito, while agreeing with the majority on the issue before the Court, had two other objections to the Amtrak statute that could raise challenges in the future. First, section 207 provides that the Surface Transportation Board may "appoint an arbitrator to assist the parties in resolving their disputes through binding arbitration."[56] While no arbitrator has yet been used in this case, the possibility that an arbitrator, usually a private party in Alito's view, might be appointed itself could violate the nondelegation doctrine.[57] This was the focus of *Carter Coal* which calls it "legislative delegation in its most obnoxious form."[58] While the government had argued that "arbitrator" meant "public" arbitrator, Justice Alito was skeptical as to the ordinary meaning of such a term. But even if he bought that argument, Alito then had problems with the use of a "public" arbitrator under the Appointments Clause.[59] His second point arises from the fact that Amtrak's board members do not take an oath to uphold the Constitution nor receive a commission, two constitutional requirements for all officers of the United States.[60] Justice Alito puts great weight on this requirement: "Both the Oath and Commission Clauses confirm an important point: Those who exercise the power of Government are set apart from ordinary citizens."[61] This sentence shows that the oath requirement is no mere formality, but a significant differentiator of public from private behavior. It also shows that the principle of inherent government functions discussed in Chapter 1 is constitutionally based. So the *Amtrak* case is latent with implicit constitutional challenges that at least two Justices

54 135 S. Ct. at 1231–32. The exception is the CEO of Amtrak; see *infra*.

55 *Id.*, at 1227.

56 122 Stat. 4917.

57 See Alito, concurring op. at 1234 (citing *A. L. A. Schechter Poultry Corp.* v. *United States*, 295 U.S. 495 (1935)).

58 *Id.*, at 1238 citing *Carter Coal*, 298 U.S. at 311.

59 Someone who exercises "significant authority," which presumably binding arbitration is, must be appointed pursuant to Art. II, § 2, cl. 2.

60 See Art. II, § 3, cl. 6.

61 Alito, 135 S. Ct. at 1234.

expect to address in the future.[62] On remand, the DC Circuit concluded that Amtrak could not promulgate "metrics and standards" for the rail industry because of its profit-making motivations and also found an Appointments Clause violation.[63] Justice Alito's concurrence made an important difference and it will be interesting to see how the Supreme Court responds.

A related Supreme Court case involves the validity of decisions by state officials under the antitrust laws. In *North Carolina Board of Dental Examiners* v. *Federal Trade Commission*,[64] the Court held that the Dental Board's decisions were not protected from Sherman Act regulation under the doctrine of state-action antitrust immunity.[65] While the sources of federal jurisdiction are different (the nondelegation doctrine does not apply to the states, but under the Interstate Commerce Clause the Sherman Act does),[66] the impact on state regulation may be the same. The question was whether the decision of the Dental Board to declare teeth whitening by non-dentists an illegal practice was entitled to a federalism exemption from the Sherman Act. The FTC had found the dentist board members' financial interest (six of the eight members are practicing dentists) disqualifying for *Parker* purposes and the Fourth Circuit agreed.[67] Even though the Constitution was not directly implicated, the legitimacy of public officials connects to the Court's findings in the *Amtrak* case. In both cases, the question is who is a public official? The legitimacy of delegations to private parties in *Carter Coal*, raised by the DC Circuit in *Amtrak*, has echoes in cases like *N.C. Dental Board*. Does an official's conflict of interest while serving on a state board disqualify her from rendering a fair and objective decision?

Even if the nondelegation doctrine does not apply, the due process clause of the 14th Amendment surely does. In *Gibson* v. *Berryhill*,[68] the Court held that due process prevents a financially self-interested board of independent

[62] Justice Thomas' lengthy concurrence in the judgment broadly argues for a newly revived nondelegation doctrine. *Ibid*, at 2140.

[63] 821 F.3d 19 (D.C. Cir., 2016); see Aaron Nielson, *D.C. Circuit Review – Reviewed: Is Amtrak "Company A"?*, NOTICE & COMMENT (May 1, 2016), available at www.yalejreg.com/blog/d-c-circuit-review-reviewed-is-amtrak-company-a-by-aaron-nielson (questioning whether Amtrak as a government entity is statutorily required to act in the public interest or in a profit-maximizing capacity given its other duties).

[64] 135 S.Ct. 1101 (2015).

[65] See *Parker* v. *Brown*, 317 U.S. 341 (1943) and subsequent cases; see also Paul Verkuil, *State Action, Due Process and Antitrust: Reflections on* Parker *v.* Brown, 75 COLUMBIA L. REV. 328 (1975).

[66] Federal separation of powers cases could only be applied to the states would be under the Republican Form of Government requirement which is not justiciable. See U.S. CONST. Art. IV, § 4.

[67] 717 F.3d 359 (4th Cir. 2013).

[68] 411 U.S. 564 (1973).

optometrists from denying a license for corporate optometrists to practice in the state. The self-interest of the deciders in *N.C. Dental Board* and *Gibson* is identical, just the legal theory differs.[69] In *Gibson*, the source of the right under due process sprang from early English common law, namely, *Bonham's Case*,[70] Lord Coke's famous dictum that no man may be a judge in his own cause.[71] Justice Kennedy stated in *N.C. Dental Board* that the state has "delegate[d] control over a market to a non-sovereign actor" and said states must show "political accountability."[72] From this book's perspective, self-interested state actors appear much like private contractors acting on the state's behalf. The missing dimension is one of *sovereignty* (something that cannot be outsourced nor exercised by compromised state officials).

*Parker* immunity itself has been interpreted by later cases in interesting ways.[73] In the *Midcal* case cited by Justice Kennedy in *N.C. Dental Board*, the requirement that the state "actively supervise" potentially self-interested boards became a key factor in *Parker* immunity. Since the Board had declared teeth whitening an unauthorized practice of dentistry without any legislative direction, the active supervision requirement failed. The duty to supervise, which Gillian Metzger has so well articulated,[74] remains an essential and nondelegable duty of government, whether under the Constitution or under the Sherman Act's federalism exception expressed in *Parker* and *Midcal*. The Court's treatment of the active supervision idea also connects to the duty to govern expressed in *Outsourcing Sovereignty*.

Justice Alito's dissent in *N.C. Dental Board* makes convincing practical points. He argues that *Parker* immunity should not be denied to state agencies, even if they were set up to frustrate competition and benefit a particular group. To do otherwise forces the Court to enter a "morass" where it will have to evaluate what is a conflict and how many Board members must be conflicted (a majority, plurality, etc.) before an agency's action is overturned.[75] For Alito,

69 The *N.C. Dental Board* Court did not cite *Gibson*, presumably because of the different source of the right asserted – antitrust versus due process. But in the *Parker* immunity context the theories are really alternative although the remedies may vary. See Verkuil, *supra* note 65.

70 8 Co. Rep. 107 (1610).

71 The Royal College of Physicians allowed only 24 fellows to practice medicine in London and was granted the power by Act of Parliament to imprison indefinitely those they determined to be practicing medicine badly or without a license. So they were indeed "interested" in the outcome.

72 135 S.Ct. at 1111–12.

73 See *California Retail Liquor Dealers Assn. v. Midcal Aluminum, Inc.*, 445 U.S. 97, 105 (1980) (establishing the active supervision test under *Parker*).

74 See Metzger, *supra* note 16.

75 135 S.Ct. at 1118 (Alito, J., dissenting).

this becomes a federalism concern, for good reason. Many state self-regulatory schemes delegate to doctors, lawyers, and accountants the power to manage their professions with little public oversight. It is enough that North Carolina set up the Dental Board of Examiners as an agency of the State.[76] Justice Alito also raises the problem of regulatory capture, but sees no role for the Court to control it. Regulatory capture is endemic to the regulatory process and it will be discussed in greater detail in Chapter 6.[77]

On the public ethics front, the Court decided *McDonnell* v. *United States*,[78] which unanimously ruled that the Governor of Virginia did not commit an "official act" necessary for conviction of bribery under 18 U.S.C. § 201(a)(3). The Court held that the district court committed error by not allowing defendants' instructions to the jury that merely arranging a meeting, attending an event, or hosting a reception are not official acts. The governor and his wife (who was separately tried) had accepted gifts from a business friend that ranged from a Rolex to the expenses for a daughter's wedding, but what was done in return failed to reach a quid pro quo status according to the Court and the case was remanded to the Fourth Circuit.[79]

This case presented notorious facts that the Chief Justice was forced to acknowledge: "there is no doubt that this case is distasteful; it may be worse than that." Even if the criminal laws were not intended to reach the Governor's conduct, the cause of political ethics has been disserved. The Chapter 1 concern about trust and corruption in American politics can only increase after these facts are understood by the public. The ethics community has already spoken out. One who should know, Jack Abramoff, called the decision naïve, and less compromised observers like Fred Wertheimer concurred.[80]

76 *Id.*, at 1119–21. He distinguishes *Midcal* as a situation involving a private trade association, not a state agency. While Justice Alito did not mention the oath requirement that he emphasized in the *Amtrak* case, it may well be the case that North Carolina Board members do not take an oath.

77 See M. Elizabeth Magill, *Courts and Regulatory Capture*, in PREVENTING CAPTURE: SPECIAL INTEREST INFLUENCE IN REGULATION, AND HOW TO LIMIT IT 419 (Daniel Carpenter, Steve Croley, & David Moss, eds.) (2014) (Dean Magill says "courts are far from the best policemen when it comes to regulatory capture").

78 136 S.Ct. 2355 (2016).

79 On remand, the Circuit Court was to decide if there is sufficient evidence after the proper instructions are given for the jury to convict; otherwise charges must be dismissed. See *id.* at 2371–72. The prosecutors subsequently dropped all charges against the former governor and his wife in September 2016.

80 See Carl Hulse, *Is the Supreme Court Clueless About Corruption? Ask Jack Abramoff*, N.Y. TIMES (Jul. 5, 2016), www.nytimes.com/2016/07/06/us/politics/is-the-supreme-court-clueless-about-corruption-ask-jack-abramoff.html.

The answer now lies with states, which need to strengthen their public ethics laws. Virginia has put legislative limits on gifts annually at $100.[81] But the state ethics committee has exempted certain items (like college football tickets) from the annual limit. More importantly, gifts from political action committees are not within the limits.[82] Since it is these gifts that are most in mind when the public reacts to legislative corruption, it appears that, as one observer has stated: "When you talk about Virginia and ethics laws, it's pretty clear it's the Wild, Wild West."[83]

81 See Laura Vozzella, *Virginia legislature adopts stricter gift standards for public officials*, WASH. POST (Apr. 17, 2015), https://www.washingtonpost.com/local/virginia-politics/virginia-legislature-adopts-stricter-gift-standards/2015/04/17/b400b6a0-e456–11e4–905f-cc896d379a32_story.html.

82 See Alan Greenblatt, *Bob McDonnell and the Illusion of Ethics Reform*, GOVERNING (Jun. 27, 2016), www.governing.com/topics/politics/gov-mcdonnell-scotus-corruption-virginia-ethics.html.

83 *Id.* (quoting Stephen Farnsworth, director of a center on leadership at the University of Mary Washington).

# 3

# The Growth of Contracting Out in Government

Leviathan by Proxy

John DiIulio, *Bring Back the Bureaucrats* (2014)

Contracting-out services across the economy have grown dramatically in the last decade. While the focus here is on contracting with government, the outsourcing movement – the "Uberfication" of the economy – affects all dimensions of the hiring process. So contracting out deserves a broad look initially. The impact of Uber reflects a shift in jobs in the service economy from employee to independent contractor status. While a few states like California have challenged the status of Uber drivers and won concessions,[1] Uber, Lyft, and related companies, in transportation and beyond, are redefining the relationship between workers and private employers. The government is not an employer of this nature, and its contractors are subject to articulated agreements, but what is going on in the economy at large will ultimately affect how government employs its workers. That may be a good thing as flexibility in employment can help government compete with the private sector.[2]

## A. THE BIG PICTURE: CONTRACTORS IN THE LABOR FORCE

Contractors are growing as a share of the national workforce as well as in government at all levels. Nationally, Lawrence Katz and Alan Krueger show

[1] Most states have accepted Uber's relationship with its drivers as independent contractors. California litigated whether Uber (and Lyft) drivers were employees, not contractors. They ultimately settled. The key issue interestingly was whether drivers could be fired "at will," the kind of question discussed in Chapter 1 concerning state employees. See Kia Kokalitcheva, *Uber's Employment Fight Just Got More Complicated*, FORBES (Mar. 4, 2016), http://fortune.com/2016/03/04/uber-driver-unemployment/.

[2] See discussion in Chapter 8.

that alternative work arrangements grew from 10.1 percent of the US workforce in 2005 to 15.8 percent in 2015. This growth constitutes all net employment growth during that period.[3] Contracting out is the largest category of alternative work arrangements and it occurs predominantly with higher-wage jobs. As David Weil has explained, large employers are shedding direct employment and reducing costs by turning to contractors outside the organization.[4] By redefining work in the service economy to make greater use of contractors, workers in traditional jobs are disadvantaged. President Obama has observed that some jobs "aren't coming back" because of lower costs and higher scalability, flexibility, industrial skills, and diligence of foreign contractors.[5]

Part of the reason for the growth in contractors is the use of technology. New technologies allow for jobs to be standardized and easily monitored. Uber and Airbnb come immediately to mind. As Neil Irwin writes, "when people working as a team need extensive experience working together, it can be tricky to contract out work. But when there are clear simple measures of how successful each person is, and a company can monitor it, the employer now has flexibility."[6] This states the parameters well: technology reduces the transaction costs to employers for finding workers under circumstances where measurement and monitoring is possible.[7] Interestingly this analysis also applies to telework, where measured and monitored performance is necessary as well, as will be discussed in Chapter 8.

None of this should come as a surprise to governments. Regressions from the Katz/Krueger study show that the use of contractors in the federal, state, and local governments rose from 6.2 percent in 2005 to 11.9 percent in 2015,[8]

3 Lawrence F. Katz & Alan B. Krueger, The Rise and Nature of Alternative Work Arrangements in the United States, 1995–2015 (RAND 2016); see also Neil Irwin, *Job Growth in Past Decade Was in Temp and Contract,* N.Y. Times A3 (Mar. 31, 2016) (published online as *With 'Gigs' Instead of Jobs, Workers Bear New Burdens*, available at www.nytimes.com/2016/03/31/upshot/contractors-and-temps-accounted-for-all-of-the-growth-in-employment-in-the-last-decade.html).

4 David Weil, The Fissured Workplace: Why Work Became So Bad for So Many and What Can Be Done to Improve It 4–5 (2014).

5 Charles Duhigg & Keith Bradsher, *How the U.S. Lost Out on iPhone Work*, N.Y. Times (Jan. 21, 2012), www.nytimes.com/2012/01/22/business/apple-america-and-a-squeezed-middle-class.html.

6 Irwin, *supra* note 3.

7 See Katz & Krueger, *supra* note 3; see also Ronald Coase, *The Nature of the Firm*, 4 Economica 386 (1937) (explaining how technology reduces transaction costs in hiring and resizing business units as a consequence).

8 Classes of worker variables in RAND and CPS data show (1) federal, (2) state, and (3) local employees. Using these variables the share of contract workers in government jumped from 6.22 percent in 2005 to 11.90 percent in 2015. *Accord* email correspondence with Lance Y. Liu (Apr. 2, 2016) (on file with author) (analyzing sector-by-sector breakdown of contracting workers in public administration).

almost exceeding the percentage growth in alternative workers generally. The largest category of alternative workers are employed by contracting-out entities and many of those are primarily or even exclusively working for governments. While it is difficult to collect contracting-out data from state governments, which do not generally keep public records of their short-term contractors,[9] the trends show movement in the direction of contractors. Since the number of state personnel shrunk significantly in the last decade,[10] it is likely that part-time contractors as well as shrinking state budgets were causal factors.

## B. CONTRACTING IN THE FEDERAL GOVERNMENT

Much more is known about contracting out at the federal level, which is the leading edge of government contractor utilization. Over many years, contractors have provided services to federal agencies in numbers that may exceed their presence in the general labor market. The current federal services contractor budget is around $250 billion. To put that number in perspective, it approximates the cost of the entire civil service.[11] Overall, therefore, contractor expenditures are about 50 percent of the total agency expenditures for personnel, but in some agencies, such as DOD, DOE, the US Agency for International Development (USAID), and NASA, the contractor costs are even higher. While the total amount spent on government contracting is leveling out, due to sequestration and budgetary uncertainty,[12] the total spent on services contracts will probably remain high into the future. A continual difficulty is translating the amount of federal spending on human capital into numbers of contractors. We know how many federal employees there are and also how much we are spending on contractors. But the number of contractors

9 See Sophie Quinton, *States Employ Temporary Workers, But Often Know Little About Them*, Stateline (Pew Trusts Apr. 13, 2016) (part-time workers abound in state government, especially in higher education where about 50 percent of teachers are temporary adjuncts), www.pewtrusts.org/en/research-and-analysis/blogs/stateline/2016/04/13/states-employ-temporary-workers-but-know-little-about-them.

10 Since 2008, the total number of state and local employees has declined by 662,000. See Center on Budget & Policy Priorities, Elizabeth McNichol, *Some Basic Facts on State and Local Government Workers* (June 15, 2012).

11 See Congressional Budget Office, Federal Contracts and the Contracted Workforce 4 (2015) (finding spending grew more quickly than inflation and as a percent of the federal budget, and that spending grew most rapidly for contracts for professional, administrative, and management services), https://www.cbo.gov/publication/49931.

12 USASpending.Gov (last visited Aug. 27, 2016) lists total contracts spending for goods and services at $439 billion in FY2015 versus $54.1 billion in FY2008. See also Donald F. Kettl, *Contracting Fairness*, before the House Subcommittee on Government Operations, Comm. On Oversight and Government Reform (June 9, 2016), https://oversight.house.gov/wp-content/uploads/2016/07/2016–07–08-Donald-Kettl-UMD-Testimony.pdf (specifying need for government to be a "smart buyer" of human services).

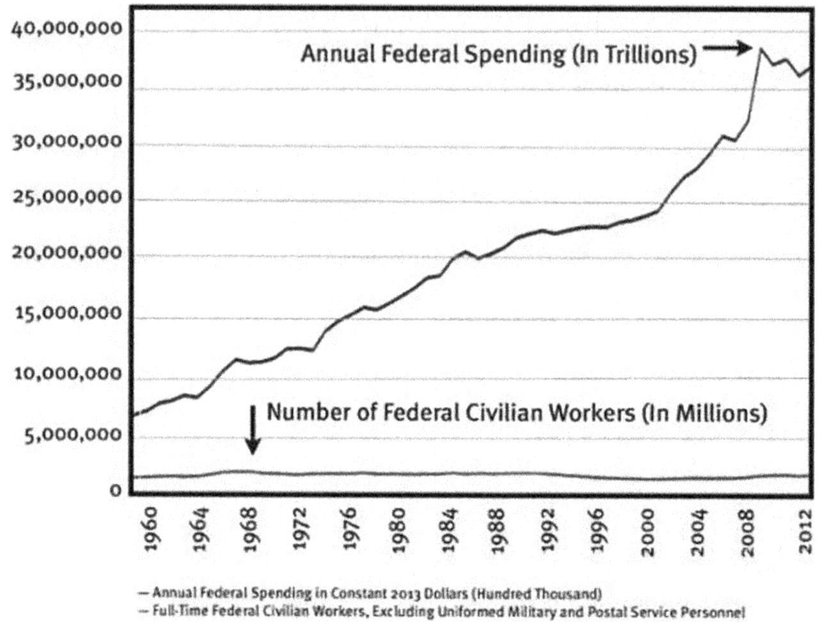


Cover image, John DiIulio, *Bring Back the Bureaucrats*, Templeton Press, 2014.

those dollars support is hard to pin down. So let's start with what we know – the size of the federal establishment. Consider this chart from John DiIulio's recent book.[13]

This chart is saying that the number of civilian government employees has remained steady (at about 2 million) since the Kennedy Administration, over 50 years ago. In reality, government employment at the federal level has been shrinking. These facts do not fit the public perception of the size of the federal government. Many would assume that as government spends more, the bureaucracy gets bigger, but the evidence is the opposite. As DiIulio shows, gross domestic product (GDP) has increased five-fold since 1960, and, assuming a correlation between the size of the economy and the need for officials to serve it, the bureaucracy remains the same size. Now think about the number of new agencies and programs created since the 1960s (start with the EPA and the Department of Homeland Security (DHS)) or other size indicators like the growth in the number of pages in the federal register.[14] If

[13] Bureaucrats (cover page).

[14] ACUS, Sourcebook of United States Executive Agencies (2012) lists dozens of agencies created since 1960. Moreover, the number of pages in the Federal Register has expanded seven-fold since 1960. See Maeve P. Carey, *Counting Regulations: An Overview of Rulemaking, Types of Federal Regulations, and Pages in the Federal Register* (Cong. Res. Serv. Nov. 26, 2014), at 17.

the GDP has increased five-fold and the number of federal register pages has increased seven-fold then who is doing all the work if the number of federal workers remains the same? The answer, of course, is contractors are expanding exponentially.

The number of government workers has not been keeping up with the growth in the economy either at the federal, the state, or the local level. In effect, the data show the Era of Big Government is over.[15] From a peak of around 7.5 percent in the Second World War, the percentage of regular payroll employment represented by the federal government dipped below 4 percent in the 1970s, and today hovers around 2 percent.[16]

One way to understand the growth in contractors is to view the triangle created by DiIulio's chart as representing an employment gap. If it is not filled by bureaucrats, the workers can come from only one source: contractors in all sizes, shapes, and forms. Unlike federal employees, who are carefully identified by headcounts ("full-time employees," or FTEs), the number of federal contractors is difficult to discern. Paul Light has made several estimates of the number of contractors that vary between 7.6 million and 12 million.[17] Since the budgets for the federal workforce and service contractors are now about equal, that could mean there are many more contractors than federal workers, given temporary and part-time personnel in the contractor workforce, or that because of cost, the contractors are far fewer in number than suggested by Light's estimates. Stan Soloway, former head of the Professional Services Council which represents contractors, takes this position and contends that given overhead and profit charges the total dollars spent per contractor actually represent far fewer of them than the 2 million federal employees.[18]

But whatever the number, it is a large one. John DiIulio calls this situation "leviathan by proxy" and includes in the "contractor" calculation state and local workers as well as for- and not-for-profit employees. Since Barack

[15] See Justin Fox, *Big Government Keeps Getting Smaller*, BLOOMBERG (Aug. 5, 2016), https://www.bloomberg.com/view/articles/2016–08–05/big-government-keeps-getting-smaller (noting that "there are almost 15 million more workers on nonfarm payrolls now than there were at the end of 2009, but 300,000 fewer government workers").

[16] See *id.* (citing figures from the Bureau of Labor Statistics, not including uniformed military and intelligence agencies).

[17] Paul Light estimated the number of contractors at 12 million several years ago. See Thomas Frank, *Government by Contract is a Disgrace*, WALL STREET JOURNAL, The Tilting Yard (Nov. 26, 2005), available at www.wsj.com/articles/SB122765980278958481 (discussing Paul Light's findings in 2005 that contractors outnumbered civil servants by four to one); see also Max Stier, *Federal Contracting System in Serious Disrepair*, THE WASHINGTON POST (Feb. 4, 2009), available at www.washingtonpost.com/wp-dyn/content/article/2009/02/04/AR2009020402605.html (reviewing Paul Light's updated estimates that at least 7.6 million contractors work alongside 1.9 million civil servants).

[18] Stan Soloway, interview with author, May 2016.

Obama's government could not be run with the numbers John Kennedy had at his disposal, service contractors, who were unknown in Kennedy's day, are now a large part of Obama and Trump's workforce.

The growth in contractors is not just a numbers game, however. DiIulio's assertion is that contractors not only serve government but create ongoing needs for their services. In effect, they help perpetuate big government (Leviathan) not only by supplying services, but by demanding them. For-profit, not-for-profit, and state and local governments form powerful interest groups that seek to protect and expand their programs. This phenomenon, well known to public choice scholars as "rent seeking," is discussed in Chapter 5 under the heading of "regulatory capture."

DiIulio's prescription is to hire 1 million bureaucrats to replace the contractors, thereby reducing the incentive to increase the size of government, while managing it more effectively. He delivers this message knowing that it is unlikely to meet with approval. But in truth, if there were 2 million federal employees 50 years ago and the economy has grown five-fold, the number is quite conservative. And it is certainly below the number of contractors currently employed, however we count them. At the policy levels, growth in federal managers would have a positive impact on the federal budget, since government officials do not have the same rent-seeking incentives as contractors (although they want to protect their jobs). The contractor lobby is also more important to Congress for campaign funding reasons than are government employees, so programs might actually be slimmed down as a result. And, of course, the degree of professionalism might also grow and with it the quality of services the public expects. Conceivably, the dismal numbers on trust in government might also move in the right direction.[19]

Selling this idea before today's Congress may be a quixotic venture, but it is a thought experiment worth engaging in. Moreover, when many countries in the world are trying to build merit-based civil service systems,[20] strengthening ours raises the bar internationally as well. That point ought not to be lost. The

[19] Chapter 1, section J, connects trust to professional government and shows how some agencies like the USPS and NPS are doing quite well on public trust measures despite the low trust in government numbers overall.

[20] See The Economist, *Civil Servants – Mandarin Lessons*, Mar. 12, 2016, at 57 ("Of the 62 countries tracked in 2010–11 by Global Integrity, an NGO, 55 had rules against 'nepotism, cronyism and patronage'. Last year Cyprus and Pakistan, among others, announced reforms intended to ensure that applicants are chosen on the basis of what they know, not whom. Countries such as Germany, Portugal and Spain pledge in their constitutions to recruit government staff based on skills. Prodded by aid donors, Afghanistan and Sudan recently promised to do likewise."), available at www.economist.com/news/international/21694553-countries-are-trying-harder-recruit-best-bureaucrats-not-hard-enough-mandarin.

civil service system, which surely needs to be modernized to account for the encrusted nature of the hire/fire process as well as the growth of alternative work arrangements, noted at the outset of this chapter, is still the best way we have to run government. Contractors can still be effective as adjuncts in this regime, but they need leadership and oversight from professional managers.

Given that the government's budget for contractors approximates that of the entire civil service, it is not surprising that some agencies have as many contractors as employees. At DOD, for example, there are 700,000 full-time contractors for its 800,000 civilian employees.[21] And there are many other agencies where the contractor-to-employee ratio approaches 50/50, if their numbers are known. Often the only way for an agency to affect contractor numbers is to translate numbers into dollars, as Robert Gates suggested when he was Secretary of Defense.[22] Despite data collection obstacles, the Government Accountability Office (GAO) lists some agencies with contractor/employee ratios even greater than the 50/50 level.

## C. THE CORRELATION BETWEEN CONTRACTOR-DRIVEN AGENCIES AND HIGH-RISK ONES

NASA, DOE, and USAID have two things in common: they have contractor/employee ratios far exceeding 50/50, and they are longtime members of GAO's high risk list for mismanagement, fraud, waste, and abuse. The Comptroller General, Eugene Dodaro, has stated that GAO has never taken a contractor-dominated agency off its high risk list,[23] even though one-third of other agencies have been removed from the list over time.[24] The Comptroller

[21] See John J. DiIulio, Jr. & Paul R. Verkuil, *Want a Leaner Federal Government? Hire More Federal Workers*, WASH. POST (Apr. 21, 2016), available at https://www.washingtonpost.com/opinions/want-a-leaner-federal-government-hire-more-federal-workers/2016/04/21/a11cf98c-fd8b-11e5-886f-a037dba38301_story.html (hereinafter *Leaner Federal Government*).

[22] See Matthew Weigelt, *Insourcing failed, DOD's Gates says. Now what?*, FCW (Aug. 10, 2010) ("'The problem with contractors – and what we've learned over the past year – is you really don't get at contractors by cutting people,' Gates said at a press conference about his department wide changes. He said contractors get the money from a contract and then hire as many as they think are necessary to do the work. 'So the only way, we've decided, that you get at the contractor base is to cut the dollars.'"). Moreover, contractors may view their personnel numbers as proprietary information which further complicates matters.

[23] See Gene Dodaro, Address before the National Academy of Public Administration, April 5, 2016. The GAO Biannual High Risk list represents 32 areas of management risk. See GAO Report 15–290 (Feb. 11, 2015) (recent areas added to the risk list include VA health care and IT acquisitions and operations).

[24] See John M. Kamensky, *The Secrets to Getting Off the GAO High Risk List*, IBM CENTER FOR THE BUSINESS OF GOVERNMENT BLOG (May 16, 2016), www.businessofgovernment.org/blog/

stated that the reason these agencies have never left the list is largely due to inadequate contractor management.[25] This oversight deficiency is caused by lack of contracting officers and outmoded technology. When agencies become overwhelmed by contractor services, we have a failure of professional government. If permanent membership on the high risk list has become an indicia of contractor-driven government, Congress should pay close attention. And all who care about effective government should be alarmed.

## D. CONTRACTOR-DRIVEN AGENCIES: DEPARTMENT OF ENERGY AND USAID

Has this agency contracted out its brain?[26]

Three major agencies have about a 90/10 contractor–employee ratio. One of them is NASA, whose well-known contractor-guided mission makes it more like a government corporation than a federal agency. The other two, DOE and USAID, will be more closely analyzed to understand how the high contractor ratios might affect their missions and operations. I was able to secure interviews with present or former key personnel of these agencies who were of great assistance in explaining how they deal with high contractor ratios and the effect they have on operations.

### 1 *Department of Energy*

DOE pretty much owns the Nobel Prize for Physics[27]

There are over 100,000 contractors at DOE and 13,000 government employees.[28] On its face, that imbalance would seem to produce management and oversight problems of major proportions. And there are stresses in the contract-awarding and -renewal process at DOE that help explain its long

business-government/secrets-getting-gao-high-risk-list (referring to a study by Don Kettl that lists three actions by agencies necessary to get removed from the list: improvements in legacy information systems; strengthened financial management systems to control resources; and strengthened contract management to ensure contractors are aligned with mission needs).

[25] Gene Dodaro, personal interview with author, June 2016.

[26] Comment from an anonymous GAO official after spending months working with someone representing the agency who turned out to be a contractor, adding "we have to start checking the color of their IDs." Interview with author, June 17, 2016.

[27] Steve Croley, General Counsel, Dept. of Energy, interview with author, Apr. 5, 2016.

[28] US Dept. of Energy, Agency Financial Report Fiscal Year 2015 at 6 (2015), http://energy.gov/sites/prod/files/2015/11/f27/DOE_FY2015_AFR.pdf.

placement on GAO's high risk list. But any analysis of management control problems must take into account the nature and duties of the contract employees. Roughly 80,000 of the contractors are in the national research laboratories like Scandia and Lawrence Livermore.[29] While these labs are under DOE control, they are populated by physicists, engineers, and other scientists who have long-term relationships with the government, who produce high-level research. Indeed, agency officials say that these "contractors" consider themselves government employees and are sometimes paid directly by the government through long-standing arrangements.

Secretary Ernest Moniz says "the Energy Department's staff and contractors are at the heart of everything we do."[30] This is an obvious effort to integrate the two workforces. Indeed, as a professor of nuclear physics at MIT, the Secretary was a contractor before going inside government, where he has been an invaluable asset both as Secretary and as a negotiator with State Department Secretary John Kerry of the Iran Nuclear Agreement.

There are contract oversight vulnerabilities, however. They appear to involve the selection of managers for the laboratories, who do change, rather than the operating arms where most of the contractors remain in place and produce, as Croley indicated, notable awards in physics. Attorneys in the DOE General Counsel's Office who were also interviewed maintain that the continuity of the scientific community makes the oversight burden manageable.

The other large group of DOE contractors (in the 20,000 range) work in nuclear waste management, where the functions and turnover are more frequent and contracting oversight is more challenging.[31] Overall, then, overseeing contractors with DOE employees seems a more manageable proposition than the 90/10 ratio initially suggests. The burdens on contracting officers, DOE officials admit, are substantial, but the conclusion that the high ratio of contractors alone does not accurately reflect the degree of risk they pose to the agency's operations seems reasonable.

[29] Author's interview with Steve Croley, General Counsel, Dept. of Energy, Apr. 5, 2016 (explaining that the bulk of the contracted personnel conduct research at the national labs, identify with DOE, and in his view form a dedicated workforce).

[30] See DOE's website on staff and contractors: http://energy.gov/about-us/staff-and-contractors.

[31] The Hanford site in south central Washington, for instance, has suffered from nuclear waste leaks that went unreported by the contractor managing the site or DOE for a year after it was discovered. The venting of toxic vapors that injured unprotected workers led to a lawsuit by the Washington Attorney General, and resulted in a series of reports by local media on the difficulties of overseeing the project. See Suzannah Frame, *Hanford's Dirty Secrets*, KING (May 19, 2016), www.king5.com/news/local/investigations/hanfords-dirty-secrets/204894383.

## 2 *US Agency for International Development*

At USAID, contractors also represent around 90 percent of the total workforce and the management problems are more complicated. For one thing, there are no equivalents to DOE's scientific laboratories where contractors have long-established and set relationships. USAID's relief missions involve work with private partners to end extreme poverty and promote democratic societies.[32] Priorities are constantly being rethought and readjusted under the influence of events (natural disasters, political upheavals, etc.), the White House, executive agencies like the Department of State, as well as Congress itself.

USAID's government workforce is often shorthanded and contractors are forced to play a central role in planning and execution. A recent agency head explained that some of his key advisors in top management decisions are contractors whose special expertise is highly valued. While he was sensitive to the need to add government employees at the professional level (and did add 4,600 to those ranks over his term)[33] the obstacles to civil service hiring (including the veterans' preference) often pushed him in the direction of contractors who could come on quickly with appropriate credentials.

The contractors in the field, however, created other problems. When the agency sought to change direction, some contractors whose programs were affected would go to Congress to object, creating pressures on USAID's professional managers.[34] Contractor influence on Congress is a well-known phenomenon (consider military contractors whose weapons are strategically produced in numerous congressional districts[35]). For USAID leadership this meant lengthy meetings on the Hill that assume valuable management time. This situation starkly presents the problem of contractor "rent seeking," which is the subject of detailed analysis in Chapter 4.

32 See USAID, MISSION, VISION AND VALUES, https://www.usaid.gov/who-we-are/mission-vision-values.

33 During my interviews I learned that an agency with rollover money at the end of the fiscal year like USAID could have, but was discouraged from investing those funds in civil service personnel. One-time money is not the way to build permanent additions to an agency's cost structure, but rollovers that occur regularly might be used for this purpose, thereby reducing the agency's personnel costs over the long run, and, as importantly, the influence of contractors on the policy process.

34 Interview with Rajiv Shaw, Former Administrator of USAID, May 20, 2016.

35 See Mandy Smithburger, *Congress Is Robbing America's War Effort to Pay for Unwanted Weapons*, WAR IS BORING (May 5, 2016), available at https://warisboring.com/congress-is-robbing-americas-war-effort-to-pay-for-unwanted-weapons-4009b56cf22e#.7ru678e92 (describing defense industry lobbyists' successful efforts to push the House of Representatives Armed Services Committee to underfund the Overseas Contingency Operations account by $18 billion in order to reallocate funds to purchase weapons systems rejected by the Department of Defense).

Heavily populated contractor agencies like DOE and USAID face special challenges in managing the mixed workforce. Overworked civil servants are particularly at risk in the contracting and contracting-oversight process. Agency personnel in these situations may overlook opportunities for competitive bidding and resort to pro forma renewals.[36] While, as the situation at DOE indicates, the ratio of contractors to civil servants does not by itself prove professional management inadequate, at USAID, on the other hand, the ratio is more problematic. Contractor/employee ratios are a useful starting point in trying to determine whether public management is performing well.

## E. PROFESSIONALLY STARVED AGENCIES: CMS AND IRS

There are many agencies who have higher than 50 percent contractor ratios, but two stand out because of the importance of their missions and the public nature of their failures: the Center for Medicaid Services and the Internal Revenue Service.

### 1 *Center for Medicaid Services*

Some agencies founder because of a shortage of professional employees to do the job, a gap contractors are forced to fill. The situation at the Center for Medicaid Services (CMS), part of the Department of Health and Human Services, is remarkable from a personnel perspective. CMS has about a 3/1 contractor to employee ratio, far below the 9/1 ratio at DOE and USAID. But that hardly tells the story. There are 5,600 employees at CMS[37] and at least 14,000 contractors.[38] Incredibly, CMS got little new staff to implement

[36] See Stephen Schooner, *The Fundamental Failure of Business-Like Government*, 50 AM. L. REV. 627 (2001) (lamenting the fact that fewer federal employees are overseeing contractors).

[37] See http://bestplacestowork.org/BPTW/rankings/detail/he70#workforce.

[38] These numbers were hard to collect. Thanks to some digging by Jim Tozzi, a former top official at OMB, the following totals were determined: CMS has eight contractors, totaling at minimum 14,000, staffed as follows:

National Government Services: 2,700
Wisconsin Physicians' Service Insurance Corporation: 3,030
CGS Administrators, LLC: 1,000+
Noridian Healthcare Solutions, LLC: 1,535
Novitas Solutions, Inc.: 2,000
Cahaba Government Benefit Administrators, LLC: 750+
Palmetto GBA, LLC: 2,100
First Coast Service Options, Inc.: 1,001–5,000

(email from Jim Tozzi, Apr. 11, 2016).

the Affordable Care Act (ACA). The agency was short on professionals who knew how to set up a website, the crucial breakdown that doomed the ACA rollout.[39] The website was Healthcare.gov which provided access to the federally facilitated marketplace (FFM) that allowed the public to compare and select insurance plans. As GAO reported, CMS employees issued task orders to the contractors developing the FFM "when key technical requirements were unknown, including the number and composition of states to be supported and, importantly, the number of potential enrollees."[40] This lack of preparation or experience was glaring for an agency with an extraordinarily complicated new mandate. CMS officials used cost-reimbursement contracts "which created additional risk because CMS is required to pay the contractors allowable costs regardless of whether the system is completed."[41] The use of cost-plus contracting by CMS was almost an admission that they were in the dark about the requirements needed successfully to complete the contract. Lack of professional personnel at CMS undermined the competency of government. The problem is not just the number of contractors overseen but whether the talent is available in-house to evaluate the efforts of contractors to do quality work.

### 2 *Internal Revenue Service*

The situation at the Internal Revenue Service (IRS) is even more challenging than CMS from an inadequate management perspective. IRS is one of the few agencies that can put a price tag on the value of their employees. IRS employees return many dollars to the Treasury for every dollar spent on their salary and benefits.[42] Do these "missing" employees have work to do? You bet. The amount of taxes owed to government that have not been collected is known. It is called the "tax gap." It currently stands at over $400 billion.[43] Remember, these are the moneys taxpayers owe, but do not pay, for a variety of reasons: some can't pay and some won't pay. It is the latter category the IRS

39 See Stephen Cohen, *Understanding the Obamacare Rollout Fiasco*, Huffington Post Blog (Jan. 23, 2014), available at www.huffingtonpost.com/steven-cohen/understanding-the-obamaca_b_4295842.html (describing rollout problems as both management and politics driven).

40 GAO, *Ineffective Planning and Oversight Practices Underscore the Need for Improved Contract Management*, GAO-14-694 (July 2014).

41 *Id.* 42 See *Leaner Federal Government*.

43 See US Internal Revenue Service, The Tax Gap (Apr. 28, 2016), available at https://www.irs.gov/uac/the-tax-gap ("A high level of voluntary tax compliance remains critical to help ensure taxpayer faith and fairness in the tax system. Those who don't pay what they owe ultimately shift the tax burden to those who properly meet their tax obligations").

should focus on. If it is assumed that 25 percent of that amount is collectible (say $100 billion) and that new employees return twenty times their cost in recoveries,[44] this could easily justify 10,000 new IRS agents. The tax gap can be viewed as a measurement of government failure that can be reduced by responsible appointments. On both a financial and management perspective, this seems like low-hanging fruit.

Lack of professional management also leads to other failures. Consider GAO's report that IRS paid $3.1 billion in identity theft refunds in 2014.[45] GAO criticized IRS for not developing a comprehensive strategy on identity theft and put the agency on its 2015 high risk list. So the case for more agents and professionals is overwhelming. From a trust-in-government perspective, how demoralizing is it for the vast majority of taxpayers to pay their share on a largely voluntary basis and see a minority ignore their obligations. This jeopardizes the tradition of voluntary compliance itself and further reduces the public perception of government competency.[46]

In what rational system could this happen? The answer is in our political system.[47] The Republican Party attacks the IRS because of allegations that it discriminated against conservative groups in its "501(c)(4)" registration of not-for-profits.[48] This has made them do strange things like prefer to fund private collection agencies (PCAs) – bounty hunters, really – rather than add qualified agents.[49] Who could rationally prefer contracting for harassing

44 See Letter from Taxpayer Advocate Nina Olson to Senator Ron Wyden (May 13, 2014), https://taxpayeradvocate.irs.gov/userfiles/file/NTA_PDC_letter.pdf (documenting a 20:1 return on investments for IRS employees in the Automated Collection System program).

45 GAO, IRS Needs to Further Improve Controls over Taxpayer Data and Continue to Combat Identity Theft Refund Fraud, GAO-16–589T (April 2016). GAO also reports that $122.5 billion was prevented in identity fraud.

46 See Catherine Rampell, Opinions, *Please Don't Tell Anyone, but Tax Cheating Is About to Rise in the U.S.*, Washington Post (Aug. 29, 2016), https://www.washingtonpost.com/opinions/please-dont-tell-anyone-but-tax-cheating-is-going-to-get-worse/2016/08/29/e66291e6–6e24–11e6–9705–23e51a2f424d_story.html?utm_term=.8819944ed36a.

47 See Editorial, *Take Politics Away From the I.R.S.*, N.Y. Times (May 15, 2013), available at www.nytimes.com/2013/05/16/opinion/take-politics-away-from-the-irs.html.

48 See Jared Bernstein, *Why the GOP Really Wants to Defund IRS – Hint: It's Not about Administrative Incompetence*, Wash. Post (Jul. 1, 2014), available at https://www.washingtonpost.com/posteverything/wp/2014/07/01/why-the-gop-really-wants-to-defund-irs/.

49 See David Brunori, *More Private Tax Collectors – A Monumentally Bad Idea*, Forbes (Dec. 10, 2015), available at www.forbes.com/sites/taxanalysts/2015/12/10/more-private-tax-collectors-a-monumentally-bad-idea/#1cf9d54a42ad (discussing private tax collection mandates imposed by the Fixing America's Surface Transportation ("FAST") Act); S. Amdt. 2421 to S. Amdt. 2266 to H.R. 22 (FAST Act) Title LII, § 52106, "REFORM OF RULES RELATING TO QUALIFIED TAX COLLECTION CONTRACTS ("of a perfecting nature")," Sen. Mitch McConnell (2015), available at https://www.congress.gov/amendment/114th-congress/senate-amendment/2421.

debt collectors rather than using professional personnel for collecting taxes? Congress experimented with PCAs on two prior occasions and as Nina Olson, the National Taxpayer Advocate, reports, the IRS lost money each time.[50] Moreover, Olson criticizes the PCA program for targeting low-income taxpayers and diverting IRS personnel from other assignments. She concludes the prior PCA programs "undermined effective tax administration, jeopardized taxpayer rights protections and did not accomplish its intended objective of raising revenue."[51] It is hard to think of a bigger outsourcing failure than the PCA program, yet Congress wants to try it again rather than add professionals with a proven record of accomplishment.

The House Oversight and Government Reform Committee decided to censure the IRS commissioner, John A. Koskinen (as a prelude to impeachment no less),[52] because he mishandled production of emails sought in the earlier 501(c)(4) investigation.[53] Mr. Koskinen, who has served in high-level roles for Republican and Democratic administrations, is the kind of professional government needs: someone who believes in government and takes on tough assignments.[54] His treatment could surely discourage others from taking on similar assignments that government needs to fill in the future. Moreover, think how hard it has been for him to effectively manage the beleaguered IRS while he prepared for impeachment hearings.

## F. CONTRACTOR RATIOS AND RATIONAL GOVERNMENT

The growth in contractors in the economy as a whole over the last decade reflects a transformation in the employer–employee relationship. But in government, contractors now represent not only numbers, but brains – brains that have been outsourced. Booz Allen Hamilton, owned by the Carlyle Group, earns about $5.48 billion per year from agencies who employ their 22,600 employees.[55] These are a cadre of highly competent talent, many of

[50] See Olson Letter, *supra* note 44, at 14–15. [51] *Id.*, at 2.

[52] See David M. Herszenhorn & Jackie Calmes, *House to Consider I.R.S. Commissioner's Impeachment*, N.Y. Times (May 23, 2016), www.nytimes.com/2016/05/24/us/politics/house-set-to-begin-irs-commissioners-impeachment-hearing.html?_r=0.

[53] See Jackie Calmes, *Head of I.R.S., Facing Censure, Relishes a Job Few Could Love*, N.Y. Times (June 14, 2016), www.nytimes.com/2016/06/15/us/politics/irs-impeachment-john-koskinen.html; see also Emmarie Huetteman, *House Calls Off Vote to Impeach I.R.S. Chief in Favor of Formal Hearing*, N.Y. Times (Sept. 15, 2016), www.nytimes.com/2016/09/16/us/politics/house-impeach-irs-john-koskinen.html.

[54] His friend Joel Fleishman asked him when he undertook the Y2K Czar job in the Clinton Administration, "Who in their right mind would want to take on a job like that?" *Id.*

[55] See Booz Allen Hamilton, Annual Report (Form 10-K) (May 19, 2016).

whom have prior government service, and one-half of whom have security clearances.[56] Since obtaining top-secret and above clearances can take up to a year, this is yet another reason why it is easier to hire contractors than civil servants. But having employees with security clearances does not mean they will be properly used. Two Booz Allen contractors, Edward Snowden and Howard T. Martin, have been charged with theft of government documents.[57] The size of Booz Allen's Washington contractor force recalls the question posed by Jack Donahue in his "warping" of government work discussed in Chapter 2.[58] Talent at the top end, rather than the middle or lower end – those who do Donahue's "custom" rather than "commodity" tasks – are the real growth area, because they yield higher salaries. Contractors, like everyone else, follow the money.

The examples given in this chapter show that it is not just the number of contractors versus government employees that matters most, but the extent to which they invade the executive level of decisionmaking. CMS and IRS need more professionals to do their missions competently. Glaring inadequacies in oversight of the contractor regime can only be overcome by infusing more talent in government itself. Rational government is not contractor government, it is professional government managing contractor services.

56 For more on the world of contractors and security clearances, see Dana Priest & William M. Arkin, *National Security, Inc.*, Washington Post (part of the 2010 series on *Top Secret America*), http://projects.washingtonpost.com/top-secret-america/articles/national-security-inc/.

57 See Matthew Rosenberg, *At Booz Allen, a Vast U.S. Spy Operation, Run for Private Profit*, N.Y. Times (Oct. 6, 2016), www.nytimes.com/2016/10/07/us/booz-allen-hamilton-nsa.html (quoting Peter W. Singer: "There will be meetings, and less than 10 percent of the people there are official US government employees as opposed to contractors").

58 See Chapter 2, note 10.

# 4

# The Consequences of Federal Contractor Government

Who's on first?

Bud Abbott and Lou Costello, *The Naughty Nineties* (1945)

Contractors and government have a long and often productive relationship. Think again of Bechtel leading a consortium of contractors to build the Hoover Dam in 1931, an amazing achievement to this day. So any attempt to evaluate that relationship must look at benefits and costs, in both their direct and social dimensions. Obvious cases for contractors are when assignments can be described clearly and costs are competitively determined.[1] In these situations, costs that self-interested agents (contractors) can impose on the principal (government) are minimized.[2] We don't need civil servants to mow the White House lawn nor the Federal Emergency Management Agency (FEMA) to produce and stockpile trailers, food, or busses for the next major hurricane. Every agency has an extensive list of those services that can and should be contracted out in order to maintain flexibility and save money.

Indeed, many other functions, Donahue's "commodity" tasks, would seem to be prime candidates for contracting out. At a White House garden reception for agency officials a few years ago, one example came to me. We were entertained by the President's own Marine Corps band in bright red uniforms playing jazz. They performed well, but not better than musicians that play in the French Quarter, for example. So it hit me, why not contract for some talent from the Big Easy for occasions like this? Why not privatize jazz bands, I naïvely thought, and save the Marine band for those occasions of state where

[1] See John Donahue, The Privatization Decision: Public Ends, Private Means (1990).

[2] See Oliver E. Williamson, The Economic Institutions of Capitalism 27–30 (1985); see also discussion in Outsourcing Sovereignty at 150–52.

they are justified? But when you look into the matter of military bands the challenge grows. Each of the services has them (the Marines have 12) and they are fully trained soldiers with career ambitions.[3] Agencies can call upon them at no cost for official events, just to keep them busy, which is something we took advantage of at ACUS (string quartet, not combo). Despite attempts to reduce their budgets, this "sacred cow" plays on. Their numbers are significant (6,500 worldwide), equal in size to the Foreign Service.[4] And their costs annually are three times the budget of the National Endowment for the Arts, which has music in its mission.[5]

This colorful and half-serious example is enough to make the point. There are many situations where contractors could do the job of government employees as effectively and at lower cost. The key is defining the product or service, costing it out and bidding it competitively. Sometimes, however, limitations on the contracting process are not captured by direct cost comparisons. Behind many government contracts are public sector values that are hard to quantify and are often hidden from view, yet they are real nonetheless.

## A. THE HIDDEN COSTS OF CONTRACTING OUT IN GENERAL

One hidden cost of contracting can be the confusion it produces on policy and management decisionmaking in government.[6] When contractors do work involving discretion and judgment at senior levels, management problems arise. By analogy, it may be acceptable to contract out management of bands but not their conductors. This is the steer, not row, concept for government that gained popularity during the Clinton/Gore reinventing government era

[3] See Walter Pincus, *Military Funds to Spare?*, Washington Post (Dec. 19, 2012), available at https://www.washingtonpost.com/world/national-security/military-funds-to-spare/2012/12/19/25facd7a-4951–11e2–820e-17eefac2f939_story.html.

[4] See Walter Pincus, *House Puts Squeeze on Military's 'Musical Arsenal'*, Washington Post (May 18, 2012), available at https://www.washingtonpost.com/blogs/checkpoint-washington/post/house-puts-squeeze-on-militarys-musical-arsenal/2012/05/18/gIQAs1WiYU_blog.html.

[5] Military bands are not cheap; their costs are into the billions. See Dave Philipps, *Military Is Asked to March to a Less Expensive Tune*, N.Y. Times (Jul. 1, 2016), www.nytimes.com/2016/07/02/us/military-bands-budget.html?_r=0; see also John T. Bennett, *Analyst: Military Bands to Cost Pentagon $50B over Next 50 Years*, The Hill (May 18, 2011), available at http://thehill.com/homenews/administration/161837-analyst-military-bands-to-cost-dod-50b-in-50-years.

[6] It is important not to draw an artificial distinction between policy and operations, as one informs the other and leaders should be able to work in both directions. See Steve Kelman, *'Policy' and 'Operations': Don't Choose One over the Other*, FCW Blog (June 20, 2016), https://fcw.com/blogs/lectern/2016/06/kelman-policy-ops.aspx (recommending that top bureaucrats work in both arenas).

as discussed in Chapter 1. But when managers do the same work, sit next to each other, and can't be distinguished, except by IDs or paycheck, confusion results over mission and execution as well as identity.[7]

## 1 *The "Who's on First?" Problem*

This can create an Abbott and Costello "Who's on first?" situation. Excuse the digression. The skit worked because there was a first baseman named "Who," so the confusion became a hilarious entanglement.[8] For a whole host of important reasons set out here, we need to know the "Who" who is running our government.

The policy influence of contractors over senior civil servants is complicated territory. Government policymaking is a non-outsourceable responsibility. The exercise of judgment is inherently governmental. Yet advice from outside sources, including contractors, may lead to better decisions (this was the case with USAID discussed in Chapter 3). So the question is, when does advice cross the line into decisionmaking? In *Outsourcing Sovereignty* contractor

7 See the quote from the GAO official in Chapter 3, note 26, who didn't realize for months that the agency official they were dealing with was in fact a contractor.

8 ABBOTT: Strange as it may seem, they give ball players nowadays very peculiar names.
COSTELLO: Funny names?
ABBOTT: Nicknames. Now, on St. Louis Who's on first, What's on second, I Don't Know is on third—
COSTELLO: That's what I want to find out. I want you to tell me the . . . fellows on the St. Louis team.
ABBOTT: I'm telling you. Who's on first, What's on second, I Don't Know is on third—
COSTELLO: You know the fellows' names?
ABBOTT: Yes.
COSTELLO: Well, then who's playing first?
ABBOTT: Yes.
COSTELLO: I mean the fellow's name on first base.
ABBOTT: Who.
COSTELLO: The fellow playin' first base.
ABBOTT: Who.
COSTELLO: The guy on first base.
ABBOTT: Who is on first.
COSTELLO: Well, what are you askin' me for?
ABBOTT: I'm not asking you – I'm telling you. Who is on first.
COSTELLO: I'm asking you – who's on first?
ABBOTT: That's the man's name.
COSTELLO: That's who's name?
ABBOTT: Yes.

assistance with the rulemaking process at EPA was outlined.[9] Presumably all agencies who do rulemaking face the same problems: deciding how much to use contractors in formulating rules. Summarizing comments, which can be voluminous, may make sense (although the agency loses direct contact with the submitters). But drafting the statement of basis and purpose which derives from the comments is another matter altogether. One assignment is a species of advice; the other is a decisionmaking function. Measuring how much influence contractors have over policy usually derives from anecdotes because so much goes on below the surface. In some agencies, from impressions I have received, the government officials are demoralized (or intimidated) by the extensive use of contractors and make little attempt to claim (or preserve) their management territory; in other agencies they fight back.

However, a recent study conducted by Professor David Lewis of Vanderbilt University sheds light on how much policy influence contractors have.[10] Agency respondents were asked about the influence various groups had over their policy decisions. As to contractors, the influence ranged from "a good bit" to "none." Some of the agencies highlighted in Chapter 3 as contractor-dominated (DOE, CMS, and DOD) were highest on the list, which is set out on the next page.

This may be viewed as good news to the extent that "none" exceeds "some"; and even "some" is better than "a good bit." Lewis summarizes the responses in the footnoted chart.[11]

The result is that 32 percent of respondents say contractors have no influence over policy, but 68 percent say "little," "some," or "more." Importantly, these

9 See OUTSOURCING SOVEREIGNTY at 45–46.

10 See David E. Lewis, Vanderbilt University, Center for the Study of Democratic Institutions, Policy Influence of Senior Civil Servants Less the Policy Influence of Contractors (2016).

11 . tab policy_contractors

| policy_contractors | Freq. | Percent | Cum. |
|---|---|---|---|
| None | 435 | 31.89 | 31.89 |
| Little | 539 | 39.52 | 71.41 |
| Some | 280 | 20.53 | 91.94 |
| A good bit | 82 | 6.01 | 97.95 |
| A great deal | 28 | 2.05 | 100.00 |
| Total | 1,364 | 100.00 | |

So, 32% say none and 68% say little, some, or more.

Data from the Vanderbilt-Princeton 2014 Survey on the Future of Government Service.

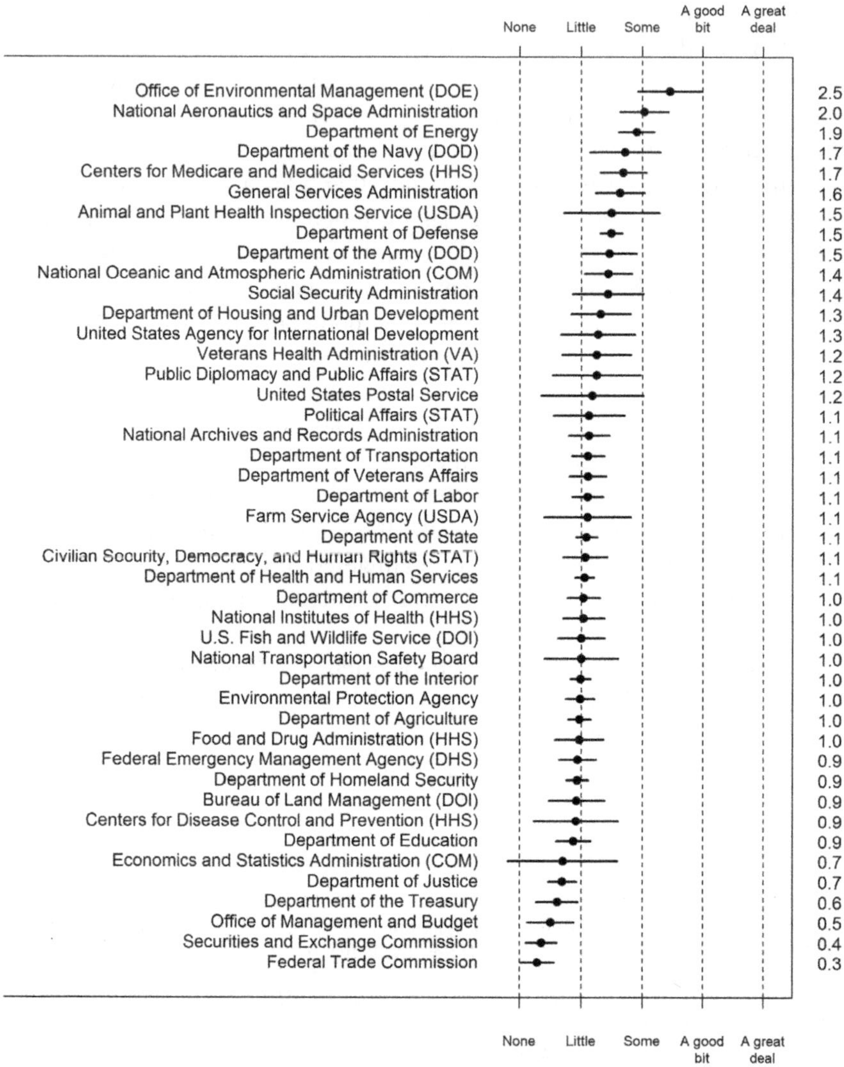


"In general, how much influence do you think the following groups have over policy decisions in [your agency]?" Contractors

*Note:* Lines denote the 95% confidence intervals. Limited to cases with at least 10 respondents excluding responses of "Don't know" and at least 30 potential respondents in the target population. Responses are "A great deal," "A good bit," "Some," Little," "None," and "Don't know." Responses are coded 0 ("None") to 4 ("A great deal"), and "Don't know" is coded as missing.

percentages go up slightly in the subsequent chart,[12] when the influence question is limited to those respondents whose jobs deal directly with decisions about procurement and contract management (74 percent say "little" to "a great deal").

Since these are particularly sensitive government functions, highlighted as agency weaknesses by GAO, these responses are of greater concern.

## 2 *Oversight Failures*

In addition, when policy and management assignments are delegated to contractors, agencies often do not impose adequate controls. GAO has determined, for example, that, while agencies often rely on contractors to operate computer systems and process information, they frequently fail adequately to oversee these contractor-operated systems.[13] While OMB has developed guidance on how to oversee contractor-operated systems, GAO found that five of six major agencies failed to implement the guidance or establish security and privacy protocols.[14]

The oversight of contractors is a large problem for agencies because they lack capable personnel to perform that role. It is one of the main reasons shown in Chapter 3 that the Affordable Care Act website rollout had such a difficult time. When government, in desperation, hires contractors to oversee contractors, the "Who's on first?" dilemma is in plain view. Who in government oversees the contractors who oversee the contractors? This was the key policy

12
```
. tab policy_contractors if job_contract ==1

policy_contr |
      actors |      Freq.     Percent        Cum.
-------------+-----------------------------------
        None |        178       26.10       26.10
      Little |        272       39.88       65.98
        Some |        163       23.90       89.88
  A good bit |         52        7.62       97.51
A great deal |         17        2.49      100.00
-------------+-----------------------------------
       Total |        682      100.00
```
Data from the Vanderbilt-Princeton 2014 Survey on the Future of Government Service, www.princeton.edu/~psrc/SFGS/

13 Gov't Accountability Office, Information Security – Agencies Need to Improve Oversight of Contractor Controls, GAO-14-612 (Aug. 2014).

14 See *id*. The agencies were DOE, DHS, State, DOT, EPA, and OPM. Only DHS met all GAO criteria.

issue emphasized by the Harvard Conference discussed in Chapter 2 and it only seems to be getting worse. To contain it, as John DiIulio says, we need to bring back the bureaucrats.

### 3 *Unknown Cost Comparisons*

The direct costs of contractors can also be "hidden" in other ways – they are simply not available for comparison. It is sensible to think that contractors can often do jobs for government more efficiently, if they are short-term and competitively bid. The direct overhead government assumes for its employees (health care, retirement, etc.) is costly (over 26 percent of an average salary) and the indirect charges, for facilities, training, etc., can, if properly allocated, exceed that total. Even if they charge more on a per-hour or -month basis, contractors can come in below the fully costed government total. But these comparisons are rarely made because the information is hard to collect, maintain, and update.

Some information on contractors' costs has been developed by the Project on Government Oversight (POGO), a public interest group. POGO has studied DOD contracting costs and concluded in a letter to then Defense Secretary Chuck Hagel that "DOD expends on contracted services nearly three times what it would cost were those services performed by civilian personnel."[15] Since DOD is required by statute to develop a cost-effective mix of public and private services, this is a troubling report, backed up by others with similar conclusions.[16] These estimates are subject to challenge, but so far DOD has not acted to rebut these conclusions. They are direct evidence of economic waste.[17]

Contractor services are more likely to be competitive with government alternatives when the bidding process is properly invoked. In theory, professional

[15] Paul Chassey & Scott Amey, *POGO Highlights GAO Report and Documented DoD Failures in Hiring a Cost Efficient Workforce* 1 (Oct. 17, 2013), available at www.pogo.org/our-work/letters/2013/pogo-highlights-gao-report.html, criticize DOD for not developing proper overhead cost models which it is required to do under 10 U.S.C. § 129.

[16] See POGO, *Bad Business: Billions of Taxpayer Dollars Wasted on Hiring Contractors* (Sept. 13, 2011), available at www.pogo.org/our-work/reports/2011/co-gp-20110913.html.

[17] Megan McCloskey, *As the Military Cries Poor, It Wastes Billions in Afghanistan*, The Fiscal Times (Jan. 21, 2016) (regarding questions raised as to the effectiveness of spending by DOD in Afghanistan: "The readiness subcommittee of the Senate Armed Services Committee didn't get many answers. 'That's the big question, and it's the right one,' was all Brian McKeon, principal deputy undersecretary of defense for policy, could offer. During two hours of questioning, he provided few specifics, allowing, 'It's a little early to say' whether the now-defunct Task Force for Business and Stability Operations had been successful").

services contracting can be done three ways: full and open; competed (two or more options); or sole source.[18] But true competitive bidding may be on the decline in government, where "repeat players" means entrenched suppliers have a renewal edge with the agencies for whom they work.[19] On the equipment side, weapons systems are usually sole sourced.[20] On the services side, in the $250 billion contractor market described earlier, competition in bidding can be affected by the complicated nature of the duties, the capacity of contractors to deliver, and the urgency of the mission. Certainly the ACA rollout fiasco at CMS is an example of cost-plus contracting producing problems. And there is one other factor to consider: the burden on the government's contractor workforce. Competitive bidding takes time and expertise, which is in short supply. The contractor specialist workload is so high that one leading expert observer compared them to legal aid lawyers with too many cases to manage.[21] This may be one reason why the Lewis chart in footnote 12 above shows a higher degree of contractor influence in procurement and contracting officer responses.

When contractors secure favored status from competitive renewals due to their prior performances, the value of contractor efficiency can be further compromised. Established and repeat players have created an asset in their status. This status becomes a protectable interest with the agencies involved. It may not amount to a property right, but contractors' relationships to government are valuable commodities. The value is both on existing and future contracts. This is where the "revolving door" helps provide continued access. Generals and Flag Officers, for example, frequently find a home across the contractor–government divide. President Eisenhower's famous concern over the military–industrial complex made the connection between established players, military hardware, and government procurement.[22] Today the issue has been extended to professional services contracts as well. As contractor services

[18] Personal interview with Stan Soloway, May 18, 2016 (Stan Soloway is the former President and CEO of the Professional Services Council, which represents the government technology and professional services industry).

[19] See Matthew Nussbaum, *How Elon Musk Exposed Billions In Questionable Pentagon Spending*, Politico (Apr. 28, 2016), available at www.politico.com/story/2016/05/elon-musk-rocket-defense-223161 (discussing the breaking of the Boeing–Lockheed joint venture, United Launch Alliance, ongoing monopoly of bidding for GPS satellite launches by SpaceX).

[20] See Government Accountability Office, DOD's Use of Class Justifications for Sole-Source Contracts, GAO-14-427R (Apr. 16, 2014).

[21] Interview with Stan Soloway, *supra* note 18.

[22] Farewell address of President Dwight D. Eisenhower on January 17, 1961.

have grown, military hardware companies like Lockheed Martin and Boeing have become big services providers.[23] And contractors like Booz Allen see their national security business grow even in the face of security failures by their employees, like Edward Snowden.

### B. HIDDEN COSTS OF REGULATORY CAPTURE

Regulatory capture is a phenomenon with a long history. It began with a concern about overt corruption in nineteenth-century regulatory agencies,[24] became associated with the "maturing" process in old line regulatory agencies in the 1950s[25] and was assumed as largely inevitable by the 1970s.[26] After the deregulation movement and the curtailing of industry-specific economic regulation, interest in the subject waned.[27] But it has recently returned to both political and academic attention. Led by Senators Sheldon Whitehouse, who said "regulatory capture assaults democracy," and Mike Lee, who called it a "moral issue of our time," regulatory capture came to Capitol Hill in 2016.[28]

A major book on regulatory capture theory appeared just before the Senate program.[29] Daniel Carpenter and David A. Moss introduced the *Preventing Capture* volume by describing the "mechanisms of capture." The first, characterized by the deregulation movement, is labeled "corrosive capture," which seeks to dismantle regulation "in the absence of public support or a strong public welfare rationale for doing so." The second mechanism is called "cultural capture," which describes more subtle interference with the public good, like

[23] Lockheed was the biggest government contractor in 2015 at $36.2 billion and Boeing was second at $16.6 billion. This total consists of military weapons like the F-35 and "services programs too numerous to list." See Aaron Mehta, *Lockheed Martin Biggest U.S. Government Contractor in 2015*, DEFENSE NEWS (May 9, 2016), www.defensenews.com/story/defense/policy-budget/industry/2016/05/09/lockheed-biggest-government-contractor-2015-defense-industry/83961520/.

[24] See William J. Novak, *A Revisionist History of Regulatory Capture*, in PREVENTING REGULATORY CAPTURE 25, 41 (Daniel Carpenter & David A. Moss, eds. 2014) (hereinafter PREVENTING CAPTURE). Novak quotes Charles Francis Adams in 1871 saying: "Who will guard the virtue of the tribunal?"

[25] See MARVER H. BERBSTEIN, REGULATING BUSINESS BY INDEPENDENT COMMISSIONS (1955).

[26] See George J. Stigler, *The Theory of Economic Regulation*, 2 BELL J. OF ECON. & MGMT. SCIENCE 3 (1971) (regulation was a commodity purchased by a regulated industry).

[27] See Richard A. Posner, *The Concept of Regulatory Capture – A Short, Inglorious History*, in PREVENTING CAPTURE 43.

[28] See ACUS Regulatory Capture Forum (Mar. 3, 2016) (agenda and overview available at https://www.acus.gov/meetings-and-events/event/regulatory-capture-workshop).

[29] See PREVENTING CAPTURE, at 16, 19.

"campaign contributions, pressure on politicians, and perhaps the 'revolving door.'"[30]

### 1 Agency Lobbying and the Revolving Door

The revolving door is the concept most applicable to agency use of contractors, since it is harder to lobby agencies (and impossible to give them political contributions). But there are often times when agencies can be approached. One is before the notice of proposed rulemaking has officially issued when lobbyists for interested parties (like drug and insurance companies in connection with rules promulgated under the Affordable Care Act or banks in terms of Dodd–Frank rules) are able to contact agency officials. Moreover, during the rulemaking process through contact with OIRA, the OMB arm that oversees executive agency promulgation of significant rules, is also permitted, although contact lists are published.[31]

Sometimes, when lobbyists cannot approach the agency directly, Congress is urged to legislate specifically against agency rulemaking authority. This seems to be what happened with the FDA where Congress, in a bill written by cigarette lobbyists, was urged to take away its jurisdiction to regulate e-cigarettes.[32]

The revolving door has a mixed reputation in capture theory. It assumes that industry officials, or their lawyers, will serve in government and then return to their private jobs and lobby their agencies, after appropriate waiting times. This is a form of influence that is traded upon regularly by the lobbying and law firms who symbolically reside, at least in DC, on "K Street." The negative view is that these former officials "peddle influence" and shape agency agendas for their clients' benefit. This is why lobbyists were banned from serving in the Obama Administration.[33] But there were numerous loopholes in this ban, from registering as lobbyists in the first place to finding ways to reach former agencies after leaving government.[34] The positive spin is that government service makes former officials better able to shape private clients'

30 *Id.*, at 27. A leading voice on money in politics belongs to Professor Lessig. See Lawrence Lessig, Republic, Lost – How Money Corrupts Congress and a Plan to Stop It (2011).

31 See Wendy Wagner, *Administrative Law, Filter Failure, and Information Capture*, 59 Duke L.J. 1321, 1380–82 (2010) (showing how industry makes many more contacts pre-NPRM than public interest groups do).

32 See Eric Lipton, *A Lobbyist Wrote the Bill. Will the Tobacco Industry Win Its E-Cigarette Fight?*, N.Y. Times (Sept. 2, 2016), www.nytimes.com/2016/09/03/us/politics/e-cigarettes-vaping-cigars-fda-altria.html.

33 See Exec. Order 13,490, 74 Fed. Reg. 4,673 (Jan. 21, 2009).

34 See Josh Gerstein, *How Obama Failed to Shut Washington's Revolving Door*, Politico (Dec. 31, 2015), www.politico.com/story/2015/12/barack-obama-revolving-door-lobbying-217042.

activities in a public interest direction. Eric Holder, now at Covington & Burling, presumably fits this category. Either way, the revolving door keeps turning, with some of its negative dimensions monitored mostly by transparency requirements, conflict rules, and cooling-off periods.

## 2 *Contractors and Rent Seeking*

But what of government service contractors? They are repeat players in the government and private sector whose ranks are populated by former government employees, retired military, or political appointees. McKinsey and Booz Allen Hamilton are long-term standouts, and large manufacturers, like Lockheed and Boeing, have now joined them. Do they engage in cultural capture? The question is highly relevant to the hidden costs of contractor versus professional government. The public choice and Stiglerian viewpoints[35] assert that government officials maximize their welfare by seeking rents, which consists primarily of preserving their jobs. But if that is true for career officials, the rent-seeking potential for contractors who work for government is far greater. Indeed, over time they achieve what is called an "expertise rent" consisting of superior knowledge gained from their repeat assignments.[36] And as Chapter 3 showed, at agencies like USAID, contractors sometimes go over the agency heads to Congress in order to preserve their programs from demise or modification. On the Buchanan and Tullock[37] public choice chart of regulatory self-interest, the incentives for contractors to preserve and grow their jobs should weigh more heavily than the civil servants' desire to keep their jobs. Indeed, on a relative basis, government employees' self-interest is far less than a contractor's, simply because of the numbers involved. Government employees, for example, might be able to preserve salaries, but contractors have a large field (now exceeding $250 billion) to play in.

## 3 *Political Contributions by Contractors*

Another cultural capture situation concerns the role of political contributions by contractor entities. There is presently no comprehensive way to know the

[35] See Stigler, *supra* note 26.

[36] See Nolan McCarty, *Complexity, Capacity, and Capture* 119, in PREVENTING CAPTURE (recommending that government strive to reduce the expertise advantage of firms by refining skills and raising pay of government workers).

[37] See JAMES M. BUCHANAN & GORDON TULLOCK, THE CALCULUS OF CONSENT: LOGICAL FOUNDATIONS OF CONSTITUTIONAL DEMOCRACY (1962); see also Reeve Bull, *Combatting External and Internal Regulatory Capture*, PROMARKET (Aug. 23, 2016), https://promarket.org/combatting-external-internal-regulatory-capture/.

amount of political expenditures by government contractors. According to Public Citizen, in 2014 barely more than a quarter of the top 15 contractors disclosed their contributions to dark money groups.[38] The Sunlight Foundation stated:

> Between 2007 and 2012, 200 of America's most politically active corporations spent a combined $5.8 billion on federal lobbying and campaign contributions. A year-long analysis by the Sunlight Foundation suggests, however, that what they gave pales compared to what those same corporations got: $4.4 trillion in federal business and support.[39]

Whether there is a connection between campaign contributions and the awarding of federal contracts is not established, but a disclosure requirement for federal contractors could provide transparency necessary to know the answer. Legislation on this issue has been defeated,[40] but there was pressure on President Obama to issue an executive order to require federal contractors to fully disclose money spent in politics.[41]

Since many federal contracts are awarded without competitive bidding,[42] the potential for influence from repeat players is evident. And one study has found a connection between contributions and contracts awarded.[43] There is a long-standing statute that prohibits political contributions directly to a candidate or political party during the time when contracts are being

[38] See Public Citizen, *An Executive Order on Contractor Political Spending Disclosure Would Reach 70 Percent of Top Companies* (Apr. 27, 2015), available at www.citizen.org/documents/Fortune-100-contractors.pdf. Dark money groups are 501(c)(4) and (c)(6) organizations that do not have to disclose their donors. See Kathleen M. Donovan-Maker & Steven L. Greenspan, *Why Dark Money is Bad Business*, N.Y. Times Op-Ed, May 10, 2016, at A23 (discussing pending Securities and Exchange Commission (SEC) rule on political disclosure).

[39] Bill Allison & Sarah Harkins, *Fixed Fortunes: Biggest Corporate Political Interests Spend Billions, Get Trillions*, Sunlight Foundation Blog (Nov. 17, 2014), available at http://sunlightfoundation.com/blog/2014/11/17/fixed-fortunes-biggest-corporate-political-interests-spend-billions-get-trillions/.

[40] The Democracy Is Strengthened by Casting Light On Spending in Elections Act, commonly known as the DISCLOSE Act and also known as H.R. 5175 (S.3628-Senate), was a bill introduced in the US House of Representatives by Chris Van Hollen (D-Maryland) on April 29, 2010 and in the US Senate by Charles Schumer (D-New York) on July 21, 2010. After a cloture vote failed 59–39 on September 23, 2010, the bill was essentially defeated.

[41] See Letter from Sen. Sheldon Whitehouse and 25 senators, "Executive Order on Political Spending by Governmental Contractors" (June 23, 2015).

[42] See Majority Staff of H. Comm. on Oversight and Govt. Reform, 110th Cong., *More Dollars, Less Sense: Worsening Contractor Trends Under the Bush Administration* 1 (Comm. Print 2007), available at http://democrats.oversight.house.gov/sites/democrats.oversight.house.gov/files/migrated/More%20Dollars%20Less%20Sense%20Final%2006–27–07.doc.

[43] See Christopher Witko, *Campaign Contributions, Access, and Government Contracting*, 21 J. Pub. Admin. Research & Theory 761 (2011).

negotiated or performed.[44] This statute has been upheld by the DC Circuit[45] against challenges posed by *Citizens United*, since it dealt with quid pro quo corruption, a subject left in place by the Supreme Court.

The theory of regulatory capture also seems to apply to these situations. In addition to revolving door issues, "cultural corruption" covers political contributions of the "pay to play" or quid pro quo variety. Many states also prohibit political contributions for state contractors, especially in noncompetitive bid situations.[46] Given their potential to cause direct corruption, it is understandable that reformers would suggest banning federal contractor political contributions altogether.[47]

The case against political spending should be made first through the transparency requirements. Transparency is one way to reassure the public, which Chapter 1 shows increasingly believes that government is corrupt. Congress has so far been unwilling to enact the DISCLOSE Act, which would require all corporations to reveal political contributions, and the Securities and Exchange Commission (SEC) has been unwilling to act as well.[48] The White House can act by Executive Order to fill this void, having in mind that information about political contributions must be kept away from contracting officials who are required not to be influenced by such information.[49]

## C. PRIVATE PRISONS AS AN OBJECT LESSON

The confluence between government contracting and political influence may be best viewed in terms of the private prison industry. This industry serves both federal and state governments and provides a product ("carceration"[50]) that has

44 See Act of July 19, 1940, ch. 64 § 5(a), 54 Stat. 772.

45 See *Wagner* v. *FEC*, 793 F.3d 1, 37 (D.C. Cir. 2015).

46 See Karl J. Sanstrom & Michael T. Liburdi, *Overview of State Pay-To-Play Statutes* (May 5, 2010), available at https://www.perkinscoie.com/images/content/2/1/v2/21769/wp-10–05-pay-to-play.pdf.

47 See Naila Awan & Liz Kennedy, The Racial Equity Impact of Secret Political Spending by Government Contractors, DEMOS.ORG (2015), available at www.demos.org/publication/racial-equity-impact-secret-political-spending-government-contractors ("Federal contracting, which should be based on a level playing field, is riddled with cozy relationships, back room deals, and pay to play arrangements").

48 A number of petitions from law professors and the Brennan Center for Justice have requested the SEC require disclosure by rulemaking of political contributions by publicly traded corporations. See DISCLOSING MONEY IN ELECTIONS, THE SUNLIGHT FOUNDATION, http://sunlightfoundation.com/policy/disclosingmoney/ (last visited Jul. 8, 2016).

49 See 10 U.S. Code § 2335, which bans agencies from requesting that political information be included in bids.

50 See MARIE GOTTSCHALK, CAUGHT: THE PRISON STATE AND THE LOCKDOWN OF AMERICAN POLITICS (2015) (describing the growth of the "carceral" state).

long been thought to be an inherent function of government.[51] Early on, John DiIulio questioned whether private prisons violated the government's "duty to govern"[52] and Sharon Dolovich, in an article discussed in Chapter 1, decried the "comparative efficiency" analysis that permitted private prisons to prevail in cost debates that leave out social consequences of carceration.[53] The 2016 Nobel Laureate in Economics, Oliver Hart, and his colleagues had earlier determined that a private contractor's incentive to engage in cost reduction outweighs nonquantifiable quality of service considerations.[54]

Private prisons certainly "significantly affect the life, liberty, and property of private persons" under OMB's definition of inherent government functions (see p. 19). Still the growth in the use of private prisons continues, as contractors have utilized the political process to secure and expand their business. This industry is the poster child for regulatory capture. Private prison companies are expert lobbyists. The leading ones (GEO and CCA) have spent nearly $25 million in lobbying efforts since 1989 at the federal and state levels.[55] Their share of the prison market (which includes immigrant detainees) has grown dramatically during this time and annual revenues are about $3.3 billion.[56] The Justice Policy Institute lists three strategies of private prisons to increase revenues: campaign contributions, lobbying, and relationships and associations.[57] These techniques, familiar to the regulatory capture literature, are in greater demand now that federal and state initiatives to reduce the prison population (legislation that the private prison companies opposed) are taking effect.

And there is increasing evidence that the industry's main asset, more efficient service, is being compromised. A recent report by the DOJ's Office of the Inspector General concluded that "in most key areas, contract prisons incurred more safety and security incidents per capita than comparable

51 The use of force is an inherent responsibility of government. See OUTSOURCING SOVEREIGNTY, at 37–41.

52 See John DiIulio, Jr., *The Duty to Govern: A Critical Perspective on the Private Management of Prisons and Jails*, in PRIVATE PRISONS AND THE PUBLIC INTEREST (Douglas C. McDonald ed.) (1990).

53 See Dolovich, *supra* Chapter 1, at note 11.

54 Oliver Hart, Andrei Shleifer & Robert W. Vishny, *The Proper Scope of Government: Theory and an Application to Prisons*, 112 Q. J. ECON. 1127–61 (1996).

55 See Michael Cohen, *How For-Profit Prisons Have Become the Biggest Lobby No One is Talking About*, WASH. POST (Apr. 28, 2015), https://www.washingtonpost.com/posteverything/wp/2015/04/28/how-for-profit-prisons-have-become-the-biggest-lobby-no-one-is-talking-about/?utm_term=.885862425153 (noting that Marco Rubio is the largest Senate beneficiary and was also a big recipient when he was in the Florida legislature).

56 *Id.* There are about 130 private prisons in the United States, with 157,000 beds, about 20 percent of the total prisoners.

57 JUSTICE POLICY INSTITUTE, GAMING THE SYSTEM: HOW THE POLITICAL STRATEGIES OF PRIVATE PRISON COMPANIES PROMOTE INEFFECTIVE INCARCERATION POLICIES (2011).

Bureau of Prisons institutions."[58] This report led DOJ to reduce and ultimately end the use of privately operated prisons.[59] Following suit shortly thereafter, Secretary Johnson of the Department of Homeland Security announced that DHS would be reviewing its own arrangements with providers of private immigration detention facilities.[60] It remains to be seen whether this action at the federal level will carry over to the state prison setting, where the industry's regulatory capture techniques have been even more effective.[61]

It is hard to reconcile private prisons with the duty to govern and supervise principles that emanate from both federal and state constitutions. It is impossible to do so when the quality of service that they promise is not there as well. Efficiency principles alone should not mask the social cost dimensions of the problem, but if they are absent, then the industry can only survive on its ability to capture the public interest. Unfortunately, private prison companies are well on the way to doing that after raising a record $100 million for Trump's inauguration.[62]

58 *Review of the Federal Bureau of Prisons' Monitoring of Contract Prisons*, Evaluation and Inspections Division 16–06 (2016).

59 See Matt Zapotosky & Chico Harlan, *Justice Department Says It Will End Use of Private Prisons*, Wash. Post (Aug. 18, 2016), https://www.washingtonpost.com/news/post-nation/wp/2016/08/18/justice-department-says-it-will-end-use-of-private-prisons/?utm_term=.c5d3c4380f58 (quoting Deputy Attorney General Sally Yates that the goal is "reducing – and ultimately ending – our use of privately operated prisons").

60 See DHS Press Office, *Statement by Secretary Jeh C. Johnson on Establishing a Review of Privatized Immigration Detention* (Aug. 29, 2016), https://www.dhs.gov/news/2016/08/29/statement-secretary-jeh-c-johnson-establishing-review-privatized-immigration.

61 Not that the state prisons don't have problems. For example, a private prison in Kansas has been caught spying on constitutionally protected attorney–client conversations. See Dahlia Lithwick, *Leavenworth's Spygate*, Slate (Aug. 22, 2016), www.slate.com/articles/news_and_politics/jurisprudence/2016/08/the_leavenworth_inmate_spying_scandal_is_intensely_troubling.html.

62 See Fredreka Schouten, *Private Prisons Back Trump and Could See Big Payoffs with New Policies*, USA Today (Feb. 23, 2017) (noting the growth in private detention centers to hold undocumented immigrants).

# 5

# State Examples of Government Failure

Just do your job

Bill Belichick, Coach, New England Patriots

The problem of government professionalism at the state level is multivaried. While not synonymous with the growth of contractors as it is at the federal level, bureaucratic competence is a significant issue in the states. The question of competence – of professionalism – is apparent in the examples of government failure that follow. Whether these failures are related to the "at will" state government employment movement, the growth in contractors, the weaknesses of the civil service system, or some other cause varies with each case. What is clear, however, is that state officials are often not performing with the degree of competence the public has a right to demand. "Just do your job," as the legendary coach says.

One problem common to the states, however, is the need for "robust contractor oversight."[1] Lax oversight wastes tax dollars, encourages fraud and abuse, permits poor contractor performance, and increases risks to public health and safety. This is a problem that states share with the federal government and it is not easily solved without investment in qualified people. The requirement for quality human infrastructure has a high payoff.

## A. THE FLINT WATER CRISIS

The situation in Flint, Michigan, illustrates two infrastructure failures. One is the trillion dollar problem of deferred maintenance of deteriorated lead water

[1] See In the Public Interest, *Standing Guard – How Unaccountable Contracting Fails Governments and Taxpayers* 1 (Dec. 2014) (describing ways states and localities can assert proper oversight over contractors); see also Indiana University School of Public and Environmental Affairs, *Government Outsourcing: A Practical Guide for State and Local Governments* (Jan. 2014) (emphasizing the need to develop clear, specific, and effective contract requirements).

pipes[2] and the other is the *human* infrastructure failure of those responsible for preserving the public health in Michigan. The latter problem is the focus here but, given that water pipes are largely under control of state public authorities nationally, other "Flints" are waiting to happen,[3] unless we fix the human as well as physical infrastructure weaknesses that surround them.

The story of Flint is best summarized by the opening sentence of the Flint Water Advisory Task Force. "The Flint Water Crisis is a story of government failure, intransigence, unpreparedness, delay, inaction, and environmental injustice."[4] This Task Force, appointed by the Governor, Rick Snyder, certainly does not mince words. There were several key moments that led to this "indictment" of government. The first was when the Governor's Emergency Manager for Flint decided to switch Flint's water supply from the Detroit River to the Flint River for economic cost reasons. According to the Task Force, the Governor's appointment of an Emergency Manager removed "the checks and balances and public accountability" that comes from local Flint officials and citizens.[5] The second cause was the failure of the Michigan Department of Environmental Quality (MDEQ) to use corrosion control chemicals when the water systems were switched. MDEQ was the agency with primary authority and its officials persistently ignored valid water quality complaints and failed to do adequate sampling required by the Safe Drinking Water Act. EPA also had jurisdiction under the Safe Drinking Water Act it could have exercised, but it deferred to state authorities.[6]

[2] Michael E. Webber, *Our Water System: What a Waste*, N.Y. Times, Mar. 22, 2016, at A23 (citing an American Society of Civil Engineers report estimating that repair and replacement of water systems nationally could cost $1.3 trillion); see also Emma Court, *America's Water Crisis is Way Bigger than Flint*, Marketwatch.com (Apr. 13, 2016), www.marketwatch.com/story/americas-water-crisis-is-way-bigger-than-flint-2016–04–13.

[3] See Brady Dennis, *Schools around the Country Find Lead in Water, with No Easy Answers*, Washington Post (Jul. 4, 2016), https://www.washingtonpost.com/national/health-science/schools-around-the-country-find-lead-in-water-with-no-easy-answers/2016/07/03/b44240fe-37c3–11e6-a254–2b336e293a3c_story.html.

[4] Flint Water Advisory Task Force, Final Report (Mar. 2016) (executive summary), hereinafter FWATF.

[5] *Id.*; see also Editorial, *When State Control Damages a City*, N.Y. Times Feb. 4, 2016, at A22 (referring to the "disastrous money-saving decision to change the water source").

[6] *Id.* EPA Administrator Gina McCarthy testified before Congress that she regretted not pushing harder but denied EPA had primary responsibility. The FWATF Report concurred with her on this point, but the EPA Inspector General did not. *See* Eric Katz, *IG Faults EPA for Not Intervening Seven Months Sooner in Flint Water Crisis*, Government Executive (Oct. 21, 2016), http://www.govexec.com/oversight/2016/10/ig-faults-epa-not-intervening-seven-months-sooner-flint-water-crisis/132544/. The main reason EPA did not intervene was the practice of cooperative federalism, which gives the states first responsibility, a practice the new head of the EPA, Scott Pruitt, will surely endorse.

Governor Snyder comes in for criticism from the Task Force for relying "almost *exclusively*" on incorrect information from state officials "despite mounting evidence from outside experts."[7] The Task Force also criticizes the Governor's Office for "inappropriate and unacceptable" public statements about the Flint crisis. There are few government officials who acquitted themselves well in this situation, but the Report praises the citizens of Flint for their persistence and courage and concludes "that the Flint Water Crisis is a clear case of environmental injustice."[8]

There have been nine criminal indictments brought by the Michigan Attorney General against five MDEQ officials, three Department of Health and Human Services officials, and the city's Emergency Manager for misconduct in office, a felony.[9] There are questions whether the criminal standards of intent can be met in these cases, although there has already been one guilty plea,[10] but the larger questions remain even if the officials are convicted. Some fear that Governor Snyder will use these criminal indictments to avoid responsibility,[11] since criminal behavior takes the conduct out of the realm of poor management. The Michigan Attorney General's staff compared their investigation to those involving organized crime and promised further indictments of higher-up officials.[12] This hyper-charged analysis may be justified, but some of the targets are state officials whose main crime may be incompetence.

The lessons of Flint from a professional government perspective are multivaried. Some contractors, such as water quality experts, did a fine job,[13] while other contractors failed to provide adequate chemicals to treat the water. The governor said during his congressional testimony that his mistake was trusting "career bureaucrats" who consistently misinformed

7 FWATF Report, Finding F-12, F-16.

8 *Id.*, at Finding F-36.

9 See David M. Uhlmann, *Can the Flint Prosecution Succeed?*, N.Y. Times, Apr. 23, 2016, at A19, available at www.nytimes.com/2016/04/23/opinion/can-the-flint-prosecutions-succeed.html.

10 See Amy Haimerl & Abby Goodnough, *6 More State Workers Charged in Flint Water Crisis*, N.Y. Times (Jul. 29, 2016), www.nytimes.com/2016/07/30/us/flint-michigan-water-crisis.html.

11 See Editorial, *Indictments Don't Absolve Snyder in Flint Water Crisis*, Detroit Free Press (Apr. 21, 2016), available at www.freep.com/story/opinion/editorials/2016/04/21/flint-criminal-charges/83293934/ ("Snyder has accepted responsibility for Flint. But he continues to dodge blame, which he'd prefer to see land at the feet of those career bureaucrats").

12 Haimerl & Goodnough, *supra* note 10 ("'You don't start at the top with organized crime,' Mr. Arena said. 'That's what we're doing here'"). The state is said to be focusing on "bigger targets." Mitch Smith, *Flint, and Michigan, Brace for More Charges in Water Inquiry*, N.Y. Times (Oct. 28, 2016), http://www.nytimes.com/2016/10/29/us/flint-michigan-water-investigation.html.

13 A professor from Virginia Tech was indeed an important source of reliable information. See *The Virginia Tech Research Team*, http://flintwaterstudy.org/about-page/about-us/.

him,[14] so professionalism may have been lacking. Still, the Governor is not an objective witness – he may be searching for scapegoats. As an elected official and also a state employee, one of the Governor's jobs is to build a sound state personnel system. This is a system where bureaucrats must not only be competent but aggressive in fulfilling their mission. Ideally, part of a governor's job is to create an atmosphere where state employees want to do well and know they will be supported when they challenge authority. A good example in this regard is Secretary McDonald at the Veterans Administration who, upon assuming the job, sought dismissal of those in the Veterans Health Service who covered up the true waiting times for medical appointments, and then sought to restructure the agency so that such lapses would not happen in the future.[15]

Lead poisoning of children in cities and especially minority areas is a national disgrace. The industry fought regulation for decades despite clear scientific evidence of its human costs.[16] The lessons from Flint that the Task Force identified are not only those of "government failure" but of "environmental injustice" which has deep and troubling dimensions.[17] There were also implications that the state's emergency manager setup deprived a locality of the benefit of its elected officials (who were minorities). The decision to use outsiders to intervene in local situations like Flint or Detroit must be carefully considered. When the purpose of the appointment was to find economic savings, then decisions like shifting the water source from the Detroit to Flint Rivers flow ineluctably from the appointment. Short-term goals seemingly overrode all environmental considerations. Flint is a minority community and the governor and Republican majority legislators are from different backgrounds. Understanding the community seems to have been overlooked in the emergency manager's appointment and in his purpose.

[14] Abby Goodnough, *Michigan Governor Tells Congress He Was Misled on Flint Water*, N.Y. Times, Mar. 18, 2016, at A20, available at www.nytimes.com/2016/03/18/us/michigan-governor-tells-congress-he-was-misled-on-flint-water.html.

[15] See discussion in Chapter 7, section C.

[16] See Gerald Markowitz & David Rosner, Lead Wars: The Politics of Science and the Fate of America's Children (2013) (discussing the history of lead poisoning regulation); see also Paul Krugman, Op-Ed, *Black Lead Matters*, N.Y. Times. (Sept. 2, 2016), www.nytimes.com/2016/09/02/opinion/black-lead-matters.html?_r=0 (emphasizing the impact on minorities).

[17] The connection between race, class, identity, location, and environmental hardship was first identified by the Council on Environmental Quality in its 1971 Annual Report to the President and has since been thoroughly documented as a severe ongoing civil rights and environmental policy concern. See United States of America. Environmental Justice Group. National Conference of State Legislatures, *Environmental Justice: A Matter of Perspective* (1995).

The irony of Flint is that any economic savings from the shift in water sources have been overwhelmed by the billions of dollars now required to put the community back together. The tragedy of Flint is that the human costs to children who face a lifetime of physical and mental problems from high concentrations of lead will never be made up. Understanding Flint from a government management perspective highlights the difficulty of doing important jobs well. These are not impossible jobs, and other city water quality management programs succeed with career bureaucrats running them.[18] Flint is an object lesson in the need to improve professionalism in providing basic services to the public.

## B. THE NORTH CAROLINA COAL ASH SPILL

In North Carolina, civil service protections were watered down by statute and a State Personnel Commission established to reduce the size of the career service.[19] Taking advantage of the law, Governor Pat McCrory reduced the professionals at the North Carolina Department of Environment and Natural Resources (DENR) from 179 to 24.[20] The General Assembly and the Governor had no love for the DENR as a regulatory agency, which was once considered one of the most powerful and independent in the southeast United States. But those qualities seem no longer to have been prized. Regulators were told by new political leadership they should focus on "customer service" for regulated industry and issue permits as fast as possible.[21] It was made explicit to DENR employees that "If you don't like change, you'll be gone."[22]

Governor McCrory's timing in marginalizing DENR was unfortunate for North Carolina. Duke Power spilled 39,000 tons of coal ash into the Dan

[18] New York City has one of the strictest lead control laws and only 2.1 percent of its children were at risk. See Michael Wines, *Beyond Flint, Lead Poisoning Persists Despite Decades-Old Fight*, N.Y. Times, Mar. 4, 2016, at A11 (published online as *Flint Is in the News, but Lead Poisoning Is Even Worse in Cleveland*), available at www.nytimes.com/2016/03/04/us/lead-paint-contamination-persists-in-many-cities-as-cleanup-falters.html.

[19] General Assembly of North Carolina, 2013 SESSION LAW 2013–382, H.B. 834

[20] Trip Gabriel, *Ash Spill Shows How Watchdog Was Defanged*, N.Y. Times (Feb. 28, 2016), www.nytimes.com/2014/03/01/us/coal-ash-spill-reveals-transformation-of-north-carolina-agency.html?smid=pl-share&_r=0.

[21] *Id.* The newly appointed Secretary had suggested oil was a renewable resource and the Assistant Secretary had as a member of the General Assembly drawn "a bull's-eye on a window in his office framing the environmental agency's headquarters."

[22] *Id.* Mid-level agency supervisors who under the "at will" system now serve at the pleasure of the Governor claimed to be "scared to death to say no to anyone anymore" under the new regime; agency personnel never considered "political creatures" before now had to go offsite to talk openly due to the culture shock at the organization.

River, coating the entire river bottom up to 70 miles downstream. DENR was unable to respond effectively. To complicate matters, the Governor had formerly worked in management roles for Duke Power, and had even continued to work there while serving as Mayor of Charlotte, NC, where Duke's headquarters are located.[23] Months before the coal ash spill, the new DENR political leadership had also reached a friendly deal with Duke Energy over pollution in their coal ash ponds, providing for a minimal fine and no provision that they be cleaned up.[24]

The legislature reacted by depriving Governor McCrory of appointment authority over the DENR.[25] It created a legislatively appointed alternative called the Coal Ash Management Commission. This led the North Carolina governor and two of his predecessors to challenge the legislative act as an unconstitutional invasion of executive powers.[26] The state Supreme Court sided with the governor,[27] and in March 2016 the Coal Ash Management Commission, which reviewed decisions made by the state Division of Environmental Quality, was shut down by Governor McCrory.[28] The North Carolina lesson is that professionals matter. The bureaucracy is essential at critical times. Reducing experienced and committed civil servants was a formula for management, as well as environmental, disaster. It is tempting to see this extreme situation in neo-spoils terms, since the replacements for the fired or retired DENR employees may have preferred to please the governor rather than serve the public interest. But it just may be that inexperienced personnel are not able to deliver the high professional standards a state should expect.[29]

[23] Jonathan M. Katz, *Duke Energy Is Charged in Huge Coal Ash Leak* (Feb. 20, 2015), www.nytimes.com/2015/02/21/us/duke-energy-is-charged-in-huge-coal-ash-leak.html.

[24] See Press Release, Southern Envtl. L.Ctr., DENR May Reinstate Suspended Coal Ash Settlement (Mar. 19, 2014), https://www.southernenvironment.org/news-and-press/press-releases/denr-may-reinstate-suspended-coal-ash-settlement (criticizing settlement for shielding Duke Power from liability under a "do-nothing" settlement deal).

[25] *Id.* N.C. Senate Bill 729, The Coal Ash Management Act of 2014, became law on Aug. 20, 2014.

[26] Mark Binker, *McCrory Sues Legislature over 'Unconstitutional' Commissions*, WRAL (Nov. 13, 2014), www.wral.com/mccrory-sues-legislature-over-unconstitutional-commissions/14178019/.

[27] See *State* v. *Berger*, 781 S.E.2d 248 (N.C. 2016) (holding that the legislative branch exerted too much control over commissions that had final executive authority and thus prevented the Governor from performing his express constitutional duty to take care that the laws were faithfully executed).

[28] Matthew Burns, *Lawmaker Wants to Resurrect Coal Ash Commission*, WRAL (May 6, 2016), www.wral.com/lawmaker-wants-to-resurrect-coal-ash-commission/15688589/.

[29] Ironically, after Governor McCrory lost his reelection bid by a thin margin to the Democratic Attorney General, Roy Cooper, the legislature tried to embed some of McCrory's political appointees by granting them civil service status. See Trip Gabriel, *North Carolina G.O.P. Moves to Curb Power of New Democratic Governor*, N.Y. Times (Dec. 14, 2016), www.nytimes.com/2016/12/14/us/politics/north-carolina-governor-roy-cooper-republicans.html.

## C. THE INDIANA v. IBM LITIGATION

A remarkable story about public/private contracting in Indiana is told in *Indiana v. IBM*,[30] a face-off between the public and private sectors. Governor Mitch Daniels (who had been George Bush's Director of Management and Budget and is now President of Purdue University) declared Indiana's welfare system "broken" and sought to employ top-flight outside talent to fix it. The result was a ten-year, $1.3 billion "welfare modernization system" with IBM chosen to take over the Medicaid, disability, and food stamp programs. The goal was to streamline the system through the substitution of professional caseworkers with computers and phone calls, a so-called "remote eligibility" model[31] already in use in Texas. The caseworker system in place was described as producing 2 million unnecessary trips a year to welfare offices, a seemingly Kafkaesque enterprise.[32]

But the fix did not work in Indiana (as it had not in Texas where it had been tried earlier[33]). After three years Indiana dismissed IBM and sued for $170 million. IBM counterclaimed for $100 million. The Superior Court opinion by Judge David Dreyer describes a "perfect storm" of misguided government policy and overzealous corporate ambition. Judge Dreyer concluded that both parties are to blame and "Indiana's taxpayers [were] left as apparent losers."[34] The Indiana Supreme Court reversed the Superior Court's ruling but left Judge Dreyer's original finding of total damages in place. On remand the state argued for offsetting damages, which Judge Dreyer denied without argument.[35] He was subsequently removed from the case by the Indiana Supreme Court at the request of the state.[36]

30 Marion Super. Ct., Cause No. 49D10–1005-PL-021451 (Jul. 18, 2012), *aff'd in part, rev'd in part on other grounds*, 51 N.E.3d 150 (Ind. 2016) (affirming trial court's factual findings and reversing lower holding that IBM had not materially breached contract because lower courts used common law Restatement (Second) of Contracts instead of contract's terms defining materiality).

31 See *Id.*, at 4.

32 See *Indiana* v. *IBM*, at 5–6; see also Matea Gold, Melanie Mason & Tom Hamburger, *Indiana's Bumpy Road to Privatization*, L.A. Times (June 24, 2011), available at http://articles.latimes.com/2011/jun/24/nation/la-na-indiana-privatize-20110624.

33 Texas' history of contracting failures in the Medicaid data centralization context, including one 2008 IBM server crash which compromised several Medicaid fraud investigations, is discussed at Chapter 5.D., *infra*.

34 *Indiana* v. *IBM*, at 1.

35 See Dave Stafford, *IBM Contests Judge's Removal Petition in Welfare-Privatization Suit*, The Indiana Lawyer (May 25, 2016), www.theindianalawyer.com/ibm-contests-judges-removal-petition-in-welfare-privatization-suit/PARAMS/article/40443.

36 See Dave Stafford, *Justices Remove Judge from Court Dispute between State, IBM*, Indianapolis Business Journal (Jul. 5, 2016), www.ibj.com/articles/59272-justices-remove-judge-from-court-dispute-between-state-ibm.

So what happened to cause the outsourcing decision to go awry between two sophisticated parties who entered into a collaborative agreement with the best of intentions? For one thing, the "healthy Indiana plan" sought to provide health insurance through a paperless process, but the recipients, who responded overwhelmingly to it, could not navigate the system effectively.[37] If this reminds you of the rollout of the federal Affordable Care Act, discussed in Chapter 4, it should. In fact it was the availability of the ACA that led Indiana to connect its system to it.

In effect, by making a total switch to remote technology from face-to-face contact, the new system confronted the digital divide.[38] The need for human intervention was inevitable. Even though caseworkers were criticized for inconsistent and noncompliant decisions, their ability to communicate with some clients allowed them to work in ways computer systems could not. Caseworkers were accused of "bending the rules," but perhaps they helped make the system work. Rule-bending to overcome "red tape" may be a kind of "workaround," sometimes necessary to keep the system functioning, a point made later in Chapter 6.C. To dig out of the problem, Indiana hired First Data Corp., another contractor, to oversee IBM's performance and then decided to cut out the middleman (IBM),[39] which precipitated the lawsuit. First Data moved to a "hybrid" system of electronic and face-to-face service, the so-called "Plan B." Subsequently, Governor Mike Pence hired additional caseworkers to meet the 26 percent increase in workload from the prior year,[40] a modest effort to "bring back the bureaucrats."

It is hard to know what might have saved the program. Perhaps, as in Texas, it was poorly thought out and too ambitious from the start. Both sides were experienced and acting in good faith, but perhaps they forgot the rules of successful collaborations. The key is to "share the discretion."[41] This is a cautionary tale about doing collaborations well. Even where sophisticated parties negotiate well, if the project is ill-conceived it cannot be made to work. Public leadership and professionalism are, it seems, necessary but not sufficient conditions for good government.

[37] See *id.* The 2008 recession increased Indiana's unemployment rate from 4.6 percent to 10.6 percent, bringing larger numbers than expected to the new system.

[38] See Council of Econ. Advisers, Mapping the Digital Divide (2015) (describing how millions of Americans still do not own or use a computer regularly and distribution of internet access is not evenly distributed across many communities).

[39] *Indiana* v. *IBM*, at 27, 32.

[40] See Brandon Smith, *Pence Calls For Hiring of 113 Additional DCS Caseworkers*, Indiana Public Media (Aug. 13, 2015), http://indianapublicmedia.org/news/pence-calls-hiring-113-additional-dcs-caseworkers-86102/.

[41] See Donahue & Zeckhauser, *supra* Chapter 1, at note 96.

### D. NEW JERSEY: CONTRACTING OUT CLIMATE CHANGE RESPONSIBILITIES

New Jersey's preparation for and response to the catastrophic Hurricane Sandy reveals the smokescreen that contractors can provide around politically charged policy decisions. Years before Sandy landed, Governor Chris Christie's national political ambitions led him to eliminate the Department of Environmental Protection's Office of Climate Change and Energy, the office charged with modeling and planning for extreme weather related to climate change.[42] As Christie would elaborate in the wake of Hurricane Sandy, climate change's influence on the severity of the storm was an "esoteric question" that he did not have time to consider. This stance stood in stark contrast to that of New York Governor Andrew Cuomo, who emphasized in his 2013 State of the State address that New York faced a 100-year flood every two years as a result of changing environmental conditions.[43] Governor Christie's need to appeal to a climate-skeptical national political base may have led him to ignore New Jersey Republicans who have taken moderate stances on climate change related issues, favoring policies such as cap-and-trade and regional interstate emissions agreements. As a result, he ceded the field of climate change (and the bureaucrats who understood it) to political expediency.

By defunding the Office of Climate Change and Energy, Christie turned away from government expertise. In 2012 New Jersey's inland flooding maps were found to be 30 years old and based on 40-year-old data, and none of them took the sea-level and meteorological effects of climate change into account.[44] Consequently, when the officials at New Jersey Transit faced the decision as to where to shelter their trains during the storm, they chose railyards in Kearny and Hoboken. Those railyards flooded, damaging hundreds of engines and causing $120 million in damage.[45] The Texas A&M Engineering Extension Service conducted a review of the state's handling of the event, and found that the Office of Emergency Management did an

[42] Kate Sheppard, *Could Chris Christie Bring the GOP Around on Climate?*, MOTHER JONES (Feb. 19, 2013), available at www.motherjones.com/environment/2013/02/chris-christie-climate-change.

[43] *Id.*

[44] Kirsten Stade, PUBLIC EMPLOYEES FOR ENVIRONMENTAL RESPONSIBILITY, *New Jersey Yet to Come to Grips with Post-Sandy Flood Risks*, Dec. 19, 2012, www.peer.org/news/news-releases/2012/12/19/new-jersey-yet-to-come-to-grips-with-post-sandy-flood-risks/.

[45] Mike Frassinelli, *Review of NJ Transit's Response to Sandy Finds Need for More Coordination, Places to Shelter Trains*, THE STAR-LEDGER (Dec. 24, 2013), available at www.nj.com/news/index.ssf/2013/12/review_of_nj_transits_response_to_sandy_finds_need_for_better_coordination_more_places_to_store_trai.html.

admirable job with the resources they had, but were limited by shortages of backup personnel and communications equipment, and inadequate prior storm surge and flood models.[46] NJ Transit's response to the observations and recommendations of the A&M team followed a similar narrative. Flood mapping and modeling was contracted out to a private weather service, and storm surge maps for critical facilities were developed by an outside engineering firm.[47] A recommendation to review outdated or incomplete portions of hurricane emergency response plans led NJ Transit's Operating Divisions to engage with an outside contractor to develop new emergency response plans.

The aftermath cleanup was also handled by contract. New Jersey's $600 million Reconstruction, Rehabilitation, Elevation and Mitigation (RREM) program was designed to make grants to beleaguered homeowners who had suffered damage from the storm to rebuild. It was handled by a number of companies, two of which performed so poorly they had their contracts to process applications terminated over a year before they were set to expire, costing the state tens of millions to settle the contract disputes.[48] The contractors were botching the program so badly that 74 percent of appeals from RREM rejections were actually eligible, and successful applicants had to wait many months before receiving any payments at all.

## E. TEXAS: PRIVATIZING BUREAUCRACY

I don't know [expletive] about procurement.

Jack Stick, Texas Deputy Inspector General

It is little surprise that the self-proclaimed "wide open for business"[49] Lone Star State would be at the leading edge of the outsourcing movement in the states. It generously provides business tax breaks to lure companies like Samsung, Hewlett-Packard, and Amazon into expanding their operations

[46] See New Jersey Transit Corporation's Hurricane Sandy After Action Report (2015), available at http://njtransitresilienceprogram.com/wp-content/uploads/2015/10/TEEX-After-Action-Report.pdf.

[47] See N.J. Transit, NJ TRANSIT Response to TEEX After Action Report (2015), available at http://njtransitresilienceprogram.com/wp-content/uploads/2015/10/NJ-TRANSIT-Responses.pdf.

[48] See Matt Katz, *Amid Criticism, NJ Quietly Firing 2nd Sandy Contractor*, WNYC News (Feb. 13, 2014), available at www.wnyc.org/story/amid-criticism-nj-quietly-fires-second-sandy-contractor/.

[49] See Texas Wide Open for Business, https://texaswideopenforbusiness.com/, last visited May 26, 2016.

into Texas,[50] while it spends billions pursuing a two-decade-long initiative to privatize as much of its public workforce as possible.[51] From 2005 to 2010 Texas' contracting budget grew almost 50 percent, from $41.6 billion to just shy of $60 billion. In 2013, that number was $161 billion – probably. The state's Legislative Budget Board of contracts has so many errors that the Board's own staff warns not to use it for serious analysis.[52] This frenetic drive to privatize has seen a history of spotty progress, ballooning budgets, missed deadlines, and poor management by state officials tasked with supervising contracts.

A 2015 report by the Texas State Auditor summarizing audits they performed on contract management at state agencies found that of fourteen audits performed from July 2012 to December 2014, only two concluded that the agencies generally complied with all the contract management requirements.[53] It further noted that half the agencies audited lacked even simple written contract management policies or procedures. The report was released in the midst of an ongoing dust-up in Austin over improper contracting awards and political influence held by the contractors over both the state legislature and politically appointed leadership at state agencies.[54] The previous month had seen both the Inspector General and chief counsel of the Texas Health and Human Services Commission (HHSC) forced to resign after it was revealed they had misled the HHSC Executive Commissioner about the nature of a $110 million contract the agency had signed with a company called 21st Century Technologies (21CT).[55] They also failed to disclose their personal ties to both the company and one of its former lobbyists, triggering three separate investigations into the agency's contracting procedures.

[50] See Louise Story, *Lines Blur as Texas Gives Industries a Bonanza*, N.Y. Times (Dec. 2, 2012), available at www.nytimes.com/2012/12/03/us/winners-and-losers-in-texas.html.

[51] See Aman Batheja, *In State Contracting, Failure is an Option*, Texas Tribune (Feb. 1, 2015), available at https://www.texastribune.org/2015/02/01/cost-overruns-and-bungles-state-contracting/.

[52] See Aman Batheja, *Lawmakers Vying to Bring Sunlight to State Contracts*, Texas Tribune (Mar. 10, 2015), https://www.texastribune.org/2015/03/10/lawmakers-vying-bring-sunlight-state-contracts/.

[53] Texas State Auditor, A Report on Recent Contracting Audits, Rep. No. 15–019 (2015) (the two positive reports were "on a design services contract and a construction contract audited at the Department of Transportation and on a marketing contract audited at the Texas Lottery Commission").

[54] See Terri Langford, *State Auditor Sees Weaknesses in Agency Contracting*, Texas Tribune (Jan. 27, 2015), available at https://www.texastribune.org/2015/01/27/sao-report-points-state-contracting-problems/.

[55] The contract was broken into a $20 million initial investment and a $90 million extension which was canceled in December 2015.

The 21CT contract to provide fraud tracking software has been a watershed event in the state's history with contractors. Starting in 2005, state agencies had been required to purchase computer products and services through a central "Cooperative Contracts" system managed by the Texas Department of Information Resources.[56] Vendors competed to be included in the system, but once selected, never underwent another bidding process. The contract with 21CT originated from a familiar problem: HHSC's newly appointed Deputy Inspector General, Jack Stick, "had a catastrophic need" to quickly stand up a program to track fraudulent Medicaid and food stamp payments.[57] Stick, who admitted "I don't know [expletive] about procurement,"[58] only had to verify 21CT was already on the "Cooperative Contracts" list before he had the agency draw up an initial $20 million contract. Except it wasn't one $20 million contract, but several contracts broken up to avoid notice, which did not itemize costs for 21CT staffers' time, instead taking the "unusual step," according to an HHSC spokesperson, of including them under "licensing fees."[59] Then, James Frinzi, a lobbyist for 21CT and former friend and business associate of Stick's,[60] announced that 21CT had plans to hire Stick after his term in government expired,[61] a claim he maintained even after being fired and sued over the remarks.

Good ol' boy networking seems to be the rule in Austin, as in other state capitals. Over the previous nine years, for instance, Bill Powers, the President of the flagship University of Texas, overrode the admissions boards' rejection of

56 See Terri Langford, *A Look Back at the Health Commission-21CT Contract*, Texas Tribune (Feb. 3, 2015), https://www.texastribune.org/2015/02/03/21ct-health-commission-recap/. Three-quarters of vendors who competed to be included in the program were accepted on their first attempt, precluding the need to compete in the future. See also Brian M. Rosenthal, *Popular State Purchasing Program Lacks Oversight, Competition*, Houston Chronicle (Feb. 2, 2015), www.houstonchronicle.com/news/politics/texas/article/State-purchasing-program-not-as-competitive-as-6052742.php.

57 *Id.* 58 *Id.* 59 *Id.*

60 The two ceased being friends after a physical altercation in 2009, but documents obtained by the *Houston Chronicle*, denounced by Stick as "bad paperwork," indicated that in 2011 they were still maintaining business relationships. See Brian M. Rosenthal, *Official in Contract Scandal had Closer Ties to Lobbyist than Disclosed*, Houston Chronicle (Dec. 31, 2014), www.houstonchronicle.com/news/houston-texas/houston/article/In-Medicaid-contract-scandal-health-official-had-5988693.php.

61 See Andrea Ball & J. David McSwane, *Questionable Texas Contract Deal was Years in the Making*, Austin American-Statesman (Dec. 20, 2014), www.mystatesman.com/news/news/state-regional-govt-politics/questionable-texas-contract-deal-was-years-in-the-/njXw8/#ad08a8c9.3886855.735630 (the *Austin American-Statesman* began the investigation into the 21CT contract deal and also uncovered audio of a meeting in which Jack Stick "tout[ed] 21CT's technology long before rivals made their pitches for the work").

dozens of undergraduate and law applicants.[62] The admitted students in many cases had no more than "dubious qualifications" but they had family or personal connections to members of the Texas Legislature or one of the more powerful lobbying firms in Austin.[63] This casual attitude towards power and influence manifested itself in state contracting. A few more examples deserve mention.

Andersen Consulting was hired in 1991 to computerize the Texas Attorney General's office child payments system for $11 million. By 1997, the deal was $57 million over budget and three years behind schedule. A decade after a state audit found the company at least partially at fault, Andersen (now Accenture) mishandled another $899 million contract managing the Children's Health Insurance Program and call centers for food stamps and Medicaid by erroneously denying benefits and causing massive backlogs. It was terminated with a $244 million payout. By 2015 Accenture's 20-year history of poor performance merited its management of most of the state's Medicaid processing and *another* $99 million contract to upgrade the Attorney General's child support payments system.[64]

Xerox was fired in 2012 from a contract to manage Texas' Medicaid dental services after it was learned the state paid more than the nine most populous states combined, $1.1 billion over eight years, for the company's single dentist to "rubber stamp" thousands of claims per month. In a 2014 lawsuit the state alleged that as a result hundreds of millions of dollars were paid for "services not performed and orthodontic benefits not authorized."[65] The facts underlying the lawsuit stemmed from a federal audit published four months before the state's final renewal of its contract with Xerox. Chairwoman of the Texas House Public Health Committee Lois Kolkhorst accused the state of "not doing... due diligence" without "the proper tools in place to monitor the

[62] See Ralph K. M. Haurwitz, *UT President Bill Powers Overruled Admissions Office, Report Says*, Austin American-Statesman (Feb. 12, 2015), available at www.statesman.com/news/news/state-regional-govt-politics/uts-powers-overruled-admissions-office-report-says/nj9WH/ (from 2009 to 2014 Powers mandated the acceptance of 73 undergraduate applicants with "sub-par academic credentials").

[63] See Jon Cassidy, *Dozens of UT Law's Least Qualified Students Are Connected Politically*, Watchdog.org (May 13, 2014), http://watchdog.org/144169/ut-law-school-hookups/ (explaining conclusions of investigation into UT Law admissions favoritism despite statute barring politically motivated or legacy-based decisions).

[64] See Batheja, *supra* note 51.

[65] Becca Aaronson, *Texas Cancels Medicaid Contract, Sues Xerox Over Allegedly Misspent Money*, Texas Tribune (May 9, 2014), https://www.texastribune.org/2014/05/09/texas-sues-xerox-recover-millions-misspent-money/.

system." It was apparent that Texas lacked sufficient state workers to oversee the contractors.[66]

Xerox would in the next two years face a consumer class action in Nevada, canceled payments from Alaska, and suit by the City of Houston for failure to manage a program to collect money from insurers and individuals who received ambulance and emergency medical services. Lacking a provider after Xerox was fired, the dental coverage of 3.8 million Texans was assigned without bidding to Accenture. Both Accenture and Xerox remain eligible for no-bid contracts based on their previous membership on the "Competitive Contracts" list. They continue to attract millions of dollars in business from the state, as they are among the only partners with the resources required to provide the state with the heavily scaled technology solutions it needs. While Texas loses billions in tax revenue, there is another, more human, cost when states pass the buck to contractors.

In 2014, the Providence Service Corporation unilaterally terminated its five-year $150 million contract with the state Department of Family and Protective Services (DFPS) to care for 1,100 foster children over "unanticipated transportation costs," giving the woefully underfunded state agency 30 days to take over care of the children. While the contractor "applauded the state's use of privatization," DFPS had recently chastised Providence for failure to keep siblings close to home and develop staff, providers, and services to care for children. DFPS Commissioner John Specia, a true believer in contracted services, told stakeholders by email he remained committed to the Foster Care Redesign (privatization) initiative and moved forward with a second rollout with another firm, ACH Child and Family Services.[67] In December 2015, US District Court Judge Janis Graham issued a 255-page opinion finding that the few workers left in the agency's Child Protective Services division were left with impossible caseloads (up to 70, with an ideal of 12), burnout, and a 57 percent turnover rate, leaving "rape, abuse, psychotropic medication, and instability . . . the norm." Specia has since been replaced by Henry Whitman, the eighth Commissioner since 2004.[68]

[66] Anne Dunkelberg, associate director of the Center for Public Policy Priorities, added "I'm not saying there's no honor among our state contractors, but we shouldn't be running our contracts on the honor system." *Id.*

[67] See Alexa Ura, *State Contractor Pulls Out of Foster Care Redesign*, Texas Tribune (Aug. 1, 2014), https://www.texastribune.org/2014/08/01/state-contractor-pulls-out-foster-care-redesign/.

[68] Lisa Falkenberg, *Texas' Foster Care System Needs More than New Leadership*, Houston Chronicle (Apr. 13, 2016), www.houstonchronicle.com/news/columnists/falkenberg/article/Falkenberg-Texas-foster-care-system-needs-more-7244747.php.

Texas is doing its procurement differently, however. In the wake of the 21CT scandal, the state legislature has pushed for bottom-up contracting oversight reform, from their performance matters to simple reporting on their existence.[69] In June 2015, Governor Abbot signed S.B. 20,[70] which requires agencies to develop a contract management database and post their contracts online, and creates a public vendor tracking system which agencies can use to rate vendors' performance. While the reforms are limited in comparison to others introduced after the 21CT scandal,[71] they provide tools to turn the public management problem around. But there is little chance they will work without a commitment to professional managers. In a state that has been almost a petri dish for regulatory capture theory, Texas needs a change in political culture more than anything else.

## F. CONCLUSION: STATES NEED PROFESSIONAL GOVERNMENT TOO

Paul Light recently studied why the federal government has had a "cascade of breakdowns," especially during the George W. Bush and Barack Obama Administrations.[72] Allowing that "government was not always so vulnerable," he isolated key failures (e.g. the Volkswagen cheating scandal, the Ebola crisis, and Secret Service misconduct) and came up with a list of causes that can be applied to the state breakdowns discussed here. They were: (1) policy (poor design or delegation); (2) resources (understaffing and weak administrative systems); (3) organizational culture (misguided missions); (4) structure (organizational thickening and overdependence on contractors); and (5) leadership. The Flint, Michigan, North Carolina, New Jersey, and Texas breakdown situations, along with the *Indiana* v. *IBM* litigation, can be evaluated in terms of the causes listed in the Light topology.

69 Different Texas agencies interpreted a law mandating information be provided on contracts worth over $100,000 as requiring anything from detailed dates, values, and terms to only requiring a public list of vendors' names. See Batheja, *supra* note 50.

70 Senate Bill 20, www.legis.state.tx.us/BillLookup/History.aspx?LegSess=84R&Bill=SB20.

71 Other bills introduced would have added a central contract management division to the state's Legislative Budget Board and curtailed the influence of the "Cooperative Contracts" program to make it harder for vendors to attain contracts without oversight but died in committee. See Batheja, *supra* note 50; SB 1053, www.legis.state.tx.us/BillLookup/History.aspx?LegSess=84R&Bill=SB1053.

72 Paul C. Light, The Volcker Alliance, Vision + Action = Faithful Execution: Why Government Daydreams and How to Stop the Cascade of Breakdowns that Now Haunts It (2015), https://www.volckeralliance.org/publications/vision-action-faithful-execution (Light's methodology was to identify 48 breakdowns since the Reagan years and have them evaluated by a distinguished panel of historians and political scientists).

Flint shows both how organizational culture and structure led government professionals to fail at several levels: the Michigan Department of Environmental Quality ignored its basic responsibility to use corrosion controls in the water system. The Flint Emergency Managers failed by emphasizing economic over safety concerns, and the regional EPA officials failed adequately to oversee the process. While contractors working in Flint failed to sound alarms about lead contamination,[73] some contractors, such as faculty from Virginia Tech, performed well, alerting the state and its governor to the depths of the problems at Flint. The other Light factor present in Flint is leadership, in particular that of the Governor who failed to understand the depth of the problem and made questionable appointments. The question for Michigan now is whether to strengthen its professional management systems (after holding those responsible accountable for their failures) or to weaken them further by turning to contractors as the default solution. The other state examples provide warnings in that regard, except for North Carolina where the demise of the state environmental workforce can be directly attributed to poor leadership at the Governor's office.

## 1 *Contractors Cannot Govern*

The state government failures in North Carolina, New Jersey, Texas, and Indiana all stem from the same motivation: improve the effectiveness of state government by hiring "expertise" from the outside in its place. Inspired by the "at will" public employment movement (perfected in the cutting-back of civil service protections in Wisconsin, discussed in Chapter 3) each of these states shrank its public workforce in a risky gamble for government efficiency. In Texas, the state has made legislative changes to enhance transparency in the contract award process, which is certainly a step forward, but the open question is whether it realizes that the answer to good state contracting lies in bolstering the state procurement workforce. Procurement is a public profession with rules and standards.[74] It must be done by professionals who are bound by rules that prevent or minimize conflicts of interest. They cannot be shackled, either by contractors or legislators, and still discharge their duties effectively.

[73] See Mitch Smith & Julie Bosman, *Michigan Attorney General Sues 2 Companies Over Flint Water Crisis*, N.Y. Times (June 22, 2016), www.nytimes.com/2016/06/23/us/flint-water-crisis-michigan.html.

[74] See The Volcker Alliance, Doing the People's Business: Key Competencies for Effective Public Procurement (2016) (outlining the 12 skill sets public employees need to manage the procurement process effectively).

In New Jersey, Texas, and Indiana, the states sought to make government "private" by in effect turning over complicated management tasks to contractors and failing both to manage the contractor procurement process and monitor their performance once they were selected. In New Jersey and Texas, the governors were politically opposed to public employees and made errors in contractor management because of that fact. In Indiana, however, Mitch Daniel was an admirable leader and experienced public manager and yet his contracting-out effort still failed. He learned the hard way that government can't be run without professional managers who are dedicated to the task.[75]

### 2 *Inherent Government Functions and the States*

All of these failures raise an interesting question for state governments: do they have a concept of inherent government functions? Not only is there OMB's Circular A-76 process but there are numerous statutes, regulations, and guidance that imbed the concept into the federal process.[76] If state governments adopted an equivalent concept, they would realize that public decisionmaking has a necessary role in the government management process.

As was set out in Chapter 2 and is a continuing theme of this book, the duty to supervise is a nondelegable duty under the federal Constitution. Since state courts incorporate the separation of powers concepts from the federal Constitution into their own constitutions,[77] this duty has as much relevance to the states as to the federal government. Conceptual thinking will not make states more careful about delegating primary responsibilities of governance to contractors unless it is connected to government failures, since the nondelegation doctrine is alive in the states and has particular resonance among conservative thinkers.[78] A carefully constructed conservative legal argument that applies nondelegation in the contractor context could give state politicians pause and offer the cause of professional government a needed boost.

[75] His successor, Mike Pence (now the Vice President), had made strides by authorizing significant performance raises for state employees. See Tony Cok, *Gov. Mike Pence Authorizes $42M in Raises for State Employees*, INDY STAR (Dec. 22, 2015), www.indystar.com/story/news/politics/2015/12/22/gov-mike-pence-authorizes-42m-raises-state-employees/77770958/.

[76] See Kate M. Manuel, *Definitions of "Inherently Governmental Function" in Federal Procurement Law and Guidance*, Cong. Research Service Report 7–5700 (Dec. 23, 2014).

[77] See Cynthia R. Farina, *Deconstructing Nondelegation*, 33 HARV. J. OF L. & PUB. POLICY 87, 88 n. 6, 96 (2010) (collecting state historical opinions on nondelegation and describing circumstances which framed post-revolutionary state constitutional drafting).

[78] See Gary Lawson, *Delegation and Original Meaning*, 88 VA. L. REV. 327 (2002); but see Eric Posner & Adrian Vermeule, *Interring the Nondelegation Doctrine*, 69 U. CHI. L. REV. 1721 (2002).

# 6

# Why Professionals in Government Matter

Nothing makes me angry like hearing a member on the floor of the House use bureaucrat as an epithet.

Steny Hoyer[1]

When Congressman Hoyer defends bureaucrats (and presumably bureaucracy) he is speaking to his congressional colleagues but also to his constituents in Maryland, many of whom work for government. Not all congressional districts are similarly composed, of course, but all districts have bureaucrats living within them, whether federal, state, or local officials. So every member of Congress has a stake in bureaucracy and making it work, even though many mock the word by adding modifiers like "inefficient," "mindless," "inflexible," or "dehumanizing" before it. The dark side of bureaucracy is forever captured in Kafka's *The Trial*.[2] But we do not live in Prague in the 1920s. While it is entertaining to call aspects of our bureaucracy "Kafkaesque," we should not confuse ourselves about when that epithet is justified.

Bureaucracy is a reality in democratic as well as oppressive societies because it is the most efficient way of organizing public and private sector institutions.[3] The corporation is the private sector bureaucracy. To Ronald Coase, the corporation was the most efficient way to deal with the problem of transaction costs.[4] The private bureaucracy has built-in advantages: it can organize, merge,

[1] Address to the 2016 National Treasury Employees Union annual legislative conference.

[2] FRANZ KAFKA, THE TRIAL (1925).

[3] See Richard A. Posner, *Bureaucracy and Efficiency*, THE BECKER-POSNER BLOG (Jan. 12, 2014), available at www.becker-posner-blog.com/2014/01/bureaucracy-and-efficiencyposner.html (bureaucracy "must be on balance an efficient means of administration or it wouldn't be so pervasive in both the public and the private sectors").

[4] See Ronald Coase, *The Nature of the Firm*, 4 ECONOMICA 386 (1937); see also Chapter 3, notes 1–6.

or dissolve relatively easily and it can attract top flight talent.[5] Government bureaucracies are not so fortunate. While they are the organization of choice when Congress wants to solve a public problem, they are hard to change, eliminate, or reorganize. In fact, Congress, which authorized presidents to reorganize numerous times between 1932 and 1984,[6] has refused to do so since, despite numerous requests from President Obama.[7] As a result, agencies and their missions have grown more overlapping, inconsistent, and entrenched, and must be managed gingerly by the White House and the bureaucracy.

What it takes to run government well is the same thing it takes to run private firms well: professional managers who have appropriate levels of competence and dedication. These professionals are bureaucrats inevitably, and they must be valued, to restate the title of this book. Whatever lies ahead, whether it be bureaucracy or adhocracy[8] (the opposite of bureaucracy), government professionals are needed to get us there. This chapter will show why bureaucrats are essential and why contractors, whatever their skill sets, cannot act in their place. To recall the hedgehog/fox metaphor, contractors can do many things well, as specialists, but they cannot be generalists in the running of government. As John Rohr states, it takes "legitimated" professionals to "run a Constitution."[9] In recent years, however, this message has been overcome by the idea that expertise in government management is either overrated or, if needed, can be purchased from the marketplace.

By joining the management structures of government at all levels, contractors have created a "blended workforce" where they work alongside government employees, often on the same assignments.[10] As Chapter 3 showed, some agencies are so heavily contracted out that they have become "virtual" agencies. Whether they like it or not, public managers are forced to share

5 Business school students line up for jobs in the corporate sector. An entire industry has sprung up around connecting MBA students with large private employers, with countless general and niche job posting sites, including Monster.com, CareerBuilder.com, Indeed.com, and many more. USAJOBS is a poor competitor on this score.

6 See 5 U.S.C. §§ 901 *et seq*.

7 In 2012, Obama requested reorganization authority to consolidate key business- and trade-related agencies into one. Congress did not act on this request. See Henry B. Hogue, Cong. Research Serv., *Presidential Reorganization Authority: History, Recent Initiatives, and Options for Congress*, CRS Report R42852 (2012).

8 Adhocracy is a term first used by Warren Bennis in *The Temporary Society* (1968). It stands for adaptive, creative, flexible, and adoptive management, based on non-permanence and spontaneity. Some of these characteristics are counter to bureaucracy, but some would be absorbed into the bureaucracy of the future. Think Uber and the Internet of Things.

9 John A. Rohr, To Run a Constitution: The Legitimacy of the Administrative State xii (1986) (noting that "legitimation has a civilizing aspect about it").

10 See Outsourcing Sovereignty 45–46 (2007); see also Charles T. Goodsell, The Case for Bureaucracy: A Public Administration Polemic 46–47 (2004) (describing contractors at EPA doing inherent government functions).

management roles with contractor surrogates. One of the favorite jokes among career officials goes like this: "we used to be afraid of the politicals; now we're afraid of the contractors."[11]

In the era of the New Public Management,[12] running government like a business invites private sector influence and authority and qualifies the case for government managers. Complicating matters are the many situations where contractors, if properly instructed, can do government work as effectively as or better than their bureaucratic counterparts. But when it comes to policymaking, the contractor role is problematic. There are several reasons for this. One is normative: professionals are a constitutionally required condition for good government (the "duty to supervise"). But invoking the constitutional arguments in Chapter 2 may seem too elevated or abstract. So compelling practical reasons must be added. What distinguishes government deciders from the rest of us? Start with the oath of office with its commitment to promote the general welfare. Only government officials are sworn in. Then consider the often overlooked values of experience, judgment, and objectivity provided by long-term players. Without institutional memory, government falters and *fails*. When I restarted ACUS after a 15 year hiatus, I searched for ACUS alumni who might be available for advice and counsel.[13] They provided the knowledge necessary for the institution to be successfully revived; no contractor, no matter how diligent, could have supplied the same level of knowledge and expertise.[14] The value of experience is hard to overstate. It is the main lesson drawn from the state examples in Chapter 5. But officials must combine experience with competence to make public institutions run well. There are no substitutes.

## A. THE OATH AS DEMARCATOR

> Those who exercise the power of government are set apart from ordinary citizens.
>
> Justice Alito[15]

[11] As told by Jim Tozzi, former OMB official and a Public Member of ACUS.

[12] The New Public Management (NPM) movement began in the 1990s. See M. S. Haque, *Revisiting the New Public Management*, 67 PUB. ADMIN. REV. 179 (2007). NPM has over time become associated with gutting government capacity. See Francis Fukuyama, *Governance: What Do We Know, and How Do We Know It?*, 19 ANN. REV. POLIT. SCI. 6–1, 6–5 (2016) (discussing literature on NPM).

[13] I was lucky to connect with the former research director, Jeff Lubbers, who was teaching at American University Law School and senior attorney David Pritzker, who had transferred to GSA.

[14] Indeed, knowing how contractors work, they likely would have looked for the same people to provide advice to the agency. I just eliminated the middle person.

[15] *Dep't of Transp. v. Ass'n of Am. Railroads*, 135 S. Ct. 1225, 1234 (2015) (Alito, J. concurring).

George Washington's Inauguration, Library of Congress Prints and Photographs Division Washington, D.C., http://hdl.loc.gov/loc.pnp/pga.03236.

Even though it may seem a formality, the constitutional requirement of the oath of office has deep meaning in our constitutional system.[16] Indeed Professor Richard Re has recently asserted that the practices surrounding the oath amount to an "underappreciated tradition of promissory constitutionalism."[17] That is an elegant way to put it. George Washington's oath of office, taken in connection with his First Inaugural Address, "in obedience to the public summons," set the standard for all those public officials who have come after him. When I was sworn in as Chairman of ACUS by Vice President Biden[18] it seemed I had crossed a line – a demarcation – between a private citizen and public official. As a Presidential Appointed Senate Confirmed official (PAS), I was on duty 24/7/365 and was automatically deemed essential in the event of a government shutdown (which, astonishingly, occurred twice during

[16] See OUTSOURCING SOVEREIGNTY at 112–14.

[17] See Richard M. Re, *Promising the Constitution*, 110 NORTHWESTERN L. REV. 299, 299 (2016).

[18] Oath taken on April 6, 2010. I also took the oath of office when I was commissioned as a lieutenant in the US Army in May 1961, so, like many in the federal government, I was an "officer of the United States" in both the military and civilian contexts.

my tenure). In addition, the Rules of Ethics kicked in and relationships with former colleagues outside government changed in significant ways.[19]

The swearing-in ceremony is a transformative moment, an impression regularly confirmed to me by current and former government officials. All federal civil servants take oaths. The requirement is stated as follows:

> Federal civil servants take an oath of office by which they swear to support and defend the Constitution of the United States of America. The Constitution not only establishes our system of government, it actually defines the work role for Federal employees – "to establish Justice, insure domestic tranquility, provide for the common defense, promote the general welfare, and secure the blessings of liberty."
>
> (5 U.S.C. § 3331)

The duty to "promote the general welfare" imposes an obligation, a trust really, in Richard Re's terms. State and local officials take the oath as well.[20] When the oath takers at all levels of government are tallied up, a cadre some 20 million strong is created whose duty, broadly speaking, is to promote the general welfare. The oath provides psychic income for those who serve in government and must forgo the real income earned by their private sector counterparts. Obviously, definitions of the public welfare are contested, when some think it is violated, others think it is being upheld. So there can be debate over its meaning, but it is a sworn requirement nonetheless, and people notice it. Former Governor McCrory of North Carolina, under fire because of his state's controversial LGBT legislation, lashed out at his opponents as follows:

> Disregarding the facts, other politicians – from the White House to mayors to state capitals and City Council members and even our attorney general – have initiated and promoted conflict to advance their political agenda and tear down our state, *even if it means defying the Constitution and their oath of office*.[21]

[19] Surely officials at the financial regulatory agencies experience these strictures more, but all of us have ethical responsibilities that can alter prior relationships.

[20] State oaths are largely patterned on the federal constitutional oath. See, e.g., Const. of N.Y. Art. 8, § 1 ("I solemnly swear (or affirm) that I will support the Constitution of the United States, and the Constitution of the State of New York, (and the Charter of the City of New York, e.g.), and that I will faithfully discharge the duties of the office of (mayor of the City of New York, e.g.) to the best of my ability").

[21] Matt Apuzzo & Alan Blinder, *North Carolina May Risk Aid with Bias Law*, N.Y. Times, Apr. 1, 2016, at A1, A3 (published online as *North Carolina Law May Risk Federal Aid*, available at www.nytimes.com/2016/04/02/us/politics/north-carolina-anti-discrimination-law-obama-federal-funds.html) (emphasis added).

That is quite a list of oath violators, but it shows the oath matters, at least in the eyes of some, when it is violated. For others, of course, it matters when it is upheld.

Almost 100 years ago Justice Holmes, who graces the cover of this book, taught us that "[m]en must turn square corners when they deal with the government."[22] Today, we might expand Holmes' dictum to say that, when dealing with the people, government officials must turn square corners as well. These "corners" are established through the oath of office.

Contractors do not get psychic income from the oath, or the extensive investigations of ability and character that precede it, even though they are compensated at levels which usually exceed their government counterparts. Do contractors miss this extra bit of validation? Some who are former military have experienced it of course, and it may stay with them. For others, it may be a loss. There was a story going around in the Iraq War days that Eric Prince, then head of Blackwater, would have his new recruits take the oath of office as a way of inspiring them. So maybe they thought it mattered. Of course, contractors feel and owe a duty of loyalty to their private employers, even when they work for government. And contractors have educational and professional qualifications that may well allow them to outperform government employees, even without the benefit of the oath. But the oath is meant to divide the public and private sectors. The requirement can be abused as it was with loyalty oaths demanded of private citizens in the 1950s.[23] However, when freely entered into, the oath can inspire those who take it and become a source of professional pride.

## B. GOVERNMENT PROFESSIONALISM AND BUREAUCRATIC AUTONOMY

Though government employees take the same oath whatever their assignments, some offer expertise in managing government. These are the professionals in government in whom we place our trust to run the Constitution, in John Rohr's phrase. Whether it is the Foreign Service, those who deliver health or retirement care, the police and fire departments or those who make sure our drinking water is safe, government officials are vital players in the public sector. At the federal level, the professional category is hard to determine with precision, but it is probably no more than one-third of the bureaucracy.[24]

[22] Rock Island, A. & L. R. Co., 254 U.S. 141, 143 (1920) (need to file properly for tax refunds).

[23] See *Speiser* v. *Randall*, 357 U.S. 513 (1958) (declaring the California oath of loyalty unconstitutional).

[24] Approximately 700,000 of the 2 million government employees have been designated inherently governmental under the FAIR Act. See Ch. 2, note 37. Since the exercise of judgment is an indica of the inherently governmental designation, this is a good proxy for professional managers.

Members of the Senior Executive Service (SES) are leaders of this team of professional managers, but they number only around 7,000.[25] If the general schedule (GS) rating system is used to define managers, some 60 percent of civil servants are within the management category.[26] In addition to these career officials, about 3,800 political appointees[27] fall into the professional management category as well, providing leadership, although by definition not long-term commitments.

Professionals are said to possess "expertise," a concept more easily touted than understood. It results from knowledge gained from experience and abilities acquired through education and training. The Supreme Court has recognized the importance of expertise in federal agencies by granting it deference or even respect,[28] but without much explanation of what it means. It was lauded and largely assumed by redoubtable New Dealers like James Landis as the necessary condition for agency government.[29]

Sidney Shapiro has attempted to define its contours.[30] He identifies many kinds of expertise, but the most salient ones for government professionals are "craft" and "political" expertise.[31] The former deals with practical reason and even instinct, and the latter deals with managing an agency in a political environment. Philip Tetlock builds on this idea by saying that "what experts think matters far less than how they think."[32] Ultimately expertise leads to professional judgment. And judgment involves the exercise of discretion. Discretion, which is inherent in most management decisions, is exercised by those who have been awarded a level of trust by society.

Trust and the exercise of discretion lead to a degree of bureaucratic autonomy. Autonomy creates a limited space within which a professional should

[25] See OFFICE OF PERSONNEL MGMT., SENIOR EXECUTIVE SERVICE FACTS & FIGURES, https://www.opm.gov/policy-data-oversight/senior-executive-service/facts-figures/#url=Demographics (last visited Apr. 19, 2016).

[26] See Gov't Printing Office, *United States Government Policy and Supporting Positions* App'x No. 1, p. 197 (2016), https://www.gpo.gov/fdsys/pkg/GPO-PLUMBOOK-2012/pdf/GPO-PLUMBOOK-2012.pdf (commonly known as the "Plum Book").

[27] See United States House of Representatives, Committee on Oversight and Government Reform, *United States Government Policy and Supporting Positions (Plum Book)* (2012) (listing all political appointment positions in the federal bureaucracy).

[28] See *Chevron U.S.A., Inc. v. Natural Resources Defense Council, Inc.*, 467 U.S. 837, 865 (1984) ("Perhaps [Congress] consciously desired the Administrator to strike the balance at this level, thinking that those with *great expertise* and charged with responsibility for administering the provision would be in a better position to do so . . . ") (emphasis added).

[29] See JAMES LANDIS, THE ADMINISTRATIVE PROCESS (1938); see also THOMAS K. MCCRAW, PROPHETS OF REGULATION (1984) (chapter on James Landis).

[30] Sidney A. Shapiro, *The Failure to Understand Expertise in Administrative Law: The Problems and the Consequences*, 50 WAKE FOREST L. REV. 1097 (2015).

[31] *Id.*, at 1113–17.

[32] See PHILIP E. TETLOCK, EXPERT POLITICAL JUDGMENT 2 (2005).

act. The idea is contested in today's political environment, to our collective disadvantage. As Francis Fukuyama explains it: "Distrust of executive agencies leads [to] demands for more legal checks on administration which further reduces the quality and effectiveness of government by reducing *bureaucratic autonomy*."[33] Yet bureaucratic autonomy is a public value. It is a "form of deference," Daniel Carpenter tells us,[34] and it extends far beyond discretion into a realm where "bureaucratic reputation" defines its limits. Carpenter identifies department and agency heads whose bureaucratic reputations permit bureaucratic autonomy to exist. In essence, these are the professionals who make government work.

This autonomy can be abused,[35] like discretion itself, and that may be a reason to check it judicially, but is not a reason to eliminate it. Democratic society needs professional autonomy, in the marketplace and in government. Government professionals provide an indispensable category of public leadership that no contractor can replicate or supplant. In society, professionalism itself is characterized by expertise, judgment, and commitment. Professionals like doctors, lawyers, engineers, and accountants are allowed to self-regulate in return for educational and career commitments.[36] Since self-regulation is a form of autonomy, it also can be abused.[37]

Government frequently turns to private boards to certify federal licensing and eligibility requirements, in effect delegating public powers to self-regulatory bodies. The entire postsecondary accreditation program run by the Department of Education relies on regional and national institutional accrediting agencies to determine eligibility for access to federal financial aid programs. These agencies enlist professional educators to make determinations which are reviewed by federal officials. The results are not always acceptable. An analysis of ten different accrediting agencies shows they apply a highly

33 Francis Fukuyama, *The Decay of American Political Institutions*, THE AMERICAN INTEREST (Dec. 9, 2013), http://www.the-american-interest.com/2013/12/08/the-decay-of-american-political-institutions/.

34 DANIEL P. CARPENTER, THE FORGING OF BUREAUCRATIC ACCOUNTABILITY 17–19 (2001).

35 The judicial review standard for setting aside agency action is "arbitrary, capricious, an abuse of discretion, or otherwise not in accordance with law." 5 U.S.C. § 706(2)(A).

36 See Dr. Matthew K. Wynia, MD, *The Role of Professionalism and Self-regulation in Detecting Impaired or Incompetent Physicians*, 304 J. AM. MED. ASS'N 210 (2010).

37 See *North Carolina Board of Dental Examiners* v. *FTC*, 135 S.Ct. 1101 (2016), discussed in Chapter 2, where the Court rejected a state board's privilege to regulate its members because of conflicts of interest challenged by the Federal Trade Commission (FTC). See Charles G. Kels, *Is Professional Self-Regulation at a Crossroads?*, REGBLOG (Aug. 17, 2016), www.regblog.org/2015/08/17/kels-professional-self-regulation/ (opinion piece on whether state licensing boards should still be composed of industry members).

uneven system of sanctions.[38] This is also a problem for professional managers in government. The question is how to introduce greater consistency into the system without undoing the network of professionals who do the work. This is an "abuse of discretion" issue that does not usually reach the courts. It must be cured administratively, by monitoring and oversight, which is all part of the bureaucratic accountability.

## C. WORKAROUNDS AND PROFESSIONALISM: HOW TO FIGHT RED TAPE

The painting on the cover by Maurice Sterne shows Justice Holmes as Don Quixote manfully fighting "red tape." Red tape has been a problem for government since the eighteenth century.[39] It will be with us into the twenty-second century. But it can be reduced through clever and perceptive management if one realizes that government is as much art as it is (management) science. And the art part is where professionalism enters the picture. Nowhere is professional expertise more needed than in cutting through the spider's web of rules and formalities that delay and trap citizens.

The federal government is in many ways like a labyrinth. Not the elaborate structure that was built by King Minos of Crete to hold the Minotaur, but one created unintentionally by decades of encrusted statutory and regulatory commands directed at hundreds of agencies and the public from many directions. Now some of these dictates are essential, some are less so and some are self-contradictory. This is what happens when rules are stacked upon one another across administrations over many years. To cure this condition, Congress sometimes enacts legislation and agencies update rules via retrospective review.[40] But the crush of current business often leaves little time for these corrective functions, and choices must be made by agencies in real time. If the stasis point becomes inaction then decisions are not made that would better the public interest. This is where bureaucracy and red tape join hands in the public's mind.[41] It is confronted by the public when seeking to achieve some

38 See Antoinette Flores, Center for American Progress, *Watching the Watchdogs: A Look at What Happens When Accreditors Sanction Colleges* (2016), https://cdn.americanprogress.org/wp-content/uploads/2016/06/16111301/AccreditorActions-report.pdf.

39 See Del Dickson, The People's Government: An Introduction to Democracy 176 (2016) (establishing the beginnings with Charles V of Spain, the Holy Roman Emperor who used red tape to bind his most important documents).

40 The project on retrospective review of rules, urged by Congress and mandated by President Obama, often stalled due to the priorities that agencies give it. See ACUS Recommendation 2014–5 and Chapter 8.

41 See generally Barry Bozeman, Bureaucracy and Red Tape (2000) (providing case examples of the difference between reasonable rules and regulations and those labeled "red tape").

result from government; but it also challenges those within the bureaucracy who must administer around it to govern effectively.

When a newly appointed political leader joins an agency, an initial challenge is to understand the agency's mission and culture. Culture includes the many rules and protocols that are embedded in the agency's practices. The problem of conflicting rules or statutes surrounding specific actions is bound to arise early in the administrator's tenure. Questions are raised and answers are sought, but these may not be apparent without deep knowledge of the situation. Who does the new leader turn to? The general counsel or division heads may also be newly appointed and unable to explain the situation. Who is next? The agency professionals. The senior career officials with experience. They are the ones who embody the agency's cultural knowledge. What might take a politically appointed chief of staff or deputy days or weeks to determine, can be learned quickly from the career staff, if their advice is sought. Newcomers may know a conflict exists, but only veterans know why. This is the essence of institutional knowledge. It is why new leaders try not to go to interagency meetings without adequate staffing, including career as well as political aides. There can be no more frightening proposition for new agency heads than the notion of "principals only" meetings.

So consider the situation where an agency head is instructed to take action and calls a meeting of key staffers to effectuate it. A path is chosen and a direction is about to be given when someone says "what about regulation XYZ?" Silence and consternation fill the room. Then the agency head or general counsel says "what's the workaround?" This phrase must be said hundreds of times a day at all levels of government. To answer that question someone is needed who thinks "outside the box," with the proverbial box being tied up in red tape. Likely a career professional who knows where regulation XYZ came from, what it was really intended to do, and why it can be avoided (or not), will be called upon. This person can be a senior official or someone a branch chief is smart enough to locate deeper in the hierarchy. Much of governing consists of identifying obstacles and finding people who can overcome them.

The alternative is "gridlock," which is red tape's alter ego, and a condition that some agencies are immersed in. Some may even believe gridlock is desirable.[42] Workarounds are designed to help prevent gridlock. They must

[42] See Emily Esfahan Smith & George Will, *When We Have Gridlock, the System Is Working*, RICOCHET (Nov. 2, 2010), https://ricochet.com/archives/george-will-when-we-have-gridlock-the-system-is-working/ ("Gridlock is not an American problem. It's an American achievement. The framers of our Constitution didn't want an efficient government; they wanted a safe government.") (quoting George Will on *This Week with Christine Amanpour* as "brilliant").

be wielded delicately, thoughtfully, and not always publicly. In a democratic society this raises suspicions about motive and fidelity of purpose, as it should. But workarounds are not exceptional; they are bureaucratic autonomy in action.

"Workaround" is a computer engineering term with an interesting definitional history. It means a bypass of a recognized problem in a system, that is meant to be temporary in order to overcome perceived workflow obstacles.[43] In some fields workarounds have been systematically studied,[44] but not in government, where they are an arcane practice. But they are not secret: a standard text on public management defines "the effective public manager [as] an expert at working around constraints to produce results,"[45] even while recognizing that workarounds sometimes result in "dysfunctional Rube Goldberg contraptions created by imaginative managers to get around systems constraints."[46] I have wondered whether collecting the successful workarounds that agencies use could produce a manual of effective government. But of course the problem is no one wants to put workarounds on the record for fear they will then have to be worked around.

## 1 *Workarounds as Optimal Abuses of Power*

> [I]n every political institution, a power to advance the public happiness involves a discretion that may be misapplied or abused.
>
> James Madison, *Federalist* 41

Government is in need of a theory of workarounds that connects them to bureaucratic autonomy, the need for professional government, and the proper exercise of discretion. Some people should not do workarounds – bank tellers, for example, or attorneys at the Office of Legal Counsel at DOJ.[47] And some laws or regulations should not be worked around, such as the Constitution or explicit statutory mandates. But many rules and regulations in government are unclear or contested and discretion has to be exercised before they are invoked. Rules and regulations may be different from statutes in this regard. The Federal Circuit recently established that the federal Whistleblower Act, which protects

43 See Collins English Dictionary Complete and Unabridged (2012).

44 See Deborah S. Debono, et al., *Nurses Workarounds in Acute Healthcare Settings: A Scoping Review*, 13 BMC Health Services Research 175 (2013) ("Workarounds enable, yet potentially compromise, the execution of patient care.").

45 Steve Cohen & William Eimicke, The New Effective Public Manager xi (1995).

46 *Id.*, at xii.

47 See Karen J. Greenberg & Joshua L. Dratel, The Torture Papers 1–3 (2005) (concerning the memo from John Yoo to Timothy Flanagan on the legality of waterboarding); see also Jack Goldsmith, The Terror Presidency (2007).

employees from being asked by superiors to violate the law, does not apply when they are asked to violate rules or regulations.[48] This sensible case drew an immediate response from some in Congress who wanted to reverse its effect by statute.[49] These are the zero tolerance for abuse of power advocates. They profess to deny, as James Madison would have it, that a potential abuse of power might be a necessary condition for effective public managers to do the public's work.

Adrian Vermeule has used the Madison quote to make a case for the Constitution as a document designed not to eliminate, but to optimize, abuses of power.[50] This bold idea made me think that a theory of workarounds might even find constitutional support. Vermeule's insight is that zero tolerance for abuse (what he calls the concept of precautionary constitutionalism) would produce a regime with unacceptably high enforcement costs, "leaving too little room for the actual functioning of government and for the welfare goods that government provides." This is especially true in the design of the administrative state where there is a "pervasive tradeoff between impartiality and expertise." The cost of perfectly enforcing impartiality, Vermeule reasons, is that there are other abuses of power that must be traded off, like those in the private sector that the government cannot reach with the enforcement institutions. And inspectors general and the like who monitor government officials must themselves be watched. The "who guards the guardians?" problem, Vermoule argues, leaves us with compromised institutions, like independent agencies that seem to ignore traditional separation of powers principles by combining the judging and enforcing of laws. And it also justifies the exercise of agency discretion (even some degree of "official blundering") against concerns that the judiciary by watching too closely will "ossify" the regulatory process.[51] Sometimes "satisficing" – settling for something that is good

48 See *Rainey* v. *MSPB*, 824 F.3d 1359 (2016), affirming the dismissal of a whistleblower claim by a State Department employee who refused a superior's order to tell a contractor to rehire a terminated subcontractor, even though the employee claimed it would require him to violate a section of the Federal Acquisition Regulation. The court relied on the Supreme Court decision in *DHS* v. *McLean*, 135 S.Ct. 913 (2015), which held that the word "law" in the "right to disclose" provision of the Whistleblower Protection Act refers only to statutes and not rules or regulations.

49 See Eric Katz, *Lawmaker: Feds Shouldn't Be Punished for Refusing to Break Rules*, Government Executive (Jun. 23, 2016), www.govexec.com/management/2016/06/lawmaker-feds-shouldnt-be-punished-refusing-break-rules/129352/.

50 See Adrian Vermeule, *Optimal Abuse of Power*, 109 Northwestern L. Rev. 673 (2015); see also Adrian Vermeule, The Constitution of Risk (2014) (his larger study of constitutional design).

51 Vermeule relies on *FCC* v. *Fox Television Studios, Inc.*, 556 U.S. 502 (2009), which upheld, against an arbitrary and capricious challenge, the agency's action to restrict broadcast of indecent content even though it did not justify that the new policy was better than the old one.

enough[52] – is good enough for government work. To my nascent workaround theory the idea of good enough has appeal – it may be the only way the government's work gets done.

## 2 *The ALJ Appointment Crisis and Cautious Bureaucrats*

While I observed and participated in discussions that called for numerous workarounds in my term of service, one experience stands out. Not all (or even most) government officials are good at workarounds. Parkinson's Law defines them as "cautious bureaucrats." Now there is nothing wrong with caution, especially when facing difficult choices, but to be cautious as a mindset can become a formula for bureaucratic paralysis. To avoid gridlock and red tape, autonomous bureaucrats, not cautious ones, are required.[53]

The Social Security Disability system provides disability payments and medical insurance (Medicare or Medicaid) to those under the retirement age who meet the definitional requirements of "disability." Applicants start before state disability agencies on written submissions and, if unsuccessful there, may appeal to the federal government. Disability cases are decided by Administrative Law Judges (ALJs) working for the Social Security Administration (SSA). There are over 14 million people on the rolls,[54] and over 2 million apply annually.[55] Over $140 billion is awarded every year. For several years, the agency has faced an enormous backlog at the ALJ stage which added years before claimants could have cases resolved and benefits distributed. People needed help and yet they were stuck on a queue that could leave them homeless, with worsening conditions, or even dead before they receive a hearing.[56] This is bureaucratic gridlock of "Kafkaesque" proportions.

52 See Herbert A. Simon, *A Behavioral Model of Rational Choice*, 69 Q.J. Econ. 99 (1955).

53 The civil service system does not encourage risk-taking since caution is the safe place to be. To encourage risk-taking, Richard Thaler reminds us that it is the boss who must show it is also a safe place by not penalizing those whose value-maximizing ideas do not always work out in practice. He calls this the "hindsight bias." Richard H. Thaler, Misbehaving: The Making of Behavioral Economics (2016).

54 See United States Social Security Admin., Monthly Statistical Snapshot March 2016, https://www.ssa.gov/policy/docs/quickfacts/stat_snapshot/.

55 See United States Social Security Admin., Selected Data From Social Security's Disability Program, last visited May 25, 2016, https://www.ssa.gov/oact/STATS/dibStat.html; see also Jerry Mashaw, Bureaucratic Justice (1983).

56 See Theresa Gruber, Deputy Commissioner, Disability Adjudication and Review, Social Security Administration, Testimony before the Senate Committee on Homeland Security and Governmental Affairs, Subcommittee on Regulatory Affairs and Federal Management 3 (May 12, 2016), www.hsgac.senate.gov/hearings/examining-due-process-in-administrative-hearings (hereinafter Gruber Testimony).

In the summer of 2015, Congress, the White House (OMB), and SSA asked the Office of Personnel Management (OPM), whose job it was to hire ALJs, to certify enough ALJ applicants annually for two years to reduce the backlog. Currently, about 1,778 ALJs decide over 800,000 cases per year,[57] and 500 more were needed (250 per year). Yet OPM's examination process only produced about 100 candidates per year. ACUS was asked to facilitate meetings between OPM, OMB, and SSA to find a way to increase the flow of ALJ candidates on the OPM register so that SSA could find the extra qualified judges. After several months of meetings, little progress was made. OPM found innumerable and not totally implausible ways to avoid streamlining the appointment process. It was then I realized we were dealing with cautious bureaucrats.

The statute requires an "examination" since ALJs are in the "competitive service."[58] But OPM had managed over the years, through a team of industrial psychologists which they employ (and the agencies pay for), to make the new tests, interviews, and background checks enormously complicated. It costs $3–4 million to create a new test and each test could only be used twice due to fear of questions circulating (even though testees were forbidden to do so). Many in the room who proposed workarounds to these cumbersome rules and practices were rebuffed by the agency's officials,[59] making it virtually impossible to add the 250 additional ALJs to the register and shrink the backlog. It was a frustrating impasse. Most in the room wanted to solve a compelling problem – faster distribution of disability benefits to deserving claimants. I remember thinking that Congress, the President (through OMB), and the agency (SSA) all want to move forward to solve a crisis, but that didn't budge the bureaucrats in OPM. Preserving the status quo and protecting turf seemed a more important outcome than solving the problem.

Since OPM wouldn't budge much (they did make some changes[60]), the SSA was forced to turn to a more controversial solution – supplementing the ALJ disability corps with non-ALJs (called AAJs). AAJ appointments do not fall within OPM's jurisdiction, since they are in the excepted, not the competitive, service and can be hired by SSA directly. But their appointment raised legal

57 See *Examining Due Process in Administrative Hearings: Hearing Before the S. Comm. on Homeland Security and Governmental Affairs, Subcommittee on Regulatory Affairs and Federal Management*, 114th Cong. (2016) (statement of Joseph Kennedy, Assoc. Dir., Human Resources Solutions, Office of Personnel Management), hereinafter Kennedy Testimony.

58 *Id.*, at 2.

59 For example, suggestions for a simpler and faster exam process, such as bar associations use, or to restrict appeals to the agency by using retests were rejected out of hand, as were ways to narrow an ALJ applicant's geographical preferences. When an idea survived an initial cut, it was met by a generic "litigation risk" response.

60 See Kennedy Testimony, *supra* note 58, at 2.

issues about whether they can do the work of ALJs that jeopardized decisions made by them. This solution was yet a bigger workaround and it met with opposition from the Congress and the ALJ unions.[61] Subsequently, the Acting Director of OPM, Beth Cobert, reconvened the ALJ negotiating team and added some new members and some progress has been achieved. The register was refreshed and expanded and more names are appearing on it. It may be that effective workarounds will emerge after more than a year of trying to achieve change, but the backlog has now passed the 1 million mark.[62]

Admittedly, all bureaucrats are not good at workarounds, and not all workarounds are good. But some are good at both doing and understanding when to support their use. These are the professionals who make government work. During my time in public service I met many of them. They need to be maintained and nurtured. Officials who can exercise Phillip Tetlock's "expert political judgment" and achieve valuable public purposes while overcoming red tape and gridlock are the "A players" that George Schultz calls for. Contractors, for all their value, cannot be experts in this sense. Professionals to run the bureaucracy and find ways around it when necessary are indispensable.

## D. PROFESSIONALISM, "AT WILL" EMPLOYMENT, AND TENURE

The qualities that make government professionals valuable include judgment, knowledge, and experience. Experience is a virtue of career employment. There are many ways to encourage careerism. In the business world "golden handcuffs" are applied. In the academic setting tenure is granted and, in government, civil service promotion standards are employed and hearing rights protect against dismissal. Concepts of tenure are contested these days. Indeed, the "at will" public employment model in many states is directed against tenure or protected service. So how does stability get preserved as a value in the public employment setting?

[61] See Jory Heckman, *Senators Say SSA's Backlog Reduction Plan Violates Due Process*, Federal News Radio (May 12, 2016), available at http://federalnewsradio.com/congress/2016/05/senators-says-ssas-backlog-reduction-plan-violates-due-process/ (quoting Senators James Lankford and Heidi Heitkamp, Chairman and ranking member of the Homeland Security and Governmental Affairs Subcommittee on Regulatory Affairs and Federal Management). The fear is that cases heard by AAJs and not ALJs would have to be reheard or challenged in court, undoing the purpose of the effort.

[62] The SSA's Office of Inspector General lists 1.1 million cases awaiting decision. See Social Sec. Admin., Office of the Inspector General, Characteristics of Claimants in the Social Security Administration's Pending Hearings Backlog, Summary 1 (2016), https://oig.ssa.gov/sites/default/files/audit/full/pdf/A-05-16-50207.pdf.

"At will" employment was the default rule at common law[63] for economic efficiency reasons, since dismissal protections deter new hires as well as prevent discharges. But while the freedom to fire gives employers maximum leverage, over the last 100 years states and the federal system have raised barriers against dismissal in order to protect workers.[64] Modern employment conditions, discussed in Chapter 3, have increased the number of temporary workers and the use of contractors to provide employees to firms and businesses.[65] Contractors are appealing options to employers precisely because they can be terminated or replaced once their tasks are completed. But in the public sector, workers generally enjoy protections against removal, a kind of tenure in office. How can these two ideas be reconciled? Start with the judiciary. Without tenure in office it is hard to see how the Rule of Law could exist since making unpopular decisions would result in dismissal.[66] Tenure does not have to be for life, as in the federal courts, but at least for a term of years, as it is in most state judicial systems where judges are elected or even appointed.[67]

Restrictions on dismissal of government officials outside the judicial context are controversial because the Rule of Law justification is not obvious. In universities tenure is long established and largely accepted for academic freedom reasons. At the K-12 level, however, teacher tenure is under attack. In *Vergara v. California*,[68] students challenged the two-year tenure statute for teachers as one aspect of an equal protection claim under the California Constitution, which guarantees a public education. The California Superior Court found the statute unconstitutional, but that decision was reversed by the Court of Appeals[69] and the California Supreme Court refused to hear the appeal by a 4–3 vote.[70] Tenure in two years is too short to give an adequate evaluation

63 See Richard Epstein, *In Defense of the Contract at Will*, 57 U. Chi. L. Rev. 947 (1984).

64 See Clyde Summers, *Employment At Will in the U.S. – The Divine Right of Employers*, 3 U. Penn. J. Lab. & Empl. L. 65 (2000). See also, e.g., Civil Rights Act of 1964, 78 Stat. 241; Age Discrimination in Employment Act of 1967 (as amended), 81 Stat. 602.

65 See Katz & Krueger, *supra* Chapter 3, at n. 3.

66 See Frank H. Easterbrook, *What's So Special About Judges?*, 61 Colo. L. Rev. 773, 776 (1990) ("Tenure liberates judges from contemporary political pressures").

67 In some states, judges are targeted during elections based on their controversial decisions. See Billy Corriher, Center for American Progress, *Partisan Judicial Elections and the Distorting Influence of Campaign Cash* (2012), https://www.americanprogress.org/issues/civil-liberties/report/2012/10/25/42895/partisan-judicial-elections-and-the-distorting-influence-of-campaign-cash/.

68 See Ian Lovett & Motoko Rich, *Closely Watched Fight Over Teacher Tenure Moves to Appeals Court*, N.Y. Times, Feb. 26, 2016, at A12 (tenure in two years under California law).

69 246 Cal. App. 4th 619 (Cal. Ct. App. 2016).

70 See Emma Brown, *California Supreme Court Leaves Teacher Tenure Law in Place*, Wash. Post (Aug. 29, 2016), https://www.washingtonpost.com/news/education/wp/2016/08/22/california-supreme-court-decision-leaves-states-teacher-tenure-law-in-place/.

of performance (one year, in essence). It is not as short as the instant tenure ALJs receive in the federal system on the theory that their decisions implicate the Rule of Law. But ALJs could serve a probationary period like other federal employees.[71]

In colleges and universities the normal time for a tenure decision is six years of service, with a decision in the seventh year, which can be extended. Since higher education evaluates both the teaching and scholarly credentials of the candidates, this timeframe is needed to collect adequate data on performance. For public school teachers, who have no scholarly duties, three or four years should be sufficient to evaluate teaching competence. But even in universities, especially state-supported ones, the pressure to reduce tenured positions has produced a significant number of adjunct faculty.[72]

As a university president (an agency head) I didn't want to see tenured positions reduced too much, because the commitment to university learning and governance is affected. Tenure is awarded to encourage investment by the brightest minds in preserving and advancing fields of study that often have no marketplace alternative. These faculty are the custodians of society's culture and knowledge and it is difficult to see how you can have a great university system without them. Academic freedom is a right under the First Amendment precisely because bold and creative ideas must be encouraged and protected.[73]

Tenure in government is a different matter, of course, but the level of commitment it produces can be analogized to the academic setting. The notion of dismissal for cause after a government official serves a probationary period is supposed to encourage commitment and independent thinking. When we ask Foreign Service officers, for example, to become experts in the language, culture, and politics of the many countries of the world, it is sensible for government to provide civil service protections against arbitrary removal. We want their best judgment in times of political stress. A State Department program called the "dispute channel" permits career employees

71 The issue with a probation period for ALJs is what happens to the decisions in their cases if they do not achieve permanent status. The answer must be that they stand as decided, just like decisions of administrative judges who do not receive automatic tenure.

72 See Alan Finder, *Decline of the Tenure Track Raises Concerns*, N.Y. Times (Nov. 30, 2007), www.nytimes.com/2007/11/20/education/20adjunct.html (citing studies showing that part- and full-time adjuncts have grown from 43 percent to 70 percent of public and private school faculties).

73 See Rachel Levinson, *Academic Freedom and the First Amendment*, American Association of University Professors (July 2007 presentation), available at https://www.aaup.org/our-work/protecting-academic-freedom/academic-freedom-and-first-amendment-2007; see also [McCarthy Cases].

to voice their objections: 51 used it to criticize Obama's policy in Syria and over 1,000 used it to object to Trump's executive order barring citizens from seven Muslim-majority countries.[74] While the Secretary of State, Rex Tillerson, must, if he disagrees with administration policy, dissent in private (or resign), the tradition of public dissent by career officials can strengthen democracy and improve policy.[75] Thus, tenure can have a decisive role to play in government.

There is an analogy to contractors in government and contractors (adjuncts) in the academy that is worth noting. Universities as well as governments can benefit from the ability to utilize contractors who meet unexpected demands (surge capacity) or perform tasks that are readily replicable (language courses, perhaps). But, when it comes to running a university or a government, expertise, institutional knowledge, and the confidence to speak out are valuable commodities. Faculty appropriately share in the governance of their institutions, and government officials do as well. When this professional judgment is unavailable or undervalued, things go wrong. At the state level, the at will public employment movement has produced a loss of professionalism. Some states, like Wisconsin, have overhauled their civil service system to make this outcome seem inevitable in the future. This does not mean that civil service procedures are properly calibrated, as Chapter 8 shows, since government's use of contractors is often wrapped up in the procedural ossification of the hiring and removal process.

## E. PROFESSIONALS AS ACTING AGENCY HEADS

Career officials not only provide leadership to those at high levels of government but are also increasingly called upon to assume acting positions at those high levels. Congressional gridlock stalls the confirmations of political appointees. Over 100 of the Obama Administration's senior jobs, one-quarter of the total, were missing permanent appointments as a result of the stymied

74 See Neal Katyal, Op-Ed, *Washington Needs More Dissent Channels*, N.Y. Times (Jul. 1, 2016), www.nytimes.com/2016/07/02/opinion/washington-needs-more-dissent-channels.html (a version of this op-ed appears in print on July 2, 2016, on page A17 of the New York edition with the headline: *Healthy Dissent in Washington*). See also Jeffrey Gettleman, *State Dept. Dissent Cable on Trump's Ban Draws 1,000 Signatures*, N.Y. Times (Jan. 31, 2017).

75 For example, Arthur Blood, Consul in Bangladesh during its war for independence from Pakistan, warned Henry Kissinger of genocide. Blood, a hero in Bangladesh to this day, was demoted but served 30 years at State after the event. See Ellen Barry, *To U.S. in '70s, a Dissenting Diplomat. To Bangladesh, 'a True Friend'*, N.Y. Times (Jun. 27, 2016), www.nytimes.com/2016/06/28/world/asia/bangladesh-archer-blood-cable.html.

confirmation process.[76] Acting career officials are often forced to fill the gap. The federal government relies on political appointees to operate agencies, but the presence of career deputies sometimes makes agency operations possible. There are over 1,200 PAS positions that are supposed to be filled through a presidential nomination and Senate confirmation process. This is an extreme problem in a divided political environment, but acting positions have always been needed. A study by Anne O'Connell found that top jobs in executive agencies and Cabinet departments had not been filled by PAS officials between 15 and 25 percent of the time, on average, between 1977 and 2005.[77] About a quarter of all submitted nominations in the Senate failed to get confirmed between 1981 and 2014.[78] On average, each of these failed nominations took 180 days from start to end. For those nominations that did get confirmed, delays increased. From the start of President Obama's administration through 2014, successful nominations took, on average, 127 days to confirm, and some of those confirmations came after previous failed nominations.[79]

Under the Vacancies Act,[80] a PAS vacancy may be filled in three ways: by (1) the "first assistant" to the office automatically; (2) the President appointing a PAS from another office; or (3) the President appointing a senior employee from the same agency. Thus, under the third prong, career professionals get to act as agency heads for a specified period (usually 210 days).[81] The Vacancy Act has limitations on acting officers if the President nominates them to the Senate for Appointment to the Office,[82] but if a career official is chosen, that conflict does not arise. So yet another need for professionals in government is that they could become de facto political appointees. Their quality, experience, and judgment are increasingly necessary in the world of contested government that shows no signs of abating.

76 See Daniel Samuelson, *Obama's Vanishing Administration*, Politico (Jun. 5, 2016), www.politico.com/story/2016/01/obamas-vanishing-administration-217344.

77 Anne Joseph O'Connell, *Vacant Offices: Delays in Staffing Top Agency Positions*, 82 S. Cal. L. Rev. 913 (2009).

78 Anne Joseph O'Connell, *Shortening Agency and Judicial Vacancies through Filibuster Reform? An Examination of Confirmation Rates and Delays from 1981 to 2014*, 64 Duke L.J. 1645 (2015). Almost all those "failed" nominations are nominations returned to or withdrawn by the President. Few are voted down. These figures include both agency and judicial nominations.

79 The list of nominees awaiting Senate confirmation is available at www.senate.gov/legislative/nom_cmtec.htm.

80 5 U.S.C. § 3345(a)(1)–(3).

81 *Id.*

82 See SW *General, Inc.* v. *NLRB*, 796 F.3d 67, 74 (D.C. Cir. 2015), 136 S.Ct. 2489 (individual who became Acting General Counsel of NLRB pursuant to Federal Vacancies Reform Act (FVRA) senior agency employee provision was ineligible to serve once President nominated him to be General Counsel and was serving in violation of FVRA when unfair labor practice complaint issued against employer). The acting head of OPM, Beth Cobert, had her position challenged because of this provision. See OIG Memo to Beth Cobert, Feb. 10, 2016.

Some career officials have achieved legendary status for their abilities to step in when the political leaders need support. David Margolis of DOJ, who died recently, was lauded by Sally Yates, Deputy Attorney General, as "the go to guy for department leaders for over 50 years."[83] I have met people like Margolis at other agencies during my years in government.[84] They are the true professionals – ones who keep government running behind the scenes and for whom there is no substitute. These jobs are truly "above the pay grade" of government contractors.

[83] Eric Lichtblau, *David Margolis, a Justice Department Institution, Dies at 76*, N.Y. Times (Jul. 15, 2016), www.nytimes.com/2016/07/16/us/david-margolis-a-justice-department-institution-dies-at-76.html.

[84] David Shonka at the FTC comes to mind, who has been called upon multiple times to serve as Acting General Counsel.

# 7

# The Civil Service and Its Reform

It is a question of making politics purer

Teddy Roosevelt[1]

The civil service system envisioned by Teddy Roosevelt has many achievements. But it needs fixing. There are many reasons to do so, one of which is implied by David Margolis' wry comment when a member of Congress asked how many people work at the Justice Department – "about 60 percent," he replied.[2] His answer surely applies to other government agencies. But it is not just discipline and motivation that are needed. This book adds another reason: curing or at least moderating the addiction agencies have to the hiring of contractors. If it can be made easier to hire and fire, to compensate, incent, discipline, and promote civil servants, agencies will be encouraged to employ the next generation of government professionals, many of whom will be their replacements. A better human capital system for the federal government can ameliorate the current talent crisis and create a professional cadre for the future.

The duty to supervise, set out in Chapter 2, compels the political branches of government to move together towards this end. While the President is admonished to take care that laws are faithfully executed, Congress also has an incentive to ensure that there are "faithful agents"[3] who run the government. Civil service reform may not be enough to make politics "purer" as Teddy Roosevelt called for, but it can help to make the political system more functional, more responsive to the demands the public places on government, and more likely to work at full capacity.

1 From RICHARD D. WHITE, JR., ROOSEVELT THE REFORMER 79 (2003).

2 Lichtblau, *supra* Chapter 6, at note 84. The quoted language comes from an answer given at a congressional hearing by the legendary Associate Deputy Attorney General and 50-year veteran civil servant.

3 See John D. DiIulio, *Principled Agents: The Cultural Bases of Behavior in a Federal Government Bureaucracy*, 4 J. PUB. ADMIN. RESEARCH & THEORY 277 (1994).

This chapter reminds us first just how important the civil service system is to government and how hard it was to create – after all, America emerged from the spoils system less than 100 years ago. Yet what we have is not perfect. To demonstrate that the present system is "broken," complaints from those using the system will be reviewed, as well as the many carve-outs from it agencies have sought over the years. There are really two systems to study: the competitive system as the civil service is known, and the alternatives to the competitive service (the excepted service). The latter are, in a sense, giant workarounds driven by the frustrating limitations of the formal system. From this perspective, the biggest system workaround is the federal contractor regime itself, which offers services and flexibilities that the civil service is presently unable to provide.

The system has been encrusted over time, building in protections from dismissal that cost the government millions in delay and time lost. To take just one high-profile example, consider the use of paid administrative leave accounts during the endless disciplinary process.[4] These situations give the system a bad name and make sensible reforms more urgent, even though these protections have been bargained for by civil service unions and are protected by the Merit System Protection Board.

Despite the fact that the same number of civil servants are employed now as during the Kennedy Administration, there are those who seek to shrink it further, either by not replacing one of three who retire or by proposing hiring freezes[5] as a way to reduce the layers of bureaucracy. This is the position of the Trump Administration. The layering problem, identified by Paul Light as "thickening," should be addressed.[6] But given that the total number of federal employees has been static for over 50 years, their number is hardly excessive overall. Reducing the civil service only invites government to hire more contractors.[7] The shortage of high-level career employees can be readily seen with the Senior Executive Service (SES) which is limited to about

4 See Joe Davidson, *Administrative Leave Accounts to Make You Cringe*, Washington Post, Apr. 6, 2016, at A13 (documenting cases of agencies putting employees on paid leave for years while their cases are investigated).

5 See Ron Sanders, *DoD's Civilian Hiring Freeze: Deja Vu All Over Again*, Federal Times (Apr. 14, 2016), www.federaltimes.com/story/government/management/blog/2016/04/14/dods-civilian-hiring-freeze-dj-vu-all-over-again/83034352/.

6 See Paul Light, *A Government Ill Executed: The Depletion of the Federal Service*, 68 Pub. Admin. Rev. 413, 415 (2008) ("The thickening of the federal government has created the tallest and widest executive hierarchy in modern history").

7 See Paul R. Verkuil, *The Case for Bureaucracy*, Op-Ed, N.Y. Times (Oct. 3, 2016), www.nytimes.com/2016/10/03/opinion/the-case-for-bureaucracy.html (discussing Donald Trump's adoption of the one-in-three replacement of retirees idea).

0.5 percent of the civilian workforce. The SES is charged with providing major leadership throughout government. Reforms to the SES will allow that crucial body of officials to manage government effectively and at the highest levels.

The overall message is that civil service reform raises a moral issue – the duty to run government efficiently and incorruptly. As citizens, we must face up to the fact that the institutional deficiencies of our current system have created a talent crisis and leadership vacuum. The civil service system must make the public believe in it. When Gallup's Jim Clifton says that "a staggering 75 percent of the American public believe corruption is 'widespread' in the U.S. government," the civil service must respond, even though he connects this malaise to the rise of Donald Trump.[8] So, that is the bad news – ineffective civil service tinged with an aura of corruption.

If there is good news, it is that the rest of the world looks to us as models in the fight against bureaucratic corruption.[9] Thus, we may be, like Churchill's definition of democracy, the worst civil service system except for all the others. We may also be at an inflection point where the incoming president can prepare the way for new consensus to emerge.[10] Certainly, one of this book's purposes is to help present these reforms to the right audiences at the right time so that political change can be forthcoming.

## A. THE TRANSFORMATIVE POWER OF THE CIVIL SERVICE

Teddy Roosevelt believed that the creation of a merit-based bureaucracy could objectively carry out the dictates of the political branches. This quest began many years ago but, given the doubt discussed above, it is still not finished. There is still need for TR's kind of idealism as we try to make the system fulfill its promise while recognizing how far we have come.

[8] Jim Clifton, *Explaining Trump: Widespread Government Corruption*, Gallup Blog (Jan. 6, 2016), www.gallup.com/opinion/chairman/188000/explaining-trump-widespread-government-corruption.aspx.

[9] See *Mandarin Lessons*, The Economist (Mar. 12, 2016), www.economist.com/news/international/21694553-countries-are-trying-harder-recruit-best-bureaucrats-not-hard-enough-mandarin (showing how meritocracy is growing in 55 of the 62 countries tracked by Global Integrity, an NGO).

[10] See Jeff Neal, *Civil Service Reform Should Be High on the Next President's To-Do List*, Federal News Radio, Apr. 21, 2016, http://federalnewsradio.com/commentary/2016/04/civil-service-reform-should-be-high-on-the-next-presidents-to-do-list/.

The Pendleton Civil Service Reform Act was passed in 1883[11] and named after Senator George Pendleton.[12] The Act provided for competitive exams instead of political appointments and introduced the merit system to government. The Act was signed by Chester Arthur, James A. Garfield's Vice President, after Garfield had been assassinated by a disappointed office seeker, which made the spoils system a viable target. It did not cover many federal employees at the outset, but over time subsequent Presidents and the Civil Service Commission established under the Act expanded its coverage to most of the federal government. As Norm Ornstein notes, it is difficult to appreciate today just what this Act meant at the time.[13] Signing it probably killed Arthur's political chances to be reelected, because Democratic bosses were angered that their patronage had been lost. "Fighting the spoilsmen"[14] took the kind of dedication that suffragettes showed in passing the 19th Amendment, and the battle for merit was not won until well into the twentieth century.

Implementing the Pendleton Act fell to leaders like Teddy Roosevelt[15] who had the tenacity to get it done. While in the New York State Assembly, TR teamed with the Democratic Governor Grover Cleveland to get the "little" Pendleton Act passed in New York,[16] over the objections of established interests in both parties. When President Benjamin Harrison named him a civil service commissioner, TR went to Washington full of enthusiasm for his reforming role. But he met concentrated resistance from other members of the Harrison Administration and the President himself. Postmaster General John Wanamaker was singled out for special derision when Roosevelt labeled him the "head devil of the spoilsmen."[17] Ironically, Teddy fared much better in his reform efforts in 1892 when Harrison's successor, and TR's collaborator

[11] 22 Stat. 403 (1883).

[12] Those familiar with Steven Spielberg's *Lincoln* may remember George Pendleton as the leader of the House Democratic opposition to President Lincoln's quest to pass the 13th Amendment. Perhaps Pendleton was so offended by Lincoln's offer of patronage jobs to gather votes that, when he returned to Congress as a Senator years later, he decided to do away with the spoils system.

[13] See Norm Ornstein, *How the Assassination of James A. Garfield Haunts VA Reform*, The Atlantic (Jul. 10, 2014), www.theatlantic.com/politics/archive/2014/07/how-the-assassination-of-james-a-garfield-haunts-va-reform/374202/.

[14] See William Dudley Foulke, Fighting the Spoilsmen (1919).

[15] See generally Roosevelt the Reformer, *supra* note 1.

[16] See "Harper's Weekly", *On This Day: Reform without Bloodshed*, N.Y. Times (Apr. 19, 2001), www.nytimes.com/learning/general/onthisday/harp/0419.html.

[17] See Doris Kearns Goodwin, The Bully Pulpit, ch. 6 (2014).

in New York, Grover Cleveland, crossed party lines and kept him on as civil service commissioner.

So it is comforting to think of Teddy the Reformer sitting in his civil service office, which has been reconstructed at the Office of Personnel Management, the institution that succeeded the Civil Service Commission. It is pictured here:

Theodore Roosevelt, Library of Congress Prints and Photographs Division Washington, D.C., www.loc.gov/item/2009631487/.

After the Pendleton Act survived congressional repeal efforts during the Wilson Administration, it became entrenched at the federal level and states soon joined the cause; among them was Wisconsin, under Robert La Follette, discussed in Chapter 5.

The Civil Service Reform Act of 1978 (CSRA)[18] was the last large reform effort. The CSRA was passed during the Carter Administration, after Watergate, when the federal bureaucracy was tarnished by the corruption of that time. The Act abolished the Civil Service Commission and spread its functions among three agencies: OPM, the Merit Systems Protection Board (MSPB), and the Federal Labor Relations Authority (FLRA). The CSRA also created the Senior Executive Service and brought merit pay to the government. The SES, a core group of government professionals, will be given separate treatment later in this chapter. The MSPB has the responsibility to hear adverse personnel actions brought by agencies against their employees. It is structured as a two-level process with employees first appearing before administrative judges (AJs) for trial in required locations and then an appeal is provided before the three-member board in DC. In FY 2015 the MSPB processed a record number of 28,509 cases.[19] The time it takes to decide these cases, and the fact that employees remain on the government payroll while they are pending, is one reason why reform efforts have been mounted and Congress has sought expedited solutions in specific areas, like the VA dismissal cases discussed in the next section.

## B. TROUBLES WITH THE SYSTEM

It was quite startling to see on the cover of *Government Executive Magazine* the headline "Can't Hire, Can't Fire – other than that everything is great with the civil service system."[20] Such irony is unexpected from a publication dedicated to the federal workforce. It makes a powerful impression. What is left to say when the system has such basic failures? Less emphatically, the Partnership for Public Service (with assistance from Booz Allen Hamilton) has also weighed in, saying the system has become "increasingly obsolete, with most of its major components last retooled more than six decades ago."[21] It is the problem of obsolescence that has led to the system becoming Balkanized,

18 Pub. L. 95–454, 92 Stat. 1111.

19 See U.S. Merit Systems Protection Bd., Annual Report for FY 2015, 15 (2016). This was a 63 percent increase from the prior year which was driven by furlough cases caused by the government shutdown in 2014.

20 Government Executive, Jan./Feb. 2015.

21 Partnership for Public Service, A *New Civil Service Framework* 13 (April 2014).

as more agencies seek separate legislative arrangements.[22] The success of the opt-out process after 40 years is quite telling – it has created a situation where the "excepted" service is now almost equal in numbers to the "competitive" civil service system.[23] "Excepted" no longer means exceptional. It really means escape from a less functional regime.

In my experience, excepted positions made hiring much easier. Attorneys (listed as excepted service under Schedule A) can be hired as easily as in the private sector, and this is also true for some technology positions. But if an agency wanted to hire a public relations specialist, or even other professionals like economists, who are not "excepted," the "structured interview" process kicks in and hiring bogs down. In my case, an OPM official appeared who made sure that all the protocols were followed during the interview process. Incredibly, questions asked of candidates had to be prepared in advance of the interview and no follow-up questions were permitted, lest the candidates not be treated equally. I sat there as someone whose professional judgment of people is fine-edged, and marveled.[24] It is not difficult to appreciate the time wasted and the reduced quality of the interview that resulted. Who would invent such a system, you might ask. A committee at OPM with nothing better to do. As Jeff Neal says, "if you ask most managers, employees, and applicants what is wrong with federal HR, they will tell you it's the hiring process."[25]

22 See, e.g. Secretary of Defense Ash Carter, Remarks on "The Next Two Links to the Force of the Future" (June 9, 2016), www.defense.gov/News/Speeches/Speech-View/Article/795341/remarks-on-the-next-two-links-to-the-force-of-the-future (announcing intent of DOD to seek direct hire authority from Congress).

23 The FedScope Data system on the federal workforce reveals that as of Sept. 15, 2015, there were 700,000 civilian employees whose positions were "excepted," or not filled by competitive examination, exclusive of national security positions which are all excepted. This number was reached by taking the total number of civil service positions and subtracting the competitive service positions and the Senior Executive Service positions. FedScope is available at https://www.fedscope.opm.gov/. There were 1,831,723 total federal employees. U.S. Office of Personnel Mgmt., Data, Analysis & Documentation: Federal Civilian Employment, https://www.opm.gov/policy-data-oversight/data-analysis-documentation/federal-employment-reports/reports-publications/federal-civilian-employment/ (last visited Aug. 27, 2016) (providing the total number of full-time non-postal employees within the federal civilian workforce as of September 2013, the most recent year for which data was compiled by OPM).

24 It made me think of the last lines of Saul Bellow's *Mr. Sammler's Planet* (1970), "we can still know a good man [or woman] when we see one."

25 Jeff Neal, *Fixing Federal HR Begins with Staffing*, Federal News Radio (Sept. 1, 2016), http://federalnewsradio.com/commentary/2016/09/fixing-federal-hr-begins-with-staffing/. Jeff Neal is the former HR director of DHS and an acute commentator on the federal hiring system.

## C. OPT-OUTS FROM THE CIVIL SERVICE SYSTEM

If the success of any system is measured by the number of adherents it has relative to opt-outs, there is much concern over the civil service system. When the number of government officials who belong to the "excepted" service now approaches the number who remain within it,[26] the need to reform the 40 year-old system seems obvious. It is interesting to analyze the reasons agencies have "voted with their feet" about the civil service system.

The earliest defectors were the financial agencies (the FRB, SEC, FDIC, the Office of the Comptroller of the Currency, CFPB, CFTC, and others) who sought freedom from GS classification and pay restrictions, so they could provide competitive compensation.[27] Since these agencies compete for talent with Wall Street and money center banks, it is understandable that higher salaries are needed. But it also reflects how outmoded the general schedules are, since many non-banking agencies need salary flexibility as well. For example, GAO has modified its salary structure by reducing the number of steps in the GS system (called pay bands).

Since Congress needs to approve of these opt-outs there is no doubt that it is aware of how the system is eroding. For example, when it created the Transportation Security Agency, it designed an entire hiring system outside of Title 5.[28] TSA employees have longer probationary periods to begin and are outside the MSPB appeals process should they be let go. As a result, they are fired more easily and at a higher rate than civil service employees.[29] In effect by permitting these opt-outs at various agencies, Congress is offering alternative systems for consideration. Without intending so, perhaps, Congress has set up intriguing possibilities for civil service reform.

[26] See note 23, *supra*.

[27] See Paul H. Kupiec, The Money in Banking: Comparing Salaries of Bank and Bank Regulatory Employees (2014), www.aei.org/wp-content/uploads/2014/04/-the-money-in-banking-comparing-salaries-of-bank-and-bank-regulatory-employees_17170372690.pdf.
Congress has lifted the GS pay scale restrictions on financial regulatory and oversight agencies through a series of legislation beginning with the Financial Institutions Reform, Recovery, and Enforcement Act of 1989 (FIRREA) and most recently through Dodd–Frank for the newly created CFPB.

[28] See Aviation and Transportation Security Act of 2001, Pub. L. No. 107–71, 115 Stat. 597, at § 111(d).

[29] See Jeff Neal, *Make It Easy to Fire Federal Workers, and Then What?*, ChiefHRO.com (Jul. 27, 2016), https://chiefhro.com/2016/07/27/make-it-easy-to-fire-federal-workers-and-then-what/ (over the last five years TSA has fired 2.9 percent of its screening staff per year, versus 0.5 percent of firings in the civil service workforce).

### *The Veterans Administration as a Case Study*

The latest agency to seek excepted status is the Veterans Administration, which has been reeling from a scandal over delays in scheduling and providing medical services at its hospitals.[30] Secretary Bob McDonald, the veteran and business-oriented leader from Procter & Gamble, contends that "VA is a business" and should not be treated like a typical government agency.[31] McDonald's efforts led the Senate to pass the Veterans First Act[32] which would reclassify VA medical directors and health care professionals under Title 38 so that the Secretary would have the power to appoint, pay appraise, and discipline many of the department's senior executives.[33] The discipline side would be taken away from the MSPB which already has been deprived of appeal jurisdiction over SES dismissals at VA.[34]

One can sympathize with McDonald's desire to make his agency more businesslike, something that many other agency heads likely feel as well. But it produces yet another opt-out from the shrinking civil service system. Agencies cut deals with their authorizing committees in Congress, and carve-outs and workarounds multiply. Moreover, under the Veterans Access Legislation of 2014, VA is authorized to use private health providers where medical services are inadequate. A recent RAND study showed that 10 percent of the Veterans' Health $56 billion budget was paid to private providers,[35]

30 See Adam Andrzejewski, *It's Not Disney World – The VA Scandal Two Years Later*, Forbes (May 25, 2016), www.forbes.com/sites/adamandrzejewski/2016/05/25/its-not-disney-world-the-va-scandal-two-years-later/.

31 See Nicole Orgysko, *Compare Us to Other Businesses, Not Federal Agencies, VA Leader Says*, Federal News Radio (May 23, 2016), http://federalnewsradio.com/ses/2016/05/compare-us-businesses-not-federal-agencies-va-leader-says/.

32 S.2921 – Veterans First Act, 114th Cong. (2016).

33 See Orgysko, *supra* note 31.

34 The MSPB administrative judges had earlier reversed VA's demotions of senior executives, much to the aggravation of Congress. See Kellie Lunney, *Senators Lambaste Agency for Reversing VA's Decision to Punish Senior Executives*, Government Executive (Mar. 4, 2016), www.govexec.com/management/2016/03/senators-lambaste-agency-reversing-vas-decision-punish-senior-executives/126440/. An earlier statute required the MSPB to decide VA dismissal within 21 days, which effectively deprived the MSPB of appeals jurisdiction over their administrative judge decisions, who, in effect, make the final decision. This statutory workaround of the general MSPB statute has such legal problems that the Attorney General refuses to defend the cases brought under it. See Joe Davidson, *DOJ Won't Defend Measure that Facilitates VA Firings*, Wash. Post PowerPost (June 6, 2016), https://www.washingtonpost.com/news/powerpost/wp/2016/06/06/doj-wont-defend-measure-that-facilitates-va-firings/.

35 Carrie M. Farmer, Susan D. Hosek, & David M. Adamson, Balancing Demand and Supply for Veterans' Health Care: A Summary of Three RAND Assessments Conducted Under the Veterans Choice Act (2016), www.rand.org/pubs/research_reports/RR1165z4.html.

so Secretary McDonald has already partially privatized VA services. But the RAND study also concludes (1) that the quality of health care delivered by VA is generally equal to or better than the care delivered in the private sector; and (2) that demand for VA health care will not exceed supply after 2020. Thus the justifications for private health care no longer seem urgent, and the VA, like other agencies, might be asked to support general civil service reform rather than special legislation to fix the management problems they face.

For many years it has been something of a fool's errand to get Congress and the Executive branch to agree upon needed changes to the Civil Service System. In a Congress that cannot pass a budget and relies on a sequestration process to fund government (that is shrinking the discretionary parts of the budget, including defense, to levels not seen in 20 years[36]) it did not seem that systematic civil service reform was possible. Moreover, if President Trump insists on shrinking government by not replacing one in three federal workers who retire, as the House Republicans have proposed in their 2017 budget,[37] the prospects for serious civil service reform do not look encouraging. The Republican Party's 2016 Platform calls for reducing federal employees' compensation and hearing rights while supporting the privatization of Veterans' Health Services and labeling the IRS "toxic."[38] After the election fever fades and the new administration is upon us, Congress and the White House might turn to this demanding issue. Building coalitions for civil service reform will be hard work,[39] but there are viable examples from opt-out agencies that could be translated into a more systemic solution. But maybe the problem is how reform is characterized. If we say "let's build on what we have done," and leave out the phrase "systemic civil service reform," perhaps progress can be made in the Trump Administration.[40]

36 See Dodaro, *supra* Chapter 3, at note 23.

37 See John J. DiIulio Jr. and Paul R. Verkuil, *Want a Leaner Federal Government? Hire More Federal Workers*, Wash. Post Opinions (Apr. 21, 2016), https://www.washingtonpost.com/opinions/want-a-leaner-federal-government-hire-more-federal-workers/2016/04/21/a11cf98c-fd8b-11e5–886f-a037dba38301_story.html.

38 Eric Katz, *GOP Platform: Cut Feds' Pay and Benefits While Making It Easier to Fire Them*, Government Executive (Jul. 19, 2016), www.govexec.com/pay-benefits/2016/07/gop-platform-cut-feds-pay-and-benefits-while-making-it-easier-fire-them/130032/.

39 See Eric Katz, *Is It Too Late for Comprehensive Civil Service Reform?*, Government Executive (Oct. 5, 2016), www.govexec.com/pay-benefits/2016/10/too-late-comprehensive-personnel-reform/132132/ (reporting on views of government HR officials).

40 Towanda Brooks, the Housing and Urban Development Office's chief human capital officer, put it well: "The first step is to assess what agencies have done. Don't start from scratch." *Id.*

## D. REFORMING THE CIVIL SERVICE SYSTEM

We need A players in government

George Schultz[41]

If one believes that "good government starts with good people," as the Partnership for Public Service (and this author) do, then it is past time to revisit the civil service system. As Secretary Schultz makes clear, the quality of government employees defines government excellence.[42] But excellence will not be easy to achieve, for several reasons. First, the government is facing a "talent crisis" as it ages without high-quality talent in the pipeline. Second, Congress is fed up with existing rules that permit abuses like "golden parachute" pensions[43] and misuse administrative leave accounts.[44] Third, the pressure of large opt-out legislation like that of the Department of Veterans Affairs makes the competitive system increasingly arbitrary in application. Congress and a new administration can take on these challenges, whether under the banner of comprehensive or tailored civil service reform.

Several transition team proposals offered by institutions like the Partnership for Public Service (PPS) and the National Academy of Public Administration (NAPA) can help to begin the process. The PPS proposal makes several basic recommendations to Congress:

(1) Create a common, yet flexible, civil service system for all government that levels the playing field for talent and preserves merit and non-partisanship principles.
(2) Replace the general schedule with a market- and performance-based hiring system that allows both higher and lower pay schedules as dictated by competition.
(3) Manage promotions through performance review boards, require continual professional training, and base salary increases on merit determination.

41 Interview with author, Aug. 16, 2016.

42 See ACHIEVING GOVERNMENT EXCELLENCE (Cary Coglianese ed.) (2016) ("With increasing demands for smarter but leaner government, the need for sound regulatory capacity – for regulatory excellence – has never been greater").

43 See Eric Katz, *Another Bonus Ban, Feds' 'Golden Parachute' Pensions and More*, GOVERNMENT EXECUTIVE (Apr. 13, 2016), www.govexec.com/pay-benefits/pay-benefits-watch/2016/04/another-bonus-ban-feds-golden-parachute-pensions-and-more/127434/ (TVA executives receive average pensions of $1 million).

44 See Davidson, *supra* note 4 (116 DHS employees placed on leave for one year at a cost of $19.8 million).

(4) Create a unified dispute resolution process for employee grievances or dismissals.[45]

This framework is carefully spelled out by the Partnership's proposals. It would do much to fix the deficiencies of the current system while making it more attractive for agencies to participate and thereby reduce the draw of the excepted service. To reduce the lure of contractors, however, emphasis needs to be placed on the availability of talent and the capacity to pay competitive salaries.[46] Moreover, the civil service still has FTE limits that must be adjusted so that the right number of "slots" are available for agencies to hire within the system. There are also questions about the Veterans' Preference, which may attract agencies to use of contractors, and about the role of public sector unions in the reform process.

### 1 *The Complicated Question of the Veterans' Preference*

There are few government commitments greater than to the veterans who have served their country. As a result, for many job categories veterans are given an edge, or "preference," in hiring, a practice which profoundly affects the composition of the government workforce. Currently 26.3 percent of federal employees in professional and administrative occupations are veterans and over 47 percent of federal hires during the Obama Administration have been veterans.[47]

The preference works in different ways depending on how agencies select candidates. In essence, if a veteran meets minimum qualifications he or she is entitled to prevail in the selection process over non-veterans. The competitive service requires that eligible vets receive an extra 5 to 10 points under the "contingency rating" system and in some situations where the job application requires an examination. This is the situation with the selection of ALJs, where the veteran points system puts them at the top of the OPM register from which agencies must select.

Still there is much confusion about how the system works. While veterans often have developed valuable skills while in the service (computer training,

45 See Partnership for Public Service, *Building the Enterprise: A New Civil Service Framework* (Apr. 1, 2014), http://ourpublicservice.org/publications/viewcontentdetails.php?id=18.

46 The Partnership recognizes that there are limits on the pay range that Congress will accept (no mid-six-figure salaries). Instead, they peg the salary ceiling at Executive Level I or the pay of the Vice President, which the IRS has authority to set. See *id.* at 22.

47 See Jeff Neal, *Category Rating – Does It Work?*, ChiefHRO.com (Jul. 6, 2016), https://chiefhro.com/2016/07/06/category-rating-does-it-work/ (describing the veterans' preference point system and explaining how "category rating" is supposed to work).

for example) in addition to their leadership skills, the minimal qualification threshold can disadvantage non-veterans with extraordinary skill sets (who must compete against them).[48] So the commitment may not always yield the best candidates and it surely complicates the hiring process.

The preference does not apply to federal employees who change agencies or to former employees who retain reappointment rights. It also applies in more limited fashion within the excepted service, such as with the hiring of attorneys. For excepted service hiring decisions, a legal opinion from the DOJ's Office of Legal Counsel says only if two candidates are equal in all respects and one is a vet, should the vet prevail.[49] This approach gives federal agencies much more discretion than the point system does.

The preference generally does not apply to contractors, who are by definition not full time government employees, although many contractors have prior military or government service. The absence of the veterans' preference encourages agency employers to hire contractors depending on the job qualifications sought to be filled. And it certainly makes the hiring process less complicated and more efficient.

There are also issues surrounding the "durability" of the preference. Does it stay with the vet throughout government service or is it exhausted after the first job in government is obtained? A provision in the Senate Fiscal 2017 Defense Authorization bill would limit the preference to the veteran's first job only.[50] The bill would also limit the advantages the preference provides to close relatives of the veteran.[51] While these adjustments have their own degree of controversy, they help regularize the use of a benefit whose complicated application may well lead agencies to seek ways around it. The presence of the preference can be one inducement to agencies to seek excepted status as the VA has done or also to use contractors, who are not permanent hires and not subject to the preference. So any way to simplify the use of the preference would be helpful to all sides: the veteran, the agency, and even the contractor community.

48 See Lisa Rein, *Obama's Push to Hire Veterans is Causing Confusion and Resentment, Officials Say*, Wash. Post (Apr. 21, 2016), https://www.washingtonpost.com/news/powerpost/wp/2016/04/21/obamas-push-to-hire-veterans-is-causing-confusion-and-resentment-officials-say/.

49 OLC Memorandum 78–45, Veterans' Preference Act (5 U.S.C. §§ 2108, 3309–3320) – Application to Attorney Positions 183 (1978) ("If all other factors are equal, or even close, the preference eligible will normally be selected over the nonpreference eligible"), https://www.justice.gov/sites/default/files/olc/opinions/1978/08/31/op-olc-v002-p0179.pdf.

50 S. 2943, 114th Cong. 2d Sess., Cal. No. 469 (May 18, 2016).

51 Kellie Lunney, *Changes to Veterans' Preference Could be on the Horizon*, Government Executive (June 3, 2016), www.govexec.com/pay-benefits/2016/06/changes-veterans-preference-could-be-horizon/128804/.

### 2 The Role of Unions in the Reform Process

This book has not found it necessary to assess public sector unions in general, since the case for professionalism involves managers or supervisors who are often not part of collective bargaining units. But any overall civil service reform effort must include union interests, since many of the reforms concern hearing rights and hiring protocols that apply to all federal employees

Public sector unions are a powerful player in government. Union members constituted almost half of all public employees and about 27 percent of federal employees.[52] It is hard to know how many of the 700,000 federal employees who are deemed by agencies as inherently governmental under the FAIR Act[53] are unionized but presumably some of them are, and this book speaks to them as well. One concern with streamlining the firing process (presumably streamlining hiring is in the unions' interests), is allegiance to the current Merit System Protection Board hearing system.

The Partnership for Public Service proposes to expedite the removal process by creating a government-wide system that uses alternative dispute resolution processes to shorten times to decision.[54] Currently there are three ways employee grievances can be heard: (1) through a union-sponsored arbitration process with appeal to the Federal Labor Relations Authority; (2) for discrimination complaints, to the EEOC and then to the courts; and (3) to the MSPB and then the courts. The Partnership plan would consolidate all grievances in a reconstituted MSPB, with arbitration replacing hearings. This "one bite at the apple" approach the PPS believes would reduce delays.[55] The unions may well object to a reduction in forum alternatives, but they should evaluate the consequences. Some agencies, like TSA, have already been exempted from the system, and others could follow. An argument articulated by Nicholas Parrillo makes a point the unions should consider:

> The greatest practical support for civil service protection often comes from lobbying and unionization on the part of protected bureaucrats themselves, but that very lobbying and unionization may serve to delegitimize civil service protection in the long run by structuring protection to serve the narrow interests of bureaucrats rather than the public, or at least contributing to the popular impression that protection is so structured.[56]

[52] See Bureau of Labor Statistics, Economic News Release, *Union Members Summary* (Jan. 28, 2016), www.bls.gov/news.release/union2.nro.htm.

[53] See Chapter 1, note 82. [54] See PPS Proposal, *supra* note 45, at 32–34. [55] *Id.*, at 33.

[56] Nicholas Parrillo, *The Salary Revolution and the Marks of Government's Distinctness: A Response to Jon Michaels*, 128 Harv. L. Rev. F. 99 (2015) (*citing* Ronald N. Johnson & Gary D. Libecap, The Federal Civil Service System and the Problem of Bureaucracy (1997)).

Parrillo's concerns are real ones, not only for federal unions, but for public sector unions generally. Reforming the grievance and removal process is of general concern when the alternative is more contractors who are not unionized. The notion that contractor government might be a preferable alternative to career service is something that should drive the civil service reform process. If unions and perhaps even contractors (who will see their roles better defined) can find positives in reform efforts, the chances of reform are heightened. These groups will surely help shape the outcomes through political channels. It would be preferable if the better policy choices were also congruent with their political influence.

## E. THE FUTURE OF THE SES AND GOVERNMENT PROFESSIONALISM

At the federal level, the SES established by the Civil Service Reform Act of 1978 bears much of the responsibility for professional government. Only 7,000 plus in number, they are an elite corps of career leaders that other government professionals look to for inspiration, experience, and knowledge. Yet the SES faces a "pivotal moment" in terms of recruiting and retaining members who are leaving government.[57] They cite as reasons for leaving the political environment, the lack of senior leadership, and organizational culture. Two-thirds of the SES is eligible to retire over the next three years, and not enough is being done to create an effective pipeline of qualified successors.[58] Indeed, given the small increment in additional pay and the added responsibilities, not all eligible candidates choose to join their ranks when recruited. It is not hard to understand why. SES members are subject to a loss of bonuses. Congress seems tone deaf to the implications of singling out the SES and not the rest of the civil service for this kind of treatment. The goal of creating omnicompetent professionals by serving throughout government on a revolving basis is one aspect of the SES experience that has not been realized (and indeed that may dissuade candidates from applying). But the idea of career executives, who can serve anywhere needed, is one that has long been a dream of government planners and is gaining

57 See Kellie Lunney, *Senior Executive Service Faces 'Pivotal Moment' on Cusp of Next Administration*, Government Executive (June 21, 2016), www.govexec.com/management/2016/06/senior-executive-service-faces-pivotal-moment-cusp-next-administration/129267/ (citing Partnership for Public Service, *A Pivotal Moment for the Senior Executive Service* (2016), http://ourpublicservice.org/issues/modernize-management/SES-report.php).

58 See Partnership for Public Service, *Building the Leadership Branch: Developing a Talent Pipeline for the Senior Executive Service* (July 2013), https://ourpublicservice.org/publications/download.php?id=29.

traction.[59] It can't be jettisoned. OPM should sell this concept as part of the SES experience.

There are signs that the SES is finally getting the attention it deserves. In December 2015, President Obama issued an Executive Order – Strengthening the Senior Executive Service,[60] which declares it to be "in the national interest to facilitate career executive continuity between administrations." The executive order demonstrates the federal government's interest in "cultivating generalist executives" by increasing the number of members who are rotating to 15 percent of the SES during fiscal year 2017. The order also looks to proactively recruit new members for SES positions. This emphasis on the SES is long overdue and it represents a crucial step in ensuring that the next Administration brings momentum to the hiring, training, and retention of the government's vital career officials.

### *The SES and Congress*

Congress must be convinced to encourage rather than continue to penalize SES members. During the VA health care scheduling crisis, Congress passed legislation that virtually deprived some 400 SES members at the VA their hearing rights on removal.[61] Under the statute, the employee was given 7 days to file a claim and the MSPB was given 21 days to decide whether to remove or discipline. These draconian time limits make it virtually impossible for VA SES members to prepare for or receive an effective hearing.[62] Even though the President signed the VA legislation, he must have had second thoughts, since the Attorney General subsequently announced that the Justice Department would not defend the statute in cases resulting from its application.[63] And

59 See Nicole Ogrysko, *Rotational Assignments an Early Success Story from SES Executive Order*, Federal News Radio (Oct. 5, 2016), http://federalnewsradio.com/ses/2016/10/rotational-assignments-early-success-story-ses-executive-order/.

60 Executive Order 13,714, Strengthening the Senior Executive Service (Dec. 15, 2015), https://www.whitehouse.gov/the-press-office/2015/12/15/executive-order-strengthening-senior-executive-service.

61 See S.2921 – Veterans First Act, *supra* note 32.

62 Several cases were dismissed by MSPB ALJs, much to the dismay of Congress. See Kellie Lunney, *MSPB Agrees That VA Senior Executive Screwed Up, But Not Enough to Fire Her*, Government Executive (Feb. 16, 2016), www.govexec.com/management/2016/02/mspb-agrees-va-senior-executive-screwed-not-enough-fire-her/125962/.

63 See Davidson, *supra* note 34. There is another bill pending, the VA Accountability First and Appeals Modernization Act, H.R. 5620, that would allow the Secretary to rescind bonuses, retirement benefits, and relocation costs under certain circumstances. The White House called it "misguided and burdensome," but did not promise to veto it. See Kellie Lunney, *White House Won't Veto Bill Making It Easier to Fire All VA Workers*, Government Executive (Sept. 13, 2016).

rather than dealing with the legal issues DOJ raised, Republicans in Congress have doubled down on these provisions by approving a House Bill to expand the concept to all SES in government.[64] While President Obama had promised a veto and the Senate had not acted, the bill could well return in the next Congress under President Trump, whose platform includes limiting hearing rights for federal officials.[65]

Much of the argument for enhanced professionalism in government this book presents is premised on a well-functioning SES leadership. Since so many SES are eligible to retire, it does little good to threaten them. Instead, everything possible should be done to keep and expand this experienced cadre of public officials. Congress must ask itself who is going to be left to run government if they leave and are replaced by novices. More contractors? The case for professionalism starts with this highly trained and experienced group of public servants.

## F. CONCLUSION

Civil service reform after 40 years is on the political agenda and there is a broad understanding about the issues to be addressed. It may be optimistic to believe the political process will permit productive change to occur, but it is not any longer foolish to think so. Indeed, Congress recently passed the Competitive Service Act of 2015[66] which permits agencies to share assessments of applicants and helps government recruit top talent.[67] While this is only a part of the reform it is a start – a harbinger of sorts – that makes the broader effort more feasible. By approaching reform as a necessary condition to control contractor government, this book offers something that those in Congress concerned about government leadership and its costs should appreciate. It will be interesting to see how the lobbying forces of contractors, unions, and other industry players play out in all of this. This makes it hard but not impossible to thread the needle on legislation, even if it is partial and consolidates gains already made. What is sought is not more money for government, but more

64 Joe Davidson, *Dubious Constitutional Effort to Cut Due Process for Top Civil Servants Spreads across Government*, Washington Post (Jul. 12, 2016), https://www.washingtonpost.com/news/powerpost/wp/2016/07/12/dubious-constitutional-effort-to-cut-due-process-for-top-civil-servants-spreads-across-government/.

65 Remember that Donald Trump's most recognizable catchphrase is "you're fired."

66 S. 1580 (114th Cong.), Pub. L. No. 114–137.

67 See Partnership for Public Service, Press Release, *Partnership for Public Service Applauds Passage of Legislation to Reform the Federal Hiring Process* (Mar. 8, 2016), https://ourpublicservice.org/publications/viewcontentdetails.php?id=947.

government for the money. Reducing the role of contractors, as the private prison situation discussed in Chapter 4 shows, has a double effect of improved performance and lower costs. That is an idea that can be sold to the right and the left, but should especially resonate with those in the middle, who must do the compromising necessary to make reform happen.

# 8

# Living with and Improving the Multi-Sector Workforce

Managing the federal workforce is an increasingly complex proposition. It takes expertise, flexibility, and dedication in order to succeed. And, whatever happens with the civil service reform proposals put forth in Chapter 7, contractors will continue to provide many of the human resources necessary to run government. But that role needs to be restrained within existing resource and legal parameters to ensure sustainable and democratic government. The nondelegable duty to supervise that drives the constitutional and sovereignty discussions of this book must still be secured. This chapter suggests how to make that happen.

## A. WHAT IS EXCELLENCE IN GOVERNMENT?

The federal workforce is termed by OMB as "multi-sector" (and by others as "blended"[1]), since it encompasses not only federal employees, but contractors, not-for-profit providers and state employees who carry out federal functions. All of these people must "report" to federal supervisors in some fashion. Often the lines of authority and even communication over this diffuse workforce are hard to manage, but the "regulators" who exercise oversight authority in these circumstances must be evaluated and held to account. They can be deemed excellent when they communicate the agency's mission adequately and achieve acceptance and participation by all concerned.[2] Those

[1] See Dan Guttman, *Government by Contract: Considering a Public Service Ethics to Match the Reality of the "Blended" Public Work Force*, 2 Emory Corp. Governance & Accountability Rev. 1 (2015).

[2] See Shelley H. Metzenbaum & Gaurav Vasisht, *What Makes a Regulator Excellent? Mission, Funding, Information, and Judgment*, Penn Program on Regulation (2015), https://www.law.upenn.edu/live/files/4721-metzenbaumvasisht ("Organizational excellence necessitates making sure different parts of an organization understand how they contribute to [the] mission").

who achieve their organizations' missions and goals are the professionals who run government.

Having been in government for a substantial period, I can appreciate the need to create excellent regulators. But excellence is not automatic; indeed, it may not even be demanded or expected. Still, it is there to be developed, even if no broad mandate for reform is forthcoming from Congress. Experienced players in government and out, many of whom are fellows of the National Academy of Public Administration and/or academics, have studied ways to improve the quality of government at this time of transition. In most cases, these proposals do not need legislation to be implemented, just the will to implement them. That will must now come from the Trump Administration after the transition process. NAPA's ten proposals for the transition are worth quoting in full:

1. Consolidate existing evidence-based decision making systems into a government-wide framework, led by the Office of Management and Budget, which integrates performance management, program evaluation, futures planning, and budgeting. Incorporate benchmarking and regular performance reviews as central features.
2. Appoint agency deputies/Chief Operating Officers and other political appointees with capacity and commitment to driving performance improvement and enhancing evidence-based decision making.
3. Empower strong Performance Improvement Officers with adequate resources to support agency Deputies/Chief Operating Officers. Where the Performance Improvement Officer has other duties, ensure there is a strong Deputy Performance Improvement Officer devoting full attention to the adoption of the integrated performance management framework.
4. Continue to drive the conduct and use of appropriately tailored, independent evaluations to improve programs. Support this effort by establishing and funding a robust evaluation and data analytics capacity in every department responsible for overseeing rigorous program evaluations and for a range of other analytical exercises related to, and useful for, performance management.
5. Enhance the accessibility, transparency, and usefulness of performance information by simplifying Performance.gov, showing clear trends in government's progress, and linking it to other, relevant sources of information about the government's performance.
6. Collaborate with Congress (i.e., authorizers, appropriators, and overseers) more closely at every stage of the performance management

process to facilitate more debate about the performance of programs and about performance management.

7. Use incentives in the grant making and contracting processes to encourage adoption by state and local government, other partners, and stakeholders of the performance management framework.
8. Institute annual OMB spring reviews to assess and accelerate progress on strategic goals. Enhance OMB quarterly priority goal reviews to assess progress and identify opportunities to improve.
9. Ensure OMB is driving the development, adoption, and implementation of cross-agency priority goals.
10. Develop a clear and concise performance management and evaluation curriculum for agency and other professionals. Enlist front-line employees, through employee forums or other means, to identify ways to improve performance and strengthen the adoption of the performance management framework.[3]

These proposals emphasize data-driven analysis, employee participation, goal setting, and collaboration with agencies, OMB, and Congress to ensure performance improvements. There is no better time than early in a presidential term to incent the professionals in government to employ these new ideas. Since every agency has already been tasked by OMB to draw up transition plans, smaller steps are ripe for implementation even if the big job of civil service reform remains ahead of us.

## B. STEPS NECESSARY TO INDUCE EXCELLENCE IN GOVERNMENT

The ideas outlined by the NAPA transition report suggest how agency professionals can achieve excellence in their professional roles. But they need help from a variety of existing agencies and institutions. Here are some priorities.

### 1 *Encourage Creativity at OPM*

The key agency for personnel innovation is OPM, whose job it is to manage the civil service. Leadership of this agency is crucial to any reforms. Beth Cobert, who served as acting director of OPM during the latter years of the Obama Administration, brought a new energy and experience to the agency. Her resume includes having served as the President's second Chief Performance

[3] National Academy of Public Administration, Transition 2016: Equipping the Government for Success in 2016 and Beyond 13–17 (2015), http://napat16.org/images/T16_Final_Report_8.15.16.pdf.

Officer and long experience in organizational management at McKinsey, a notable government contractor. The next administration's appointee should be someone who can build on her efforts. The important thing is to choose a leader with the skill to collaborate with agencies to achieve systemic change. In my view, OPM's assignment is pretty clear. It consists of two words: "recruit" and "retain."[4]

OPM has long had a reputation for being a stickler for regulations and a less than enthusiastic delegator. This was my experience when I tried to help OPM figure out how to hire more ALJs for the Social Security disability program discussed in Chapter 6. As Jeff Neal, former Chief Human Resource Officer at DHS, has said, "OPM has not done a comprehensive look at their regulations to try and find every possible way to make civil service better within today's laws."[5] Cobert tried to meet this criticism by having OPM put its efforts behind a hiring excellence campaign that sought to "bust the myths" behind its cumbersome hiring regulations.[6] This kind of initiative, by opening up agencies to new approaches within the regulatory status quo, can bring results. But in order to achieve some regulatory breakthroughs, it needs to be more proactive.[7] There are many new ideas OPM could incorporate once the myths are busted. For example, Shelley Metzenbaum, an academic and former OMB management official, has suggested numerous hiring ideas that OPM could adopt (or endorse).[8]

- Fix internship and graduate programs – "energetic graduates who want to work in government have a ridiculously hard time getting hired."
- Fix the Presidential Management Program, which has low placement levels.

4 See Elizabeth K. Kellar, *The Growing Urgency of Government's Quest for Talent*, GOVERNING (June 21, 2016), www.governing.com/columns/smart-mgmt/col-challenge-recruiting-retaining-state-local-government-workforce.html (to meet the recruiting challenge, governments should become "learning organizations").

5 See Neal, *Civil Service Reform Should Be High on the Next President's To-Do List*, FEDSMITH (Apr. 22, 2016), www.fedsmith.com/2016/04/22/civil-service-reform-should-be-high-on-the-next-presidents-to-do-list/.

6 See OPM, *Hiring Excellence* (July 2016), https://www.opm.gov/policy-data-oversight/hiring-information/hiring-excellence/.

7 For example, Myth Buster #1 suggests that agency hiring managers can be involved in the hiring process while avoiding the appearance of impropriety (the myth was to the contrary), but it doesn't suggest ways to expedite the cumbersome hiring process. *Id.*

8 See Shelley H. Metzenbaum, *Untying the Knots in the Federal Hiring Process*, THE VOLCKER ALLIANCE BLOG (May 29, 2014), https://www.volckeralliance.org/blog/2016/jun/untying-knots-federal-hiring-process.

- Make greater use of the Intergovernmental Personnel Act (IPA),[9] which allows for temporary assignment of personnel between the federal government, nonprofits, colleges and universities, and state and local governments.
- Establish cross-agency hiring authority. While this initiative requires legislation, it would allow an agency that identifies multiple cybersecurity specialists, for example, to share their resumes with other agencies seeking the same kind of talent.

In my experience, these sensible ideas could do much to improve hiring and retention of outstanding government employees. The IPA, in particular, which was utilized to good effect at ACUS, helps an agency bring into government service for short periods the kind of experts from academia and think tanks who are otherwise unavailable. The Innovation Fellows program discussed in the next section is a good example of this idea. Smart, tech-savvy young people want to serve in government and make a difference, but they don't want to spend 30 years doing so.

And the IPA works in both directions, government employees can improve their skills (and learn the latest technological advances) by spending six months at a university department or a laboratory. Budget limitations often prevent agency training programs from being implemented, but this one is readily available for the cost of covering the job vacated for a short time.

Finally, USAJOBS, government's hiring face, needs an overhaul. It is difficult to navigate and discouraging to use. Often job applicants will go through a detailed application process only to learn, after much time, that their skill set does not meet the job requirements, and there it ends, with no suggestion about what might work.[10] Why not create a LinkedIn for government that lets people in and out of government advertise their skills and interests to find the right match?

There are many ideas like these that could be implemented efficiently by an OPM driven by competence, collaboration, and customer orientation.[11]

9 Intergovernmental Personnel Act of 1970, 84 Stat. 1909.

10 Writing for the VA's own in-house blog, one disabled veteran explained that the USAJOBS platform is so divorced from conventional hiring practices that after hundreds of applications across a variety of career fields, "The result was always the same. I would get an e-mail back containing some arrangement of the following phrases: Not Eligible. Minimum Qualifications Not Met. Not Selected. Stop me if these sound familiar." Phil Walls, *Why I Couldn't Get a Federal Job*, Vantage Point (Jun. 25, 2012), www.blogs.va.gov/VAntage/7292/why-i-couldn%E2%80%99t-get-a-federal-job/. Many similar stories exist, and there are several websites and forums dedicated to helping outsiders understand how USAJOBS works.

11 Moreover, OPM doesn't have to innovate alone. There are agencies ready to help and provide ideas. DHS has developed a strategy to invite employees to take jobs "in and out" of government, which sounds much like the IPA idea. See Nicole Ogrysko, *DHS: 'We're Not Looking for the*

President Trump must provide the proper leadership for OPM, and the White House Personnel Office should make the OPM Director a priority, as much of a priority as the President makes the appointment of the Director of White House Personnel. Great political hiring decisions are essential to successful government, and the Office of White House Personnel needs determined leadership. The political appointment process is crucial to getting an administration started. Timely decisions and communications make the system work and can determine the effectiveness of the President. OPM, properly led, can help to make great career (or even temporary) appointments.

### 2 *Fix the Technology Gap*

Developments in technology have bypassed government, leaving it with an outdated hardware system that is costly to scrap and even more costly to maintain. GAO reports that the government spends $89 billion annually on IT, but 75 percent of that amount goes to outdated legacy systems.[12] The floppy disk still lives in government platforms, many of which are over 50 years old. Nuclear systems are run from a 1970s IBM computing platform (with 8" floppy disks), social security systems use a programming language called COBOL dating from the 1950s, and the Treasury's business and individual master tax files are about 56 years old. GAO's 2015 high risk list contains numerous examples of problems caused by agency IT acquisitions and operations problems.[13]

The best hopes for improved technology acquisition and performance center around two basic ideas: strategic sourcing and improved contractor management. Don Kettl, in testimony before the House Subcommittee on Government Operations,[14] explained how "category management," which breaks down equipment purchases across the entire government, can improve the price and quality of products and create more beneficial relationships with suppliers. This is an initiative that OMB's Office of Federal Procurement Policy has been working on. The rewards for improved contractor management, Kettl explains, can produce immediate acquisition benefits. Noting that half of the functions in GAO's high risk list revolve around contractor management problems, Kettl shows how IRS revolutionized its information systems by relying on carefully managed expert contractors.

*30-Year-Career Employee'*, Federal News Radio (July 5, 2016), http://federalnewsradio.com/hiringretention/2016/07/dhs-not-looking-30-year-career-employee/.

12 GAO, *Federal Agencies Need to Address Aging Legacy Systems*, GAO-16–696T (2016).

13 GAO, *High Risk Series: An Update*, GAO-15–290 (2015).

14 See Donald F. Kettl, *Contracting Fairness*, before the House Subcommittee on Government Operations, Comm. on Oversight and Government Reform (June 9, 2016), https://oversight.house.gov/wp-content/uploads/2016/07/2016–07–08-Donald-Kettl-UMD-Testimony.pdf.

Acquisitions can only be made effectively with well-trained and informed professionals managing the process. Spending for IT wisely across government can use the $89 billion budget more strategically and recalculate the percentages spent on new versus legacy systems.

### a. Hire Techies as Innovation Fellows

Legacy technology hardware problems need qualified technically trained personnel to solve them. The question then becomes how to close the technology hiring gap. Part of the problem is cultural: low pay, the absence of a real community, and the lack of clear evidence of progress.[15] Another real fear is being called to account by a Congress whose members are themselves often not technically literate. Being abused for responding to questions with answers that are not adequately understood is a special burden for the tech community.

A bright spot on the tech hiring front, however, has been the Innovation Fellows program, established in 2012, which was formalized by President Obama's Executive Order in 2015.[16] It is designed to create "entrepreneurs in residence." The appointments are for one year and are highly competitive. The program has sent hundreds of top innovators into government, many of whom stay on in other positions. The program is run by "18F," the digital arm of the GSA (which is located at 18th and F Street, NW).[17] It has had numerous successes, such as creating open data initiatives, innovative contracting tools, and innovation toolkits. Innovation Fellows are currently assisting the VA with its modernization program, but there are many agencies (IRS, SSA, Treasury) waiting for help as well.

This initiative can be taken to scale by OPM and used to spur applications from IT innovators to work throughout government. The fellows' one-year terms may be seen both as a limitation and an attraction of the program. Government must adjust to the new millennium workforce, where short-term assignments and numerous job changes during a career are becoming the norm.[18] For those who want to stay in government long-term, the initial experience as fellows allows them to transfer to a career position. This kind of creative hiring approach can spread beyond the world of IT. It is not the

15 See Colby Hochmuth, *The Technology Gap in Government, Explained*, FEDSCOOP (Apr. 29, 2014), http://fedscoop.com/technology-gap-government-explained (remarks of Ashkan Soltani).

16 Executive Order 13,704, Presidential Innovation Fellows Program (Aug. 17, 2015).

17 See 18F, *Building the 21st Century Digital Government*, https://18f.gsa.gov/.

18 Nicole Ogrysko, *DHS: 'We're Not Looking for the 30-Year-Career Employee'*, FEDERAL NEWS RADIO (Jul. 5, 2016), http://federalnewsradio.com/hiringretention/2016/07/dhs-not-looking-30-year-career-employee/.

only field where "in and out" may be an attractive option. Other professionals like lawyers, economists, engineers, and accountants, might be attracted to government service if it were not tied to a long-term commitment. The Peace Corps model of two years of service may become more generally attractive.[19]

#### b. Utilize Old Technology Effectively: The Case of Video Hearings

Sometimes technology opportunities are right in front of agencies and they fail to see them. Not cutting-edge technology necessarily but available technology systems that can replace manual or personnel-heavy alternatives. My experience with the use of video technology to conduct adjudications is instructive in this regard. One technology innovation on which ACUS worked with SSA migrated a portion of the 800,000 face-to-face disability hearings before ALJs to video hearings. Done on a voluntary basis, this effort has resulted in about 25 percent of all disability cases being heard by video (over 200,000 per year) and the results have been overwhelmingly positive. Since much is at stake for claimants in these hearings, the Conference wanted to ensure that video alternatives were not only efficient, but also efficacious from a fairness perspective. The cost savings from travel and scheduling became clear immediately and for an agency the size of SSA amounted to tens of millions of dollars annually. The fairness issue was a little harder to measure, so we decided to compare outcomes (claimant success and failures) before ALJs in face-to-face hearings against those in video hearings. When no statistically significant differences were found, the fairness hurdle was safely passed.[20] The video technology has become so advanced that the hearing process – video quality of judge and witnesses – is if anything superior to that which occurs in a face-to-face hearing. And the convenience factors, remote witnesses, court reporters, translators, as well as judges and claimants have made converts on all sides. For example, law firms with large social security disability practices now set up video facilities in their offices for the convenience of clients.

ACUS hosted a video demonstration project in 2014, led by Fred Lederer at the William & Mary law school (and managed by Amber Williams), for many of the over 100 agencies who adjudicate claims and benefits, and published a best practices recommendation in support of the

[19] Of course, the more this becomes a practice, the more important "revolving door" restrictions managed by the Office of Government Ethics become. See Chapter 4.A, *supra*.

[20] See ACUS Recommendation 2011–4, *Video Hearings* (2011). The outcomes of cases in grant and denial percentages between video and face-to-face hearings were within statistically comparable ranges. A further fairness opportunity is achieved by making video hearings voluntary, but if they are equally outcome neutral even that requirement could be revisited.

video hearing process.[21] In the largest adjudicatory agencies, like the VA's Board of Veterans' Appeals Disability Program and the DOJ's Executive Office of Immigration Review Hearing Program, there was widespread recognition of the benefits of video adjudications. Yet there was opposition from lawyers, in immigration cases particularly, who felt that face-to-face adjudication was the only fair way to conduct hearings, whatever the delays might cost their clients.[22] The lawyers' views on the need to make credibility determinations in a face-to-face setting puts a faith in that method of truth finding that is not supported by evidence. In fact eyewitness misidentification (in lineup procedures) is a major source of false convictions.[23] In fact, video testimony properly administered can produce as good or better accuracy than in-person decision systems.

Some agency ALJs also resist this technological advance. Efforts to explain the virtues of video hearings to several regulatory agency chief ALJs were met with the standard lawyer's objection that the only fair process was looking the witness in the eye in order to determine truth. That professional "bias" really has many answers – first and foremost is that any judge who thinks looking at the witness directly will determine truth is deluding herself. Moreover, most cases do not turn on witness credibility issues anyway, so it is often not a relevant consideration. But it is hard to change attitudes inculcated in people since law school. Many of these objections reminded me of those from cautious bureaucrats discussed in Chapter 6, for whom refusal to change is based on the fear of the unknown.

It is important that OMB make the use of video hearings in agency adjudications a management priority and move agencies in that direction. In these days of sequestration and shrinking budgets, hundreds of millions in savings at no loss in fairness is within reach for many adjudicatory agencies. From a management perspective, this falls into the category of obvious moves.

### 3 *Insourcing and Circular* A-76

When President Obama came into office, one of his first acts was to reverse the contracting-out initiatives of his predecessor. He suggested that "contractors may be performing inherently governmental functions," and

21 See ACUS Recommendation 2014–7, Best Practices for Using Video Teleconferencing for Hearings (2014), https://www.acus.gov/research-projects/best-practices-using-video-teleconferencing-hearings.

22 See ABA Comm. on Immigration, Reforming the Immigration System 2–26, 2–27 (2010), www.americanbar.org/content/dam/aba/publications/commission_on_immigration/coi_executive_summary.authcheckdam.pdf.

23 See The Innocence Project, *Eyewitness Misidentification*, www.innocenceproject.org/causes/eyewitness-misidentification/.

proposed rebalancing the federal workforce by "insourcing" rather than continue to outsource.[24] The Bush Administration had encouraged the idea of competing government jobs with the contractors, a practice that outsourced more and more jobs.[25] Congress followed with legislation that pushed the idea of insourcing.[26] These signals were picked up by Secretary Robert Gates in 2009 and DOD's insourcing program began. It was designed "to rebalance the Department's workforce and reduce reliance on contracted services, while increasing government performance, oversight and control of critical functions."[27] This program can include both inherently governmental positions and those that are not so identified but are subject to long-term contracts or are part of the agency's core competency.

The next chart shows how it works (in DOD organizational land).[28] The DOD program has upset established relationships with its contractors[29] and reconfigured the federal workforce. Its success is hard to measure in detail,[30] but the initiative has spread to other agencies where the numbers, though modest, are worth noting.[31] Results at DHS were suboptimal largely because of the difficulties of the civil service hiring system,[32] which is a theme central to the arguments in this book.

24 See President Barack Obama, Government Contracting, Mar. 4, 2009, at 2, available at www.whitehouse.gov/the_press_office/Memorandum-for-the-Heads-of-Executive-Departments-and-Agencies-Subject-Government.

25 The Bush OMB instructed agencies to implement the FAIR Act by competing commercial activities delivered by government officials with the contractors. See OMB Guidance, June 14, 1999.

26 See National Defense Authorization Act for FY 2008, P.L. 110–181, § 324, 122 Stat. 60–61 (Jan. 28, 2008) (codified at 10 U.S.C. § 2463) (insourcing at DOD); Omnibus Appropriations Act 2009, P.L. 111–8, § 736, 123 Stat. 689–91 (Mar. 11, 2009) (codified at 31 U.S.C. § 501 note) (insourcing imposed on civilian agencies).

27 See Office of the Under Secretary for Personnel and Readiness, *DoD Insourcing Initiative Clearinghouse* (Apr. 6, 2009), http://prhome.defense.gov/RFM/TFPRQ/Insource/.

28 *In-sourcing Contracted Services – Implementation Guidance*, Attachment 1, at 4 (May 28, 2009), www.asamra.army.mil/scra/documents/DepSecDef%20Memo%2028MAY09%20In-sourcing%20Implementation%20Guidance.pdf.

29 See The Business Coalition for Competition, *Federal Insourcing Policy: Damaging the Private Sector; Growing the Public Sector* (2011) (insourcing is stealing private sector jobs).

30 Reports indicate that DOD insourced 17,000 jobs in 2010, more than one-half of which were done solely on a cost savings basis. See Pratap Chatterjee, *Insourcing: How Bringing Back Essential Federal Jobs Can Save Taxpayer Dollars and Improve Services*, Center for American Progress (Mar. 28, 2012), https://www.americanprogress.org/issues/general/report/2012/03/28/11326/insourcing/.

31 E.g. US Customs and Border Patrol estimates savings of $27 million in taking 200 contractor jobs in-house. See Alice Lipowicz, *Converting Contract IT Workers to Employees Saved $27M, Official Says*, Federal Computer Weekly (Feb. 22, 2011), https://fcw.com/articles/2011/02/22/converting-contract-workers-to-employees-saved-division-27m-official-says.aspx.

32 See Max Cacas, *Napolitano Blames Hiring Process for DHS Contractor Glut*, Federal News Radio (Feb. 25, 2010). Secretary Kelly also faces similar problems as he adds 10,000 new agents and 5,000 border guards.

**PROCESS FOR PRIORITIZING AND REVIEWING CONTRACTED SERVICES FOR IN-SOURCING**

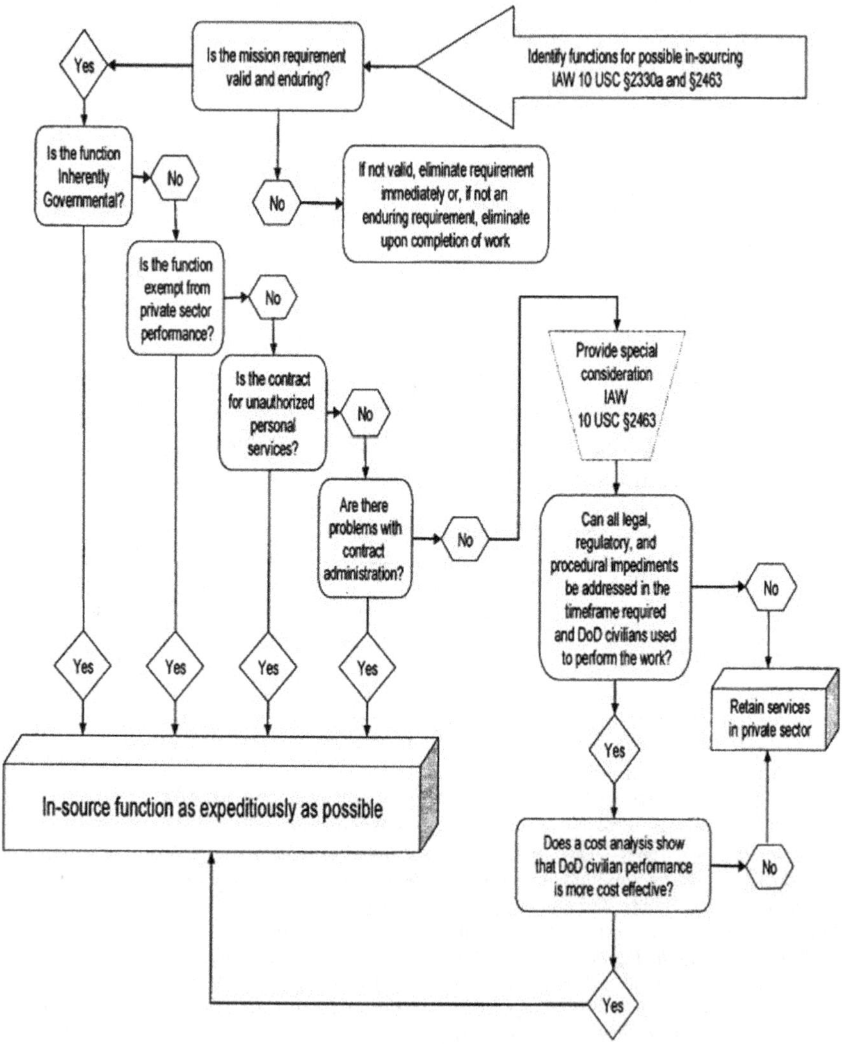


The reallocating of government jobs from contractors to government employees is one of the most direct ways to reduce the growth of contractor government. In effect, government takes two steps at once by adding government employees and reducing contractors. Importantly, the insourcing program applies to three categories of jobs: those that are inherently governmental, those that are "close to" inherently governmental, and those where the public sector performance is more "cost effective" than the private sector. While it is important to focus on inherently governmental and "close to" inherently governmental functions, "critical functions" where the agency is at risk of losing control of its operations are also crucial. The policy letter is set out on the next two pages.[33]

Obama's OMB directed agencies to conduct pilot human capital analyses of programs where they are concerned about the use of contractors,[34] and Congress reinforced their obligations to do so.[35] The powers that OMB possesses through this insourcing legislation as well as through its long-standing Circular A-76 authority have helped stem the tide of contractor government.

More can be done, especially since Congress has been behind the effort. The implementation difficulties at the agency level reveal a lack of commitment to the task. While the questions are complicated and existing relationships are upset, the agency benefits in the long run by recovering positions. One opportunity to explore is for agencies to convert existing contractors who are performing well into government employees. Some agencies have "direct hire authority" and can hire "any qualified person" without engaging in the competitive civil service process.[36] But others cannot, making the hiring task that much more difficult. Guidance from the White House would be crucial in this regard. In addition, agencies engaged in insourcing jobs can expect to be challenged in court by contractors whose services are terminated (or whose employees are moved into government).[37] The Justice Department also needs to provide legal support to encourage reluctant agencies to confront these legal challenges.

As was discussed in Chapter 4, contractors who have engaged in regulatory capture will find insourcing an existential threat. They can be expected to fight hard to keep contracts in place. This is another reason why good contractor management (and drafting skills) are necessary for government to work effectively.

33 Office of Federal Procurement Policy (OFPP), *Performance of Inherently Governmental and Critical Functions*, Policy Letter 11–01, 76 Fed. Reg. 56227, 56234 (Sept. 12, 2011).

34 See Peter R. Orzag, Director, OMB, M-09–26, Managing the Multi-Sector Workforce (July 29, 2009), https://www.whitehouse.gov/sites/default/files/omb/assets/memoranda_fy2009/m-09–26.pdf.

35 See Duncan Hunter National Defense Authorization Act for FY2009, P.L. 110–417, § 321(a)(1)–(4), 122 Stat. 4411 (Oct. 14, 2008) (OMB required to review existing definitions of inherently governmental functions to make sure they are not contracted out).

36 See US Office of Personnel Management, *Direct Hire Authority (DHA) Factsheet*, https://www.opm.gov/policy-data-oversight/hiring-information/direct-hire-authority/#url=Fact-Sheet.

37 See Kate M. Manuel & Jack Maskell, Congressional Research Service, *Insourcing Functions Performed by Federal Contractors: Legal Issues* (2013).

| Function | Work that is inherently governmental and therefore must be performed by federal employees | Work that is closely associated with inherently governmental functions and that may be performed by either federal employees or contractors |
|---|---|---|
| Budget development | The determination of budget policy, guidance, and strategy, and the determination of federal program priorities or budget requests. | Support for budget preparation, such as workforce modeling, fact finding, efficiency studies, and should-cost analyses. |
| Policy and regulatory development | The determination of the content and application of policies and regulations. | Support for policy development, such as drafting policy documents and regulations, performing analyses, feasibility studies, and strategy options. |
| Human resources management | The selection of individuals for federal government employment, including the interviewing of individuals for employment, and the direction and control of federal employees. | Support for human resources management, such as screening resumes in accordance with agency guidelines. |
| Acquisition planning, execution, and management | *During acquisition planning:* (1) determination of requirements; (2) approval of a contract strategy, statement of work, incentive plans, and evaluation criteria; (3) independent determination of estimated cost based on input from either in-house or contractor sources or both. | *Support acquisition planning by:* (1) conducting market research; (2) developing inputs for government cost estimates; and (3) drafting statements of work and other pre-award documents. |

| Function | Work that is inherently governmental and therefore must be performed by federal employees | Work that is closely associated with inherently governmental functions and that may be performed by either federal employees or contractors |
|---|---|---|
| | *During source selection:* (1) determination of price reasonableness of offers; (2) participation as a voting member on a source selection board; and (3) awarding of contracts. | *Support source selection by:* (1) preparing a technical evaluation and associated documentation; (2) participating as a technical advisor to a source selection board or as a nonvoting member of a source evaluation board; and (3) drafting the price negotiation memorandum. |
| | *During contract management:* (1) ordering of any changes required in contract performance or contract qualities; (2) determination of whether costs are reasonable, allocable, and allowable; (3) participation as a voting member on performance evaluation boards; (4) approval of award fee determinations or past performance evaluations; and (5) termination of contracts. | *Support contract management by:* (1) assisting in the evaluation of a contractor's performance (e.g. by collecting information, performing an analysis, or making a recommendation for a proposed performance rating); and (2) providing support for assessing contract claims and preparing termination settlement documents. |

While the process involves time, effort, and some degree of risk for agencies that are otherwise overworked, insourcing should be on the agenda of OMB and OPM in the Trump 'do more with less' era. Moreover, as long as the insourcing effort is cast in terms of financial savings to government, this effort, which Congress has accepted in the past, may avoid the political thickets awaiting many of the new President's initiatives.

## 4 *Improve Coordination among Agencies*

For political reasons, the federal government is characterized by organizational overlap that no private regime would tolerate. Both fragmented and overlapping delegations of power to agencies are commonplace and arguably intended. When he was Comptroller General, David Walker observed that "[v]irtually all of the results that the federal government strives to achieve require the concerted and coordinated efforts of two or more agencies."[38] This means that agencies who share "regulatory space," in contexts like food safety, financial regulation, or border regulation, must either work together or at cross purposes. Yet, collaboration is often the hardest thing to achieve. Agencies are mission driven. Too often that drive creates a kind of regulatory myopia where only one mission matters, not the collective missions of the other agencies involved in the same space. Government officials are expected to understand (and sometimes create) the missions of their agencies, but they are often less versed in the connected missions of sister agencies. They sometimes forget the larger mission – which is to make government work. For bureaucrats, focusing on mission is essential, but it can produce nearsightedness that blurs the bigger picture – that of solving overlap problems.

There are notable success stories of regulatory cooperation,[39] but often the White House needs to establish interagency coordinating bodies just to get things done. For example, the White House Office of Energy and Climate Change Policy facilitated the joint rulemaking between EPA and the Department of Trade (DOT) which produced new fuel efficiency and greenhouse gas standards.[40] This effort and others led ACUS to adopt a recommendation entitled "Improving Coordination of Related Agency

[38] GAO, GGD-00-95, *Managing for Results: Using GPRA to Help Congressional Decisionmaking and Strengthening Oversight* 19 (2000).

[39] See Jodi Freeman & Jim Rossi, *Agency Coordination in Shared Regulatory Space*, 125 HARV. L. REV. 1131 (2012); see also ACUS Rec. 2012–5 (Improving Coordination of Related Agency Responsibilities) (June 15, 2012).

[40] See Jody Freeman, *The Obama Administration's National Auto Policy: Lessons from the Car Deal*, 35 HARV. ENVTL. L. REV. 343 (2011).

Responsibilities,"[41] which called upon agencies and the White House to assume responsibilities for resolving jurisdictional disagreements, to include sharing information, soliciting conflicting views, and avoiding duplication. It was clear from the outset that the level of cooperation needed to conduct joint rulemaking and other policy ventures is not instinctive to agencies. Collaboration can only come about with effort on all sides. Under the Government Performance Results Modernization Act (GPRMA),[42] implemented by OMB, incentives are provided for cross-cutting budget allocations to help induce agencies to work together on a variety of projects, including joint rulemaking. But GPRMA is not self-executing. GAO has found that, in the context of Dodd–Frank Act implementation, a majority of agencies still have not developed internal policies on coordination, many years after the statute was enacted.[43]

The GPRMA process facilitates coordination through designated Performance Improvement Officers (PIOs) who are specifically charged to do so. OMB is required to develop long-term outcome-oriented goals for a limited number of management improvement areas, such as finances, human capital, information technology procurement/acquisition, and real property.[44] These are areas of core agency authority and if the goals are pressed by OMB many of the barriers that keep agencies from cooperating can be removed.

ACUS studied implementation efforts and found that sometimes barriers are created by agency general counsels who find legal impediments to cross-agency collaborations. It recommended the use of tools such as interagency agreements, memoranda of understanding, and other protocols that can minimize barriers and facilitate cooperation. GPRMA also creates the Performance Improvement Council (PIC) which facilitates agreements and helps measure cross-agency performance goals. The PIC is located within GSA and is composed of agency PIOs and OMB officials. By setting up ways to collaborate and placing direct responsibility on professional managers (PIOs), GPRMA provides a technique for cross-agency management.

The Act also requires the development of an agency-wide performance plan, as well as individual agency plans, and sets up quarterly agency reviews. Enhanced transparency is meant to be achieved by use of performance .gov, a single website devoted to posting performance goals and progress

[41] ACUS Recommendation 2012–5 (June 15, 2012). [42] 45 P.L. 111–352, 124 Stat. 3866 (2011).

[43] See GAO-12–151, *Dodd-Frank Act Regulations: Implementation Could Benefit From Better Analysis and Coordination* 25 (2011).

[44] See ACUS Recommendation 2013–7, GPRA Modernization Act of 2010: Examining Constraints To, and Providing Tools For, Cross-Agency Collaboration, 78 Fed. Reg. 76,269, 76,273 (2013).

toward realizing them.[45] Furthermore, the Act requires that such goals be established in collaboration with Congress, which provides valuable connections to key congressional committees and staff that President Trump should benefit from.

## 5 *Encourage Retrospective Review of Agency Rules*

Few objectives in government are harder to achieve than agency reevaluations of the rules they have promulgated. It stands to reason that rules become inadequate or even counter-productive over time and that they must be revised, strengthened, or eliminated. Yet the tendency is for agencies not to look back, but to forge ahead with new initiatives that pile on more regulations and draw the ire of regulated parties and the general public.[46] President Trump proposed a "one in two out" rule that would shrink agency rulemaking. The UK has also experimented with the idea. The mission to reexamine prior work faces numerous obstacles, including resource and time constraints as well as psychological barriers.

Agency officials, whose budgets have been virtually frozen due to sequestration requirements, must deal with new rules first, many of which are required by statute to be implemented. Financial rules under Dodd–Frank are a good example of this category.[47] In addition, agencies, like individuals, tend to give their prior work high marks – they become invested in existing rules.[48] This is why a system of pure agency "self-review" might yield suboptimal results. At the same time the regulated community, usually large entities, become adjusted to rules and may not be eager to change them. Investment in compliance can be a kind of barrier to entry.

45 Unfortunately, the Performance.gov website is failing to achieve the goals set for it under GPRMA. A GAO report concludes that the site is not meeting federal requirements. See Gov't Accountability Office, *PERFORMANCE.GOV: Long-Term Strategy Needed to Improve Website Usability*, GAO-16-693 (2016). The Trump Administration needs to devote the necessary resources to fix this portal which is crucial to interagency collaborative efforts.

46 See generally Peter H. Schuck, *Why Government Fails So Often and How It Can Do Better* 57–60 (2014). Professor Schuck's comprehensive work explores the agency motivations that stand in the way of effective retrospective review.

47 See Puneet Kollipara, *Wonkbook: 4 years later, Dodd-Frank is still only halfway implemented*, Washington Post Wonkblog (Jul. 21, 2014), https://www.washingtonpost.com/news/wonk/wp/2014/07/21/wonkbook-4-years-later-dodd-frank-is-still-only-halfway-implemented/.

48 See Reeve T. Bull, *Building a Framework for Governance: Retrospective Review and Rulemaking Petitions*, 67 Admin. L. Rev. 265, 280–81 (2015) (explaining in behavioral economics terms the bias agencies and individuals have towards their own ideas, the "not invented here" bias).

President Obama tried to create "a culture of retrospective review"[49] through several Executive Orders which showed promising results. Executive Order (EO) 13,563 directed executive agencies to reassess existing rules which have become "outmoded, ineffective, insufficient, or excessively burdensome,"[50] and EO 13,610, reported on elimination of "billions of dollars in regulatory costs and tens of millions of hours in annual paperwork burdens."[51] These results show what is possible when the President takes charge of a program. It also shows that political appointments, in this case Cass Sunstein as head of OMB's Office of Information and Regulatory Affairs (OIRA), can make a real difference. Sunstein's knowledge of behavioral economics and administrative law made him ideally suited to the task.[52] His successor, Howard Shelanski, was comparably qualified.[53] The Trump Administration needs to appoint someone with those kind of credentials.

President Trump is placing regulatory reform officers in agencies who can do retrospective rulemaking as well as implement rule reduction proposals. Certainly instructions given to new agency leaders when they take over (citing the Obama EOs as examples) is one way to move forward. To assist in agency compliance, instructions should include the suggestion in ACUS Recommendation 2014-5 that when formulating new regulations agencies should build in methodologies facilitating data-driven retrospective reviews in the future. The advantage is that data collected for justifying rules *ex ante* can be much more accurate when they are updated and applied to a rule *ex post*. Few subjects are likely to gain more bipartisan support than the retrospective review of rules, so long as review is not seen as a one-way ratchet to weaken or eliminate rules. A balanced approach to the review process contemplates both tightening as well as terminating rules when they are given a second look.

49 Joseph E. Aldy, *Learning from Experience: An Assessment of Agency Rules & the Evidence for Improving the Design and Implementation of Regulatory Policy* 47–48 (Nov. 17, 2014), https://www.acus.gov/sites/default/files/documents/Aldy%2520Retro%2520Review%2520Draft%252011-17-2014.pdf.

50 76 Fed. Reg. 3821 (Jan. 21, 2011); see also EO 13,579, 76 Fed. Reg. 14,587 (June 21, 2011) (applying to independent agencies).

51 77 Fed. Reg. 28,469 (May 14, 2012).

52 See Cass Sunstein, Simpler: The Future of Government 180–84 (2013) (highlighting successful retrospective review efforts). And, of course, *Nudge*, which he co-authored with Richard Thaler. Nudge: Improving Decisions about Health, Wealth, and Happiness (2009).

53 Office of Information and Regulatory Affairs, *OIRA Leadership*, https://www.whitehouse.gov/omb/oira/leadership (Mr. Shelanski was previously the Director of the Bureau of Economics at the FTC, and he has also served as Chief Economist of the Federal Communications Commission and as a Senior Economist for the President's Council of Economic Advisers. He has been a member of the faculties of Georgetown University (since 2011) and the University of California at Berkeley (1997–2009).).

## 6 *Level the Ethical Playing Field*

Contractors often carry out assignments that are identical to those performed by civil servants; indeed they may sit next to one another and be indistinguishable except for their identity badges. For example, despite what the A-76 chart on inherently governmental functions shows, "the determination of the content and application of regulations" is often contracted out. Yet while the job descriptions may be identical, the ethics regimes are quite different. For government employees, ethics requirements cover their financial interests, use of government resources, outside activities, and post-employment restrictions. Contractors are not so bound.[54] They may have ethical obligations to their private employers, but often far fewer ethical duties to the government for whom they are working. The degree of this ethical mismatch between contractors and civil servants varies by agency, leaving the overall ethical landscape uneven at best and suggesting that reforms are in order.

The Administrative Conference looked into this situation and, after hearing from all interests and carefully analyzing the responses, proposed a recommendation dealing with contractors' personal conflicts of interest and use of non-public information, the two areas of most concern. The recommendation focused on ethical issues involving contractors performing activities that "approach" being classified as "inherently governmental functions."[55] These would include activities where contractors advise on policy matters or participate in procurement functions, sensitive areas that are at the heart of concerns over contractor government. For example, information received from working on procurement matters may be used to a contractor's financial advantage, whereas the government official in the next chair clearly could not so benefit. The ACUS Recommendation asked the Federal Acquisition Regulatory Council (FAR Council) to promulgate model language for use in agency contracts. The language has been drafted and proposed to apply government-wide. However, it is still sitting on the list of FAR provisions "pending" resolution relating to the definition of "closely associated with inherent government functions."[56]

54 See ACUS Recommendation 2011–3, *Compliance Standards for Government Contractor Employees – Personal Conflicts of Interest and Use of Certain Non-Public Information* (2011), https://www.acus.gov/sites/default/files/documents/Recommendation%202011–3%20(Contractor%20Ethics).pdf) (preamble).

55 See *OMB Circular A-76: Performance of Commercial Activities* Attachment A § B.1.a.; OMB, *Work Reserved for Performance by Federal Government Employees*, 75 Fed. Reg. 16,188, 16,190 (Mar. 31, 2010).

56 See Case No. 2013–022, Part no. 3.11, 52 203–16, www.acq.osd.mil/dpap/dars/opencases/farcasenum/far.pdf.

The issues of contractor functions that are "closely associated" with inherently governmental ones (set out in the OFPP chart at pages 142–43) are complicated, but three years to study should be enough time for the FAR Council to resolve them. Certainly from the public's perspective, having these ethical issues resolved would be reassuring, even though their resolution cannot justify the use of contractors to perform those duties in the first place. But given the impracticability of insourcing all jobs that are inherently governmental or closely associated thereto, these second-best solutions are preferable to the existing gaps in ethical practices.

## 7 *Let's Play (Government) Moneyball*

One of the benefits of the GPRMA process is that agencies are required to set priorities and report progress on a regular basis through the (hopefully improved) Performance.gov website.[57] Agencies collaborate under the GSA's Performance Improvement Council and work with congressional committees to review and critique results. This sets up a structure for innovation in government that had not existed before. Now the question becomes how best to implement these new performance goals. What is needed is a commitment to evidence-based and data-driven analyses. As Don Kettl has noted, "if we are going to have better government, we need better evidence."[58] And, he adds, we need competent professionals to follow where the evidence leads.

In *Moneyball for Government*,[59] the authors of various chapters are paired on a bipartisan basis by the editors Jim Nussle and Peter Orzag to suggest ways to improve government performance. The editors recommend the adoption of three principles that can improve outcomes: (1) build evidence about programs that work; (2) invest in evaluating these programs to ensure that they work; and (3) disinvest in those programs that don't measure up. Robert Gordon and Ron Haskins, Obama and Bush II OMB officials, suggest a bipartisan moneyball agenda that drives home the use of data and evidence across agencies. They recommend a Chief Evaluation Officer for every agency, whose job is to "define [program] success in terms of measurable, transparent outcomes."[60] They

57 The NAPA transition proposals also discuss simplifying the Performance.gov website. See page 131.

58 *Escaping Jurassic Government: How to Recover America's Lost Commitment to Competence* 118 (2016).

59 (Jim Nussle & Peter Orzag eds.) (2014). The title draws from MICHAEL LEWIS, MONEYBALL: THE ART OF WINNING AN UNFAIR GAME (2003), which describes how Billy Bean, general manager of the Oakland Athletics, used statistics and data analysis to improve the record of his small market baseball team.

60 *Id.*, at 85.

suggest that agencies set aside 1 percent of their budgets for program evaluation purposes[61] and "build human capital government."[62]

These suggestions are sensible and doable, but agencies will object to budget set-asides because of sequestered and diminishing resources. Certainly, the Chief Evaluation Officer duties could be folded into the PIO position created under GPRMA. Indeed, the connection between the GPRMA agency reporting requirements and the data analysis suggestions seems obvious and beneficial. Of course, Gordon and Haskins' call for building human capital is at the heart of the ideas advanced in this book.

The authors emphasize the need for closing the average pay gap, which has widened to 18 percent, between the government and the private sector for employees with advanced degrees. This is also a concern which has been addressed in Chapter 7 of this book. The talent necessary to play moneyball does not come cheap, but the use of short-term appointments such as the innovation fellows program may permit some creative budgetary alternatives. In addition, talented contractors may also be called upon. For example, Aid Data, a consortium run by William & Mary and Brigham Young University[63] is doing evaluation studies for USAID and the World Bank on the effectiveness of foreign aid programs using evidence-based research and employing academics and students. They could also be tasked to assist in the more general moneyball efforts throughout government. Evaluation theory has its own society (the American Evaluation Association) and its own journal,[64] so the field is established and in a position to assist government at all levels.[65]

## 8 *The Pros and Cons of Telework*

The federal government has latched onto the technology of virtual commuting with enthusiasm. But it is a complicated management tool that should be used cautiously. Government often turns to it for the wrong reasons, as when GSA mandates telework for two days a week for its employees as a way to reduce traffic congestion.[66] Marissa Meyer, CEO of Yahoo, described the trade-offs well when she explained why she revoked Yahoo's telecommuting policy: "people are more productive when they are alone, but are more

[61] *Id.*, at 89. [62] *Id.*, at 96. [63] See AidData.org.

[64] See, e.g., Lydia I. Marek, Donna-Jean P. Brock, and Jyoti Savla, *Evaluating Collaboration for Effectiveness: Conceptualization and Measurement*, 36 Am. J. of Evaluation 67 (2015).

[65] At the municipal level, Bloomberg Philanthropies has a program to help mayors foster innovation as financial resources tighten, which may have lessons to teach the federal agencies.

[66] See Mike Causey, *Changing Face of Teleworking*, Federal News Radio (Jan. 21, 2016), http://federalnewsradio.com/federal-report/2016/01/changing-face-of-teleworking/.

collaborative and innovative when they're together."[67] I think her phrasing is especially applicable to government employees who work for an institution where collaboration (among and within agencies) is a necessity but is in short supply, as part 4 of this chapter shows.

The federal government made a big push for telework under the Telework Enhancement Act of 2010[68] which saw benefits such as: recruiting and retention of staff, reduced energy use, and reduced travel and real estate costs.[69] OPM has been monitoring telework data on an agency-by-agency basis and reported the results on Telework.gov. OPM reported that one-half of employees were eligible and over 300,000 telecommuted in 2013.[70] The advantages of workplace flexibility are significant and should help those with family obligations. It may also encourage the hiring of talented millennials who are comfortable with the idea. Indeed, it is difficult not to encourage the practice while the DC Metro undergoes extensive repairs in the coming years.

There are also difficulties with implementing Marissa Meyer's productivity advantage for solitary workers. When the Patent and Trademark Office (USPTO) permitted its examiners to write reports from home, it failed to monitor their time effectively. A Department of Commerce Inspector General's report concluded that USPTO supervisors had permitted over 288,479 unsupported hours over a 15-month period resulting in $20 million in wasted overtime.[71]

The costs to collaboration and innovation that many government managers I have interviewed express are not to be discounted. In my agency, telework was used carefully. But in many agencies empty halls signify lost opportunities to interact. Interactions often produce new ideas and creative solutions (the famous water-cooler chats) which cannot occur in the isolation of homebound work. So if telework is done selectively (one day per week, or two days per month) it might provide some productivity benefits. But broader use can undermine morale, reduce productivity, and suppress creativity.

67 See Christopher Tkaczyk, *Marissa Mayer Breaks Her Silence on Yahoo's Telecommuting Policy*, FORTUNE (Apr. 19, 2013), http://fortune.com/2013/04/19/marissa-mayer-breaks-her-silence-on-yahoos-telecommuting-policy/.

68 H.R. 1722, Pub. L. No. 111–292, 111th Cong. (2010).

69 See GAO, https://blog.gao.gov/2015/12/10/five-years-of-the-telework-enhancement-act-of-2010/, WATCHBLOG (Dec. 10, 2015), https://blog.gao.gov/2015/12/10/five-years-of-the-telework-enhancement-act-of-2010/.

70 See OPM, 2014 STATUS OF TELEWORK IN THE FEDERAL GOVERNMENT REPORT TO CONGRESS (FISCAL YEAR 2013) 44, Table 26 (2015), https://www.telework.gov/reports-studies/reports-to-congress/2014-report-to-congress.pdf.

71 Dep't of Commerce, OIG Investigative Report No. 14–0990, *Analysis of Patent Examiners' Time and Attendance* (2016).

### C. CONCLUSIONS: WE CAN MAKE GOVERNMENT WORK BETTER

This chapter may appear to concede that the broad civil service reforms proposed in the prior chapter are impractical or politically unfeasible. But there is room for both. The ideas proposed here should be implemented whether or not broad change is legislated. They should not be considered as compromising on the underlying needs for reform of government employment practices at all levels.

Under President Trump, the management needs and processes of the government should be on the agenda of an early Cabinet meeting. Indeed, it would be ideal if the use of the Cabinet as a management tool were also on the agenda. The Cabinet meeting brings together the President's top officials, yet it has withered as a policy tool in the Obama years, in favor of White House czars and other special assistants.[72] If the Cabinet is part of presidential priorities like civil service reform it can interact productively and then hand off the project to appropriate personnel at the White House, GSA, OMB, and OPM. Whatever happens, the message should be sent that the civil service needs to change and improve to serve the nation well.

[72] See Albert R. Hunt, *Why Doesn't Obama Use His Cabinet More?*, Bloomberg View (Feb. 10, 2013), https://www.bloomberg.com/view/articles/2013–02–10/why-does-obama-keep-his-cabinet-all-stars-on-the-bench-.

# 9

# In Sum

## *Reprofessionalize Government*

To adapt Trump's favorite phrase, it is time to make government great again. Greatness is defined not by the size of government, but by its quality, and quality is driven by professionalism. This is not a difficult proposition to understand, and it applies to politics itself. Members of Congress have a stake in professionalizing their roles also. As Peter Wehner notes: "Our low regard for politics is leading us to undervalue the craft of governing."[1] A civil service that has not grown for 50 years cannot be shrunken further without inviting less professional government. During the campaign, Donald Trump's call to replace only one of every three retiring federal workers echoed a plan initially proposed by Paul Ryan.[2] Trump then called for government to address improper payments and collect unpaid taxes. Who is going to carry out these instructions? Private collection agencies by contract? We saw in Chapter 3 how poorly that idea has worked. The contractor illusion must be shattered.[3] Reducing the size of government arbitrarily only serves to weaken it. Such an effort would be self-defeating and counter-productive. Ensuring the right balance between contractors and career officials is a characteristic of an effectively run government. Reducing the professionals imbalances public leadership, reduces the quality of services, and costs more.

We need the best talent to run government. Obstacles in the way of achieving this goal are political and also self-inflicted by the limitations of

[1] Peter Wehner, *In Defense of Politics, Now More Than Ever*, Op-Ed, N.Y. Times (Oct. 29, 2016), www.nytimes.com/2016/10/30/opinion/campaign-stops/in-defense-of-politics-now-more-than-ever.html.

[2] See Eric Katz, *Trump Revives Familiar Plan to Cut Federal Workforce*, Government Executive (Sept. 7, 2016), www.govexec.com/federal-news/fedblog/2016/09/trump-cut-federal-workforce-through-attrition/131352/.

[3] *See* Paul R. Verkuil, *The Case for Bureaucracy*, Op-Ed, N.Y. Times (Oct. 3, 2016), www.nytimes.com/2016/10/03/opinion/the-case-for-bureaucracy.html.

the civil service system documented here. Reform should preserve and enhance professional management, including its tenure-like characteristics, where appropriate, while also limiting its cumbersome and accreted procedural barriers to removal and retention. This message is particularly salient for "at will" public employment states where the ability to remove career employees jeopardizes the supply of professional managers who can deliver quality performance. But that message now needs to be sent to Congress as well, where a bill submitted in the last days of the 114th Congress seeks to permit agencies to fire new employees "without notice or right to appeal."[4] This bill is sure to gain new adherents in the Republican Congress and the Trump Administration.

The examples provided at the federal and state agency level set out many reasons why our professional government is in need of restoration. Government performance failures are connected to the quality of management. Shrinking government or disincentivizing the career service is not the solution. Beating up on the bureaucracy for political effect does not make it go away. Privatization can reduce its size, and contractors, properly employed, can help make it more efficient, but it will still be bureaucratic when we are done. The way to value bureaucracy is to reprofessionalize it.

## A. SIGNS OF PROGRESS

Forces on both sides of the political spectrum have to be convinced, of course, and this has always been a difficult collaboration to achieve. Nonetheless, there are some indicators of progress worth noting. One is the bipartisan Competitive Service Act of 2015[5] that enables agencies to share their vetted lists of best qualified candidates to more quickly fill mission critical positions in specialized fields like cybersecurity.[6] That this legislation passed during the height of the political season is significant recognition of the need for "A-level" talent in government. Its premise, respect for quality professionals, offers a necessary perspective for a more general approach to civil service reform. An appreciation of the need for able professionals has long been missing from the reform debate. Moreover, the recognition of the need

[4] Promote Accountability and Government Efficiency Act, H.R. 6278, 114th Cong. (2016), introduced by Todd Rokits (R-Ind.); see Eric Katz, *A Last-Minute Push for Turning Feds Into At-Will Employees*, GOVERNMENT EXECUTIVE (Oct. 4, 2016), http://www.govexec.com/pay-benefits/2016/10/last-minute-push-turning-feds-will-employees-emerges/132104/.

[5] S. 1580 (114th Cong.), Pub. L. No. 114–137.

[6] See Sen. Rep't 114–143, 114th Cong., 1st Sess., Comm. on Homeland Security and Gov. Affairs to accompany S. 1580 (Sept. 15, 2015).

for quality hires will address other concerns about reform, such as excessive procedural protections from dismissal that impair the ability to raise the quality of existing personnel. If the conservatives can be sold on quality then maybe the progressives can be reached on process. But the compromise cannot be radical civil service reform which denies the need for process at all.[7] If a compromise process regime is offered, the public sector unions need to step forward. As Nick Parrillo has noted, "the greatest practical support for civil service protection often comes from lobbying and unionization on the part of protected bureaucrats themselves . . ."[8] Public sector unions have grown in strength and now exceed the number of union members in the private sector.[9] With this strength came the ability to affect public expenditures and add procedural protections. Now opportunities for compromise should be sought.

Consider the California teachers tenure case *Vergara* v. *California Ass'n of Teachers* ("CAT").[10] The case involved a challenge to tenure terms under the California Constitution. The union successfully defended its two-year tenure rule in court and has so far refused legislative attempts at compromise. In the course of winning in the California Supreme Court by a 4–3 vote that upheld the appellate court's dismissal of the case, the CAT lost two liberal judges who might otherwise be on their side. Justices Liu and Cuéllar dissented because of excessive procedural protections against teacher removal. They noted that California is one of five states with a two years to tenure rule and that to remove anyone who did not meet it required a complex process: written statement of hearing rights; written statement of unsatisfactory behavior, with 90 days to correct; then written statement of charges; 30 days to request hearing (after 60-day period); and *then* judicial review.[11] The teachers unions are powerful political players nationwide, but they should consider the effect of pushing for unreasonable ends – like extremely short tenure times. As Chapter 8 discusses, tenure is a reasonable goal, but it must be administered in a reasonable fashion. Meeting halfway on tenure or civil service hearing protections at the federal

7 See Stephen E. Condrey & R. Paul Battaglio, Jr., *A Return to Spoils? Revisiting Radical Civil Service Reform in the United States*, PUB. ADMIN. REV. 425 (May/June 2007); see also Chapter 8.

8 Nicholas R. Parrillo, *The Salary Revolution and the Marks of Government's Distinctness: A Response to Jon Michaels*, 128 HARV. L. REV. FORUM 99 (2015).

9 See Daniel DiSalvo, *The Trouble with Public Sector Unions*, 5 NATIONAL AFFAIRS 3 (2010) (discussing state and local public sector unions).

10 See *Vergara* v. *Cal. Teachers Ass'n*, – Cal.Rptr.3d –, 2016 WL 4443590 (Aug. 22, 2016).

11 The trial court thought this process could take two to ten years (and cost the school board $50,000 to $450,000 per case) with teachers left on the roll in the interim. See *Vergara* v. *Cal. Teachers Ass'n*, 209 Cal.Rptr.3d 532 (Aug. 22, 2016) (dissenting opinions of Justices Liu and Cuéllar).

level can benefit both sides politically – and the public generally. It may just be that the Trump Administration can make civil service reform proposals that the legislative process can turn into compromises that are in the public interest.

## B. HOW TO MOTIVATE BUREAUCRATS

Incentive structures are particularly complicated for government employees, since so much of their compensation is provided by steps in systems that rely more on time in grade and passive annual performance reviews ("meets expectations" is the default rating). Financial incentives are not very well funded and hard to administer. In addition, the federal government has gone years without an overall pay raise.

### 1 *Set Reasonable Goals, not Self-Defeating Ones*

So how else to motivate? Perhaps it is best to flip the question – how *not* to motivate bureaucrats? This brings to mind what happened at the Veterans Administration, when numerous VA hospital officials falsified data on the real waiting times veterans experienced for doctors' appointments.[12] Part of the reason this happened was that then Secretary Shinseki, under pressure to reduce the times, placed unreasonable deadlines on his hospital officials, which made it an ineffective and even perverse management exercise. Shinseki was a resolute military leader, who spoke truth to power during the Iraq War,[13] but the pressure he put on his staff to perform scheduling miracles without enough doctors adequately to staff the hospitals was bound to fail. Impossible orders create false compliance. This is no way to motivate people. Motivation must give employees challenges that can be met. This is the essence of professional government.

This is not a management failure unique to government. It is what went wrong with the Wells Fargo situation, where 5,300 employees were fired because they set up unwanted (or even unknown) accounts for their customers in an attempt to meet impossible new account demands.[14] The bank settled

[12] See discussion in Chapter 7, pages 120–21.

[13] He angered Secretary of Defense Rumsfeld by testifying that several hundred thousand troops would be needed in post-war Iraq.

[14] See Michael Corkery & Stacy Cowley, *Wells Fargo Warned Workers Against Sham Accounts, but 'They Needed a Paycheck'*, N.Y. TIMES (Sept. 16, 2016), www.nytimes.com/2016/09/17/business/dealbook/wells-fargo-warned-workers-against-fake-accounts-but-they-needed-a-paycheck.html.

with the Consumer Financial Protection Bureau for $185 million[15] and faces numerous lawsuits from its employees.[16] Attention then turned to the bank's leaders who placed unreasonable demands for the creation of new accounts on their employees.[17] When John Stumpf, the bank's Chairman and CEO, testified before the Senate Banking Committee the senators adamantly pressed him on why senior management officials were not terminated or their bonuses recovered ("clawed back").[18] Many of the people fired were earning $12 an hour and were required to participate in the bogus credit card program as a way to meet incentive goals. The scheme went on for five years or more before being brought to light. A management team that drives unrealistic sales goals is almost complicit in the subsequent fraud that occurs. Setting incentives that are unreasonable produces failures, for both employees and management. This is a fact that led to Mr. Stumph's resignation.

This situation is reminiscent of the cheating Chicago school teachers discussed in *Freakonomics*.[19] The incentive system there (bonuses for improving students' test scores) led to widespread teacher manipulation of the students' test scores, something that might have been anticipated by good managers. But the data collected to prove cheating also showed the opposite, how good teachers who actually improved students' test scores could be identified. Arne Duncan, as head of the Chicago School System, used these data to reward and incent properly, a management technique he presumably took with him during his service as Secretary of Education under President Obama.

The question of how to motivate government bureaucrats then is the same as how to motivate those in the private sector (bankers at Wells Fargo by this example). Choose the right incentive techniques, ensure that they are not

[15] CFPB Press Release, *Consumer Financial Protection Bureau Fines Wells Fargo $100 Million for Widespread Illegal Practice of Secretly Opening Unauthorized Accounts* (Sept. 8, 2016), at www.consumerfinance.gov/about-us/newsroom/consumer-financial-protection-bureau-fines-wells-fargo-100-million-widespread-illegal-practice-secretly-opening-unauthorized-accounts/.

[16] See Mike Snider, *Ex-Wells Fargo bankers sue over firing amid fraud*, USA TODAY (Sept. 26, 2016), www.usatoday.com/story/money/2016/09/25/ex-wells-fargo-employees-sue-over-scam/91079158/.

[17] See Susan Ochs, OP-ED, *In Wells Fargo Scandal, the Buck Stopped Well Short*, N.Y. TIMES (Sept. 15, 2016), www.nytimes.com/2016/09/15/opinion/in-wells-fargo-scandal-the-buck-stopped-well-short.html.

[18] See Michael Corkery, *Elizabeth Warren Accuses Wells Fargo Chief of 'Gutless Leadership'*, N.Y. TIMES (Sept. 20, 2016), www.nytimes.com/2016/09/21/business/dealbook/wells-fargo-ceo-john-stumpf-senate-testimony.html.

[19] See STEVEN D. LEVITT & STEPHEN J. DUBNER, FREAKONOMICS: A ROGUE ECONOMIST EXPLORES THE HIDDEN SIDE OF EVERYTHING 25–29 (2009) (explaining how an algorithm could be designed to find cheating by teachers manipulating answers to thousands of math tests).

misused, and reward accordingly. But do not send signals that results (new accounts opened or number of appointment days) are the only thing that matters. Integrity and respect for customers and citizens count for a lot also. These are teachable skills for the managers who are professionals in their fields.

### 2 *Positive Motivation Works*

And finally, try some praise and recognition. The Partnership for Public Service awards its Service to America Awards ("Sammies") annually to high-achieving public servants that are culled from hundreds of deserving candidates. Pictured here are the 2016 winners.[20]

These government officials make citizens proud. Their achievements are remarkable and provide some balance to the debate about how well the bureaucracy performs.[21] And they are backed up by hundreds of semi-finalists and thousands of former winners and runners-up who can be found on the PPS website. This is the kind of motivation that government needs more of and that politicians need to recognize. To be sure, many in Congress do acknowledge the achievements of the professional government, but their voices should be heard when it counts, as it does in these times.

[20] Photo from Partnership for Public Service, Service to America Medals, https://servicetoamericamedals.org/ (last visited Oct. 5, 2016) (photo at https://servicetoamericamedals.org/assets/homepage/homepage-sammies-winners-16_2.jpg). These awards have been made since 2002.

[21] See Ruth Marcus, *And the Oscars for Good Government Geeks Go To*, Wash. Post (Sept. 23, 2016), https://www.washingtonpost.com/opinions/and-the-oscars-for-good-government-geeks-go-to-/2016/09/23/2666552a-81b2–11e6–8327-f141a7beb626_story.html?utm_term=.5c8c91942c36.

### 3 *Try Double Bottom Line Thinking*

One way to approach the motivation of bureaucrats is to look at the theory of "double bottom line" investing.[22] The power of impact investing is that it satisfies two human needs: to do good and to do well. It is guilt-free investing. Similarly, incentive structures for employees are a means of investing in their futures and connecting them to the organization's goals. Incentive structures have both social goals and financial ones. For the Wells Fargo employee it is a combination of customer service and bonuses for new accounts. For the bureaucrat, it can be the same: service to the public (as an ethic) as well as number of public served (if you are at the Social Security Administration or IRS, for example). The social return is easier to ensure for those in government, since many of them are there because of their belief in service. The way to motivate bureaucrats is to make them part of a team of achievers that is led by managers who understand human nature, have a respect for people, and know how to incent and inspire. These are the leaders who will reprofessionalize government.

## C. LISTEN TO CONTRACTORS

This suggestion may come as a surprise to those who consider a theme of this book to be controlling contractors or reducing their influence. But contractors know their agencies from the inside, and they strive to improve performance. My experience from interviewing leaders at major government contracting firms is that they also want to see government work better, which is why they are employed in the first place.

Remarkably, the Professional Services Council (which represents four hundred contracting companies) has weighed in on the transition.[23] Some might think this is arrogance or chutzpah speaking, and it certainly shows a confidence about the centrality of the contractors' role in government. But it also is quite revealing. The PSC agenda calls for an "on demand" government (one that is responsive, resilient, flexible, and less hierarchical). While this would often call for the use of contractors to meet emerging or fast-developing needs (think FEMA), this is exactly how contractors should be used. The problem

[22] See Judith Rodin & Margot Brandenburg, The Power of Impact Investing 7 (2014) ("At the heart of impact investing is the presence of dual objectives – the desire actively to achieve positive social or environmental results as well as financial ones").

[23] Professional Services Council, PSC 45: An Agenda for the Next President of the United States (2016), www.pscouncil.org/c/other_content/An_Agenda_for_the_45th_President.aspx.

we have now is that contractors have become part of the permanent federal workforce.

The PSC says: "Refocus government on core (inherently governmental) missions while leveraging industry through outcome-based contracts to deliver non-core services."[24] I couldn't have stated it better. This book wants professionals to perform and manage core services. The PSC Agenda also calls for better contractor management and for a "focus on results – not process – in government contracting."[25] Bravo to this one as well.

It is reassuring that the contractor community has views about improving government and is willing to share them with those who must manage the transition. Perhaps the PSC can help to recover inherent government functions through the insourcing process described in Chapter 8. The PSC suggestions go a long way to restoring professionalism in government (while leaving plenty of jobs for the contracting community). I even wonder whether the contractors might join with the public interest sector (PPS and NAPA) and the public sector unions to push for civil service reform. This type of coalition could surely move Congress.

### D. RETURN JOBS TO GOVERNMENT

The idea of "insourcing" explored in Chapter 8 has considerable potential for returning jobs, especially ones that are inherent or close to inherent government functions. While progress should continue in that regard, more progress can be achieved by reducing the number of contractors unilaterally.

The Obama Justice Department, by phasing out the regime of private prisons, sought to reduce the number of contractors in government substantially while adding some federal prison employees to make up the difference.[26] Moreover, since President Obama commuted the sentences of thousands of nonviolent drug offenders held in federal prisons, the need for prisons and prison beds may be reduced as well.[27]

The larger trends, including state and federal prison admissions, are declining as well. As of 2012, for example, the number of releases from prisons exceeded the number of admissions for the fourth straight year.[28] This trend,

[24] *Id.*, at 12. [25] *Id.*, at 13. [26] See discussion in Chapter 4.

[27] See Jelani Cobb, Comment, *A Drawdown in the War on Drugs*, THE NEW YORKER (Aug. 29, 2016), www.newyorker.com/magazine/2016/08/29/a-drawdown-in-the-war-on-drugs ("Last year, the Justice Department reported the first decline in the federal prison population in thirty-three years . . .").

[28] BUREAU OF JUSTICE STATISTICS, PRISONERS IN 2012: TRENDS IN ADMISSIONS AND RELEASES, 1991–2012 (updated 2014), www.bjs.gov/content/pub/pdf/p12tar9112.pdf.

which is only accelerating, builds support for state and federal reclaiming of the operations of their prisons. No wonder the private prison industry turned to Trump.

The trend to insourcing or reducing the need for contractors altogether had some other detours. Under legislation passed in 2015, Congress required that the IRS outsource debt collection to private collection agencies (PCAs).[29] The use of PCAs failed in prior efforts for a variety of reasons, including abusive collection practices. The effort was opposed by the Taxpayer Advocate, Nina Olson, and the National Treasury Employees Union, which proposed retraining IRS employees who were about to lose their jobs as paper tax return processors.[30]

This outsourcing effort is difficult to understand, except as part of the Republicans' dislike of IRS generally. The use of PCAs who failed in the past rather than strengthening the capacity of government officials will likely lead to similar failures of management down the road.[31]

## E. THINK PRAGMATICALLY, LIKE HOLMES

In the spirit of Justice Holmes, we need to think about government pragmatically.[32] While I have posed normative (constitutional) values for maintaining a professional government, the politics of the matter call for pragmatic thinking. It may be that I have a psychological aversion to extremes, but much of this book is directed at finding the balanced solution. The economists have refined this quest into a principle (moderate growth, low inflation), but those of us in the public law and administration field are not so far along. This book tries to move in that direction. Virtually all of the solutions are premised on pragmatic understandings of available choices. Use contractors more sparingly, but don't eliminate them. Reform the civil service, but don't gut it. Live with "at will" employment, but preserve experience and seniority. Reduce the size of government, but don't "drown" it. Use business principles, but shape them for government. This kind of reversion-to-the-mean thinking

[29] See Eric Katz, *IRS Begins Privatization of Long-Term Tax Debt Collection*, GOVERNMENT EXECUTIVE (Sept. 27, 2016), www.govexec.com/management/2016/09/irs-begins-privatization-long-term-tax-debt-collection/131890/.

[30] *Id.*

[31] Nina Olson, the Taxpayer Advocate, has pointed out that PCAs will be going after those receiving Social Security Disability payments which the IRS had chosen not to pursue. She also worries about the training and procedures manuals used by PCAs, which are not subject to FOIA disclosure. Email exchange with author, Sept. 28, 2016.

[32] *See* RICHARD A. POSNER, THE ESSENTIAL HOLMES xi, xii (1992) (discussing Holmes' pragmatic approach to law through contract theory and, more broadly, legal realism).

helps define what is practical and possible, and drives solutions to problems once they are understood. Pragmatic thinkers believe in ideas, but are doubtful about ideologies.[33] I am always hopeful that arguments well made can persuade, so long as people remain faithful to the cause of democratic governance. Even doubters in this administration must come to recognize that the bureaucracy is their government and disparaging it will neither make it go away nor perform better. The warning of Frank Fukuyama, referred to earlier, still seems the best way to close: "The belief [or ideology] that government is unfixable will otherwise lock us into an equilibrium where poor quality government becomes a self-fulfilling prophecy."[34]

33 See Louis Maynard, THE METAPHYSICAL CLUB: A STORY OF IDEAS IN AMERICA (Introduction) (2002).

34 Francis Fukuyama, *Governance: What do We Know and How Do We Know It?*, 19 ANN. REV. POLIT. SCI. 42 (2015).

# Index